Diamonds from the Dugout

115 Baseball Legends Remember Their Greatest Hits

By **Mark Newman,**
Foreword by **Brooks Robinson**

Diamonds from the Dugout:
115 Baseball Legends Remember Their Greatest Hits

Published by Blue River Press
Indianapolis, Indiana
www.brpressbooks.com

Distributed by Cardinal Publishers Group
317-352-8200 phone
317-352-8202 fax
www.cardinalpub.com

ISBN: 978-1-68157-067-9

Cover Design: Glen Edelstein, Hudson Valley Book Design
Book Design: Dave Reed
Cover Photo: Jeff Curry — USA TODAY Sports
Editor: Dani McCormick

Printed in the United States of America

21 20 19 18 17   1 2 3 4 5

CONTENTS

FOREWORD

BROOKS ROBINSON

You're going to find a lot of my friends in the pages of this book, and that is one of the best things to happen in a life spent in or around the wonderful game of baseball.

In addition to growing a large family of my own, I have been fortunate to make a lot of wonderful friends along the way. Being the president of the Major League Baseball Players Alumni Association for many years has kept me in touch with many of them. As I look through their stories that you will see here, I have been eager to see what hits *they* chose. Some of their hits brought back memories for me as well, and I know that each of them will be nostalgic as well as motivational when you turn the pages.

My longtime teammate Jim Palmer talks about his own first hit, which just happened to come in his first of 268 Major League wins for our Orioles on May 16, 1965. I'd like to tell you I was on the field to see that one, but I had to miss close to a few weeks around that time thanks to a Hank Aguirre fastball. That happened during a game at home against Detroit on May 8, 1965, the year after I received the American League Most Valuable Player Award. I had singled off Aguirre in each of my first two at-bats that day, and when I came up against him in the bottom of the fifth, Bob Johnson had just hit a solo homer off of him. Aguirre proceeded to hit me and John Orsino in back-to-back at-bats, and it broke my thumb. I managed to finish that game, played the first game of a doubleheader the next day, and then pinch-hit and scored the winning run in the 12th inning of the nightcap. I didn't like to be out of the lineup, but I had no choice, so I guess when I came back, the best pitcher in Orioles history was in the books with a home run.

That 1965 season, the Yankees finally faded back into the pack, and the Twins won the pennant. But the next year was ours, the first World Series title for the Orioles. And during that summer of '66, I was honored to be named MVP of an All-Star Game for the first time. We were at the brand-new Busch Stadium in downtown St. Louis, right next to the Arch. It was 105 degrees and humid, a tough day, but I grew up in Arkansas with summer heat. I had three hits, including a triple off Sandy

Koufax in the second inning, scoring the game's first run. Ron Santo drove in Willie Mays with a single in the fourth for the National League, and it stayed a 1-1 game for a long time. I led off the top of the 10th with a single off Gaylord Perry, got to second, but was stranded there when Jim Fregosi struck out. Now we're in the bottom of the 10th, and here comes Maury Wills, who had replaced Willie Stargell in the lineup on a double-switch in the eighth. Well, Maury sent us all home, I got my MVP award despite being on the losing team, and you can read just how much that walk-off hit meant to him in this book. Our paths would just happen to cross again later that October, when we swept the Dodgers.

I remember another big game that was a 1-1 tie before the home team won in the 10th. That was in 1969, Game 4 of the World Series against the Mets. We were hoping for a win to make it a 2-2 series split and make sure we could take the series back to Baltimore. Tom Seaver was working on a shutout in the ninth, but Frank Robinson and Boog Powell both singled to put Orioles on the corners. That brought me up, and I drove one to right-center. Ron Swoboda somehow made a diving catch that might have saved the series for them, because even though it tied the game as a sacrifice fly, Seaver then got out of the inning and the Mets won to take a 3-1 series lead. I had seen enough of Swoboda at that point, I guess, but when you read what he has to say in this book, you will see why he wasn't quite done in that World Series.

Fortunately, we won a second championship the following year, and I guess that 1970 World Series is what cemented my reputation at third base among sportswriters and fans. I have always been humbled by and thankful for any such praise, especially from peers. After a few more seasons, I shared my life story in an autobiography titled, *Third Base Is My Home*. In that book, I talked a lot about how important it always was to me that I became more than just a good fielder. In that same 1970 World Series, in fact, I was 9-for-21 (.429) with a pair of homers and six RBIs. We had a great all-around team with maybe the best starting rotation ever, one that produced four 20-game winners the following year. The Orioles were in the World Series three consecutive years, 1969-71, and I was proud of our run and my own contributions.

I have been fortunate to play with and against some of the best hitters in the business. I am glad to see Frank Robinson sharing his favorite hit here as well. I played in a different league than Pete Rose for our entire careers, but I saw enough of his bat in all those All-Star Games. I guess you could say third base is pretty well-represented in these pages. There's Mike Schmidt, George Brett, Wade Boggs, Chipper Jones, David Wright, Aaron Boone, and Evan Longoria. And don't forget my friend

Tony Perez, because even though he spent most of his career as a first baseman for the Big Red Machine, he was my counterpart at third base during that 1970 World Series.

Cal Ripken Jr., meanwhile, was a shortstop and a third baseman, and it has always been an honor to call him a friend and a fellow lifetime-Oriole alum. Maybe the greatest moment of all of our baseball lives was when he took the field at Camden Yards that night in 1995 to break Lou Gehrig's record of 2,130 consecutive games played. Cal started with Baltimore four years after I retired, and then spent 21 seasons with the Orioles. Over that time, he had 3,184 hits in the regular season. You'll see that the hit he selected had a lot to do with his father, and that relationship with his dad was just another of the many things we have in common.

I can proudly say that my father had a large role in me becoming a Major Leaguer, teaching me many of the kinds of lessons that are abundant here. Go back to the very beginning, when he cut off an old broomstick just short enough so I could swing it like a bat. I hit a rubber baseball back to him at first, but then I graduated to rocks. There were thousands of them behind our house, and I made those woods my own field. He gave me my desire to do the best I could every day, and he let me know the importance of moving past today's game and being ready once the next national anthem is played. I learned from him to correct my mistakes but not dwell on them. One of the lessons I learned involved the hit I shared here, and I appreciate having the chance to answer. The hit I chose was not discussed in previous books, including that autobiography, but it is important today to relay what I learned in those times.

My first 40 years were about learning to be a ballplayer, then becoming an everyday ballplayer, and then building a family while striving to accomplish everything I could in a long career as a ballplayer. My next 40 years were about life after being a ballplayer. It has been important for me to stay in touch, to help players who came before me and after me, and to pool together our abilities to help make a difference in the lives of others. I suppose it may seem surprising that a guy who has two fielding statues around Camden Yards—where I am either in a defensive-ready posture at third base or about to throw across the diamond—is writing the foreword for a book about the one hit that mattered most to more than 100 baseball legends. It would have made my former manager Paul Richards happy, because one day in 1958, when I was just trying to last a full season in the Majors without needing more seasoning down on the farm, he gave me confidence when he told writers: "Someday, Brooks is going to help us at the plate just as much as he does with the glove." I finished with 2,848 hits in the regular season and another 44 in the postseason. It was like hitting rocks with a broomstick back home in Arkansas.

Like the great shortstop Ozzie Smith said in discussing his hit here, being asked about hitting is very much appreciated. I think you are going to enjoy spending time with many of my friends like The Wizard in these pages. Thanks for being a fan and for wanting to soak in so many of these wonderful life lessons that Baseball has to offer.

ACKNOWLEDGEMENTS

This was a journey many decades in the making, and I have had countless family and friends to thank along the way for their support. First and foremost is the never-ending encouragement and inspiration from my wife Lisa and our blended grand slam of kids: Matthew, Benjamin, Joshua, and Rachel.

For a boy who at the age of two saw both his first Major League game and his first baseball news story involving a hit—the one that broke Jim Kaat's teeth, as the legendary pitcher recalls here—I must thank my mother for taking me on a train to Minnesota and setting me on course. Thanks also to her sister Sue and especially to my uncle Johnny Goryl, a Minnesota Twins infielder at the time and a lifetime baseball legend, for making that seat in the Twins player wives' section possible. Always call your Mom.

Thanks to Tom Doherty, head of Cardinal Publishers Group, who shared a vision for this project. I was extremely lucky to have an editor like Dani McCormick, who not only shared a love for the Indy 500 growing up but also made me focus on each sentence like it was a fastball coming at you. Props to the intern who titled this book.

My own history-making teammates at Major League Baseball Advanced Media have kept me inside the game and around legends for the better part of two decades, and a special thanks to Dinn Mann for having me on his team of journalists almost since the start of MLB.com.

Thanks to Brooks Robinson for so many great memories when I listened to baseball on a transistor radio, and then for all he did to make the world a better place after retiring. He eagerly gave me the first hit for this book and I appreciate him handling the foreword like as if it were just another routine 5-3 assist.

Two key players to thank are Mike Tackett and Maury Gostfrand, longtime friends and respected leaders in their fields. Mike, my first Indiana University newspaper sports editor whose book *The Baseball Whisperer* is a must-read, suggested that I take all the lessons within these stories and make them the connective tissue of the book. Maury got me over the hump in finding just the right publisher.

Thanks to B.B. Abbott, Shana Wilson, Nikki Warner, Max Carter, Jen Masuda, Sabrina Strauss, Marisa Wayne, and the Baseball Hall of Fame library staff. To Dusty Baker, for all those times chatting by the

Giants' cage to teach me baseball and for his thrilling story here. To Rob Engelbrecht, my Rural Junior League coach in Evansville, for his mimeographed sheets teaching us where to throw the ball in certain situations, and for driving us in his VW hippie van to Cincinnati to see the Big Red Machine.

Thanks to John Rawlings, who hired me not once, not twice, but three times in my career—something like an immaculate inning. Also to Dick Zitzmann, who sat with J.R. and me for those two priceless hours with Stan Musial and Tony Gwynn for our roundtable discussion that led to the popular "Man to Man" cover story in *The Sporting News* and material for this book.

My father took me to Evansville Triplets games at Bosse Field, coached my first youth team, and encouraged me to make a difference. My grandmother took me to the library regularly as a boy, and my discovery of Matt Christopher books made a foundation for this.

I appreciate the contributions of those who were happy to answer in proxy for those who sadly could not: Vera Clemente, Bob Costas, James Caan and Chris Gwynn. Thanks to guest appearances by Juan Marichal, Bo Jackson, Tom Brokaw, Joe Piscopo, Arsenio Hall, and Bud Selig.

This is a book of numbers as well as the lore and lessons, and amongst that multitude of arcane statistics, any mistakes are mine. Thanks to my byline readers over 40 years, and for the hits that keep coming every day and night.

Diamonds from the Dugout

115 Baseball Legends Remember
Their Greatest Hits

INTRODUCTION

This journey began at the age of two, when I was sitting with Harmon Killebrew's kids in the Minnesota Twins players' wives' section and a smash off a Detroit bat knocked out pitcher Jim Kaat's teeth while my own were still erupting. I did not notice it at the time, of course, and, to be honest, I never even knew the details of that first Major League game until midlife, when I began working on this book and my mother explained it in detail. She described the sound of that horrifying moment of a Minnesota summer and how Kitty Kaat's wife was hysterical beside all of us, including my cousins and aunt, who was married at the time to Johnny Goryl, an infielder on the 1962 Twins (and later their manager). You see, baseball hits are like heartbeats, sometimes passing without real fanfare and sometimes very closely monitored and even celebrated.

Hits and heartbeats accumulated. The teenage years, barreling baseballs into cornfields of Southern Indiana, and traveling in a coach's hippie van with friends to Cincinnati to watch Pete Rose, Johnny Bench, Joe Morgan, and Tony Perez hit everything; they later told me all about their favorite hits in this book. As a sportswriter, I was watching Joe Carter's famous homer land right in front of me, there for a Junior Griffey milestone, there for Cal Ripken's 2,131st consecutive game, there for 20-plus World Series and the end of the most fabled curses, there to weigh hits on Hall of Fame ballots, there for historic performances and ordinary scratch singles on a slow summer day. As a father, I was telling my son to wait here in our seats behind the Cardinals dugout while I go stake out the left-field seats in hopes of catching Big Mac's 62nd home run in 1998, there to teach three boys how to see it and hit it. These things have gone on my whole life—these hits, these heartbeats—so at last it was time to find the true meaning in them, in life.

This book is the result of that journey and the answer to a nine-word question that began innocently enough. Nearly a decade ago, I asked the great Brooks Robinson: "What hit meant the most to you and why?" Anyone who knows Brooksie will recognize his manner of reply: nice, thoughtful and humble—the sort of ballplayer fans have idolized the most over generations. He proceeded to tell me about a lesson in humility that he had experienced as a prized rookie out of Arkansas; the one hit that meant the most to him out of nearly 3,000 overall hits in his career was the one that made him see inside and become a model of consistency. His answer made me want to ask another legend the same thing, and eventually after asking this question for years, more than 100 of our favorite legends, including more than 40 Hall of Famers, had contributed to a completely different kind of pursuit of a hit, the hardest thing to do in sports.

Combine these answers with a lifetime spent around baseball immortals, and you have what I hope is not only a book filled with surprising and cherished baseball stories, but also a motivational work filled with lessons for success that can help anyone seeking higher achievement in life. It is organized through stories shared by Derek Jeter, Stan Musial, Ken Griffey Jr., Pete Rose, Carl Yastrzemski, Rickey Henderson, Mark McGwire and more than 100 legends. You will even find the occasional pitcher like Jim Palmer, Ferguson Jenkins, and Jim Kaat himself, who told me more about that fateful day in 1962 and about a big hit *he* had shortly after that. Abraham Lincoln had a story to share with a bat in his hand, whether apocryphal or not, and it just reminds us how long this has gone on. Hits and heartbeats accumulate.

Their impassioned—and often surprising—responses are wide-ranging teachable moments that have been sorted and grouped into chapters by motivational techniques. Their lessons are the connective tissue of this book. The extraction, sorting, and naming process for those lessons was the biggest challenge in putting this together. The actual gathering of stories was comparatively easy and a labor of love. For me, it was more like a hobby, like collecting baseball cards when I was younger. I was collecting stories, and I am simply displaying my cool collection here.

All of us want to be inspired in some way, and because I run marathons in my spare time, my own reading interests gravitate toward biographies, motivational tomes, and quotable classics—anything to push myself. Ask the right questions in life and you may be surprised where the answers take you in your journey. It became clear early on in this process that there would be plenty of surprises among the respondents. Carlton Fisk, Mike Piazza, Joe Carter, Luis Gonzalez, Aaron Boone and McGwire are all known for iconic hits . . . but when asked to choose one hit that mattered most to them, their answers were unexpected and useful tools for learning. Don't go with the flow.

Darryl Strawberry was at Spring Training as a wiry Mets phenom learning how to carry himself when I first interviewed him for *The Miami Herald* in the 1980s, and he was talking about the secret to being prepared when I interviewed him again as a legend looking back on it all. His hit came against the Cardinals. Brock was representing the same team one day in 1964 when he delivered a hit that he now associates with atonement. Dodgers great Maury Wills revealed for the first time that he felt "blackballed" by fellow National League players who voted for All-Stars, and "retribution" was the motivation behind his most important hit.

I have tried to take every possible opportunity to ask this important question in my spare time, because I found that the more I asked it, the more it became clear that what matters most is why that particular work of art was more meaningful than any other to the master who created it. This was way beyond sports. For a corollary, just consider the many modern experts who are so quick to tell you which Van Gogh painting was his greatest, which Ella Fitzgerald song was her best, and which of Michelangelo's creations mattered the most. I can guarantee that you would be surprised by the response if you could go back in time and ask masters such as those which work actually was the finest in that person's own estimation. During a tour of the Sistine Chapel while in Rome for the 2016 marathon, I discovered, much to my surprise, that Michelangelo, who considered himself more of a sculptor than a painter, had taken on the four-year ceiling project with reluctance, as the will of Pope Julius II was too strong. "The School of Athens" is my favorite fresco in the Sistine Chapel, painted by his rival Raphael, depicting Michelangelo begrudgingly signing His Holiness's contract for the commission, and with Raphael's own likeness inserted to the far right. What it shows: You may not love your "greatest work" over others. There were only a handful of obvious hits in the responses to my question—from the Ozzie Smith to Bucky Dent to Chris Chambliss to Edgar Martinez—yet in each case there is a lesson to learn if you want to be your best in any endeavor worth pursuing.

During a conversation with Luis Gonzalez, I told him that he had followed a trend started by Fisk in this project. The Hall of Fame catcher was not going to give me the 1975 World Series Game Six homer that so many others remember for him waving it fair. This was going to be a book filled with surprises, and instructive ones at that.

"Yeah, it's just one of those things. It's an exciting time for players to be able to find what's in themselves," Gonzalez said. "I'm curious to see how the book comes out, to see all the different hits people chose."

1

FOCUS ON WHAT YOU WANT

Visualization, patience, anticipation, and readiness are essential ingredients for a definitive hit. Edgar Martinez and Derek Jeter saw what they wanted and made it happen. For Roberto Clemente, it was a way of life; he was utterly certain that he would die young and had to get his 3,000th hit as soon as possible. For Orlando Cepeda, it meant waiting out the great Don Drysdale, knowing there might be a lesser reliever to face later in a historic big-league debut. Johnny Bench predicted a crucial home run for the Big Red Machine, and Tim McCarver believed a pitcher would throw the same pitch twice in a row in a key World Series moment. Roy White knew for the first time in his career that he would hit a home run his next time up, so he started planning for it. Will Clark, who once gave me a tongue-lashing for not thinking before asking a question, also encountered someone's wrath as he began to think ahead.

EDGAR MARTINEZ

Edgar Martinez squeezed the tarred bat handle tightly in his hands, saw what he wanted to do, hoisted and twirled the Louisville Slugger high in his batting stance, and then slashed at an 0-1 pitch. The ball rocketed into the left-field corner and all of Seattle except Mount Rainier erupted. Ken Griffey Jr. came around from first to score the winning run, and as he popped up from his slide, Alex Rodriguez, a 19-year-old substitute shortstop who had been on deck after pinch-running in the eighth inning for Tino Martinez, jumped into his arms and started the dogpile celebration. Don Mattingly walked off the field for the final time as a player and slowly collected his equipment from the dugout racks with Bernie Williams right behind him. On one end of the New York Yankees' bench sat Wade Boggs, then a 14th-year veteran, removed for a pinch-hitter late in the game and wondering if he ever would win it all. On the other end sat Derek Jeter, too young to be on the postseason roster but brought along to learn, and he took in the celebration scene and looked at teammates' reactions as if he knew that day would come for him and Boggs just one year later. Between them, a young catcher named Jorge Posada watched the Mariners celebrate as well, wanting it.

Those nine legends were all caught in a frozen moment of Major League Baseball history that became forever known as "The Double" in the Northwest, clinching Game Five in the 11th inning of a thrilling 1995 American League (AL) Division Series at the Kingdome, and they just happened to be among the more than 100 greats who would become part of this journey over a decade to discover the secret lessons of what hit matters the most and why. Martinez joined the list in early 2017, just a couple of months after he took another big step forward in the annual Hall of Fame balloting, earning votes like mine for the first time amid the changing perception created by advanced statistics. There is a Cooperstown speech in his future, and it will include The Double he hit off Jack McDowell. "My double in the last game of the series against the Yankees in 1995 meant the most to me because we were able to advance in the playoffs," Edgar said. "I believe our success that year led to us being able to keep the team in Seattle. There had been talk of the Mariners moving to Tampa, but after that postseason, we were here to stay . . . and I can still call Seattle home."

Edgar provided one of the most valuable lessons of any respondent in this book. His two-run double in the bottom of the 11th finished a series that was filled with dramatic performances. The fans at the old Kingdome held up "Refuse to Lose" signs that night, and nearly four out of every five fans in western Washington were tuned into the big game. Dave Niehaus, the Mariners' late Hall of Fame broadcaster, described his call of that game as his own "seminal moment." It went like this:

"The stretch and the 0–1 pitch on the way to Edgar Martinez. Swung on and lined down the left field line for a base hit! Here comes Joey! Here is Junior to third base—they're gonna wave him in! The throw to the plate will be late . . . the Mariners are going to play for the American League championship! I don't believe it! It just continues! My oh my! Edgar Martinez with a double, ripped down the left field line, and they are going crazy at the Kingdome!"

It is such a contrast of styles, those seminal moments. On the one hand, you had a beloved broadcaster defining himself in the most boisterous and excitable way imaginable. And on the other hand, you had a beloved All-Star seeming so calm, so composed, so unnerved by the enormity of the moment. I told Edgar that I had watched that at-bat so many times and always wondered what he was thinking as he squeezed that bat handle and looked out at the world, so relaxed.

"I struck out the previous at bat against McDowell with a spit finger, and I was confident he would go with that pitch again," he said. "I had learned a few years earlier that by focusing on what you want and not on what you want to avoid, you gain the focus and confidence to succeed."

Although the Mariners were eliminated by Cleveland in the next round, the excitement over the Mariners and The Double prompted Washington's state legislature to approve a deal for a retractable roof facility for the '99 season, and that would become Safeco Field.

Edgar's focus on what he wanted and not what he wanted to avoid will be words to remember for anyone seeking success in business and life. And so will that laser-focused vision of the rookie shortstop who watched it all from the Yankees' bench that night. . . .

DEREK JETER

Courtesy of Sarah Fryefield

Derek Jeter's 3,000th hit meant a lot to him,
but the most meaningful hit is the next one you're going to get

My own favorite Derek Jeter hit was the one in Game Four of the 2001 World Series, in that electric setting of Yankee Stadium in the nervous days post-9/11. A city needed him that night in many ways. Game Four started on Halloween, and it lasted into the 10th inning. At midnight, the scoreboard in center field read: "Attention Fans, Welcome to NOVEMBER BASEBALL." It was the first time that any non-exhibition baseball game had been played in the month of November (I would work the next such example at Philadelphia in 2009), and moments after fans saw that message, Jeter went to the opposite field with a 3–2 pitch from Arizona closer Byung-Hyun Kim for the walk-off homer that tied the series at 2–2. A fan in the stands held up a sign with the words "Mr. November." Broadcaster Michael Kay picked up on it and called Jeter by this name, referencing the sign, and the rest was history. Most Yankees fans you talk to would put that moment near the top of their list of favorite Jeter hits, along with his 3,000th and the walk-off hit in his final at-bat at Yankee Stadium.

But I thought it best to ask him what he considered his most memorable hit.

The day before the Yankees won the 2009 American League (AL) pennant, they had just arrived in New York after a long cross-country flight from Los Angeles, where they had played the Angels in Game Five of the AL Championship Series. Jeter was putting on that grey sweatshirt with the sleeves cut off and heading out to batting practice, and I asked him what hit was most special to him.

Jeter responded with all the reaction time of a swing at a Major League fastball—faster than anyone I asked.

"The next one you're gonna get."

Not exactly what I was hoping for, but that was pretty sweet. In fact, even his father was impressed by it. I relayed that answer to Charles Jeter when we were all together just days later for the presentation of the Roberto Clemente Award. Charles was understandably proud of his son as he looked on, sitting with wife Dorothy and daughter Sharlee in the front row, at a pinnacle moment in Derek's professional life.

"He said that? Ha—that sound like him," Charles said. "That's a good one. I'll have to use that one sometime."

Ever faithful to the case, I had not stopped at that, though. After all, you really do want to know what one hit Derek Jeter remembers most in his career, right? I stood there at his locker wondering which direction he was going to go.

"First hit's probably the one that stands out the most," he finally said. "Anytime you get your first anything, it's better. Relief. I went 0 for 5 my first game. So I think anytime you get the first. You at least got *something* to show for it."

That happened on May 30, 1995. Jeter was batting ninth, and he struck out with two men on his first time up to make it 0-for-6 in the outset. Leading off the fifth and facing starter Tim Belcher again, Jeter drilled a single through the left side of the infield, and he soon scored his first Major

League run on a Jim Leyritz hit. Not content with that, Jeter again led off the seventh, and again he singled, this time up the middle, and again he scored, this time courtesy of Paul O'Neill. The Yankees lost, but Jeter was off and running, and from that point forward, it was about the next hit you're gonna get.

Before he walked through the clubhouse tunnel out to the batting cages for the 170th regular batting practice session (excluding All-Star Game) of that season, I asked him how much he loves hitting. It's what he had mostly done in his life.

"You love hitting when you feel good at the plate," he said, living in his moment. "It's a challenge. You don't love it all the time."

The Yankees retired Jeter's number on Mother's Day 2017. He held a news conference after the ceremony, and for the final question, a reporter mentioned that fans had been talking about their favorite Jeter memories on and off the field. "Do you have a favorite?" he was asked. It was not a question about one hit, but it was close, because no one will ever forget his final hit at Yankee Stadium. He stepped to the plate with the score tied at 5-5 in the bottom of the ninth that night, and said goodbye with a clean walk-off single.

"It's tough, because it's a little unfair," Jeter replied to that question, thinking of that last home game as a whole event rather than as a game-winning hit. "It's the freshest memory I have, because it's the last game I played here at Yankee Stadium. Which is ironic, because it's the only game I've played here that didn't mean anything. But the way that the fans reacted and the relationship that I've had with them for twenty years, it felt as though it was a playoff-type atmosphere. I feel selfish saying that, because we were eliminated, but that was a special moment for me, and I'll never forget that last game."

That could mean he holds his final hit most dear. There would be so many other choices, including a homer for number 3,000 or some postseason magic, to talk about in his golden years. But again, the protocol here is to ask just once. Trying to keep up with further milestones and pose the question again would be unfair. I am pretty sure Jeter would tell you it is "your next one" anyway.

ROBERTO CLEMENTE

I got to know Vera Clemente well from being with her for each annual presentation of the Roberto Clemente Award, baseball's ultimate honor recognizing community leadership. She carries on his legacy faithfully, much like Rachel Robinson has done for Jackie, always giving of her time and spreading his sense of purpose. Vera is a beautiful person and just being around her makes you feel good inside and want to go out and get more involved in helping others.

On the morning of Game Two at the 2011 World Series, we were at the Loyola Academy, a St. Louis school for youths, four out of five coming from homes under the poverty line. They had read up on Roberto, an assignment for kids wherever Vera goes. She spoke to them with Hall of Famer Lou Brock. Then Vera and Lou were transported over to the St. Louis Children's Hospital, where they participated in the dedication of a Starlight Fun Center mobile video gaming unit.

After that event, I spent some time with Vera and I told her that if Roberto were alive today, I would ask him what hit had meant the most to him. "You mean of his whole life?" she asked. "I know that the 3,000th was important for him. The last one. Finishing with an even 3,000 was important for him."

Why was it important?

"He was saying that he felt he was going to die young, always," she said. "He would die young. Since he was young, he would say that—that he was going to die young. Then in 1972, since he was very close to that mark, he said, 'If I don't do it this year, I will do it never.' He was thinking something would happen to him. 'If I don't do it this year, I know I won't get to 3,000,' he said. He always was thinking ahead, always ahead of time. He had an idea that something would happen."

Vera reflected back to when the Pirates "were in Philadelphia, and for him to have the hit in Pittsburgh, they put him on the bench." Indeed, Clemente went 1-for-2 in that final road game at the Phillies on September 28, and it was the top of the sixth, with future Hall of Famer Steve Carlton protecting a 2–1 lead at home. Clemente had led off the fourth with a single in his last time up, but as Vera recalled, her husband was removed for pinch-hitter Bob Robertson, who proceeded to strike out. It would be win number 26 of 27 on the season for Carlton, who was in his first year with Philadelphia after a big trade from St. Louis, and he would win the National League's Cy Young Award.

Maybe Clemente would have delivered number 3,000 in that game and cost Carlton one of those wins. It was not going to happen, though, because they wanted Clemente to get the milestone back home. He wanted it as fast as possible, before he died, according to Vera.

The rest of the story is common baseball knowledge.

Clemente went 0-for-4 against Tom Seaver in the homestand opener against the Mets on September 29, and then the next day was in the lineup on a misty and overcast day at Three Rivers Stadium in Pittsburgh. There were only 13,117 fans on hand to see something truly special, but it was the tail end of a season that was not playoff-bound, college football was on TV in a football town, and money was tight all around. Clemente, after striking out in his first time up against Jon Matlack, reached out from his customary stance far away from the plate and hammered an outside curve against the left-field wall.

It was the 3,000th hit of his career, and it would be his last.

Here is how broadcaster Felo Ramirez made the call for an island hero's native audience:

"A double for Roberto Clemente against the wall! No-no-no! No-no-no! A double for Roberto Clemente! Completely clean double against the wall. On the pitch from Jon Matlack. Ladies and gentlemen, the fans are going crazy here in Three Rivers Stadium! Everyone is on their feet. Great emotion. They are giving Roberto Clemente the ball. He takes off his hat. He greets the public and receives the congratulations of the shortstop, Jim Fregosi. By his action, the shortstop is greeting him as the best. The fans are on their feet. The enthusiasm is huge here in Three Rivers. We are seeing a historic event, a historic event in baseball."

After that half inning, Clemente walked regally back to his position in right field, which he owned. He was showered by applause and confetti from the fans. Number 21 tipped his cap to acknowledge them, and *Clemente* author David Maraniss would note that "over time it would seem that his gesture had a deeper meaning, that he was saying farewell. Indeed, number 3,000 was the final hit for Clemente. The prophecy that he had consistently conveyed to Vera came true. He died on that subsequent New Year's Eve when the ill-equipped plane carrying himself and relief supplies to Nicaragua crashed in the Atlantic Ocean. The Baseball Writers' Association of America (BBWAA) cast aside the usual five-year wait period and immediately voted Clemente into the Hall of Fame. Clemente would go on to symbolize goodness and grace, the namesake of the annual award (one I write about every year) given to a Major Leaguer who personifies not only excellence on the field but especially off the field. Vera and their children carry on his mission, building the Roberto Clemente Sports City in Puerto Rico per his dream, and whenever she speaks to children she tells the story of how her husband died and what he had meant. Until asking her, I did not know exactly what 3,000 had meant to him.

ORLANDO CEPEDA

Baseball Digest, front cover (April 1962)

Hall of Famer Orlando Cepeda cites his first hit as his most meaningful

It was Opening Day, April 15, 1958, Seals Stadium in San Francisco, and it was a time unlike any other in Major League Baseball history. Two longtime rivals, the Brooklyn Dodgers and New York Giants, were now officially the Los Angeles Dodgers and San Francisco Giants. The Show was on the West Coast for the first time, and it just happened to be Orlando Cepeda's debut.

It would have been a memory of a lifetime for anyone, participating in that historic first game before 23,448 fans at the Giants' new temporary home against their rivals. On the mound for the Dodgers was a blossoming star, Don Drysdale, one of many future Hall of Famers in the ballpark, including the rookie he was facing. Cepeda, a brute force from Puerto Rico starting at first base, grounded out to third in his debut in the second inning. In the bottom of the fourth, Cepeda flied to left.

Fortunately for the rookie, Drysdale was getting roughed up elsewhere. He was chased later that inning with the Giants ahead, 4–0, and charged with his fifth and sixth runs when Willie Mays singled to the right side. Then with one out in the fifth, Drysdale was out of the picture and Cepeda achieved a lasting moment against the pitcher who replaced him that game.

"My first big-league hit, Opening Day, I hit a home run off Don Bessent," Cepeda said in 2011. "My first big-league hit? Incredible. I'll never forget that. I'll never forget that game. It was my biggest thrill, my first game in the big leagues."

Another thing that made it so memorable: Cepeda was 1-for-17 at the start of his career. If not for that homer in the debut, it might have all seemed over his head. After his first four games of scuffling, he registered three three-hit games over his next four. It was the start of a fruitful career that would include World Series appearances with the 1962 Giants and the 1967–68 Cardinals ("El Birdos"), and it would lead me to drive with him one day in early 1994 to his Buddhist temple in San Francisco.

At that time, I was writing a story for *The Sporting News* about a player's 15th and final hope on the BBWAA Hall of Fame ballot. I was not yet a voter, but I was unquestionably campaigning for him, believing his career had been worthy, that he had paid enough for a drug-possession charge from earlier in life. He was a changed man. He took me to his Buddhist temple, where he had recently learned chanting and inner peace.

"I'm normally very calm," he said while driving around San Francisco then. "I've been through a lot in my life. This is just bugging me. It's hard. Real hard. It's in my mind. In the beginning I said, 'I can deal with that,' but it's in my mind. I'm a human being. It's like when I used to play for the Giants, and I'd wake up the day of a game and say, 'Gibson's pitching tonight. I got to hit tonight.' It's right here," he said, pointing to his forehead. "Right now, everything around me is Hall of Fame, Hall of Fame, Hall of Fame."

Cepeda did not receive the required 75 percent of ballots in that 15th try. But five years later, the Veterans Committee righted a wrong, and the Baby Bull was inducted in the Class of 1999; not just any class, but one of the two or three greatest classes ever, also featuring former players Nolan Ryan, George Brett, Robin Yount, Smokey Joe Williams, umpire Nestor Chylak, and manager Frank Selee.

JOHNNY BENCH

"Probably in Cincinnati Reds history, it was the home run in the playoffs in '72 against the Pirates that tied the game in the ninth, and we went on to win the playoffs in that inning and got into the World Series. For Cincinnati Reds fans, that was voted the number one, so I'd have to say that was pretty special."

Arguably the greatest all-around catcher ever, Bench played his entire 17-year Major League career with Cincinnati. I sat with him in Manhattan on a Saturday morning during the 2012 season, talking baseball as he was in town to deliver a message about skin cancer on behalf of MLB. I told him that my first Major League game as a fan—that I can *remember* (technically my first game attended was at age two while sitting with Twins players' wives during the 1962 game at Minnesota where Jim Kaat's teeth were knocked out)—had been as a 13-year-old boy at Riverfront, having made the trip there from Southern Indiana along with my baseball team. I remembered that day, and when I asked him what he remembered about any one single hit, that blow about 40 years earlier—October 11, 1972—was the one that came to mind.

"Dave Giusti was pitching for the Pirates. Nobody hit Dave Giusti. He was an automatic save," Bench said, referring to the right-hander who had just come on for the ninth for the reigning world champs to close out a clincher. There were 41,887 fans there that day at Riverfront. Giusti was all set to face the 4-5-6 meat of Sparky Anderson's Reds lineup, and Bench was leading off.

"I told somebody in the third inning that I was going to hit a home run to make a difference," Bench recalled. "I led off the ninth inning, so I pulled one foul on the first or second pitch, I pulled it foul and it would have been out of the ballpark. I just pulled it a little bit down the line. Then came Al Michaels's great call: '. . . change hit into the air to right field, back goes Clemente to the wall, she's gone.' Every time they play that, it sends chills when I hear it. There's still an echo that was in Riverfront Stadium for a long time from the fans, they made it extra-special."

Michaels, the legendary broadcaster, started his career announcing Reds games from 1971–73, and that call is most definitely remembered around Cincinnati. It went:

"The pitch to Bench . . . change hit into the air to deep right field … back goes Clemente . . . at the fence . . . It's gone! Johnny Bench, who hits almost every home run to left field, hit this one to right and the score is tied!"

The Reds proceeded to win that game when pinch-runner Hal McRae scored on a Bob Moose wild pitch. They would go on to lose the World Series for the second time in three years, the first of Oakland's three consecutive Fall Classic victims from 1972–74, but Bench and the Big Red Machine would solidify their greatness by repeating as world champions in 1975–76. He was Most Valuable Player (MVP) of that '76 sweep of the Yankees, and while there would be enough hits to recall in that one, it was that at-bat against Giusti that still does it for him to this day.

TIM MCCARVER

Long before he became known to generations of baseball fans as the Hall of Fame voice of Major League Baseball's jewel events, Tim McCarver played in three World Series for the Cardinals—1964, 1967, and 1968. To a 22-year-old catcher, nothing could match the thrill of hitting a three-run home run off Yankees reliever Pete Mikkelsen in the 10th inning to help ace Bob Gibson preserve a complete game in Game Five of the '64 Fall Classic, a seven-game triumph. Here is what he had to say about the hit that mattered most to him:

"I remember missing a 3–1 pitch, I hit hard down the first base line, and I thought to myself just very briefly: 'I won't get that pitch again.' Then when I stepped in the box, I said, 'Yes I will, he's gotta throw that pitch.' And I hit a home run. But initially I thought I wouldn't get another, because I hit a low scorcher down the first-base line, and I thought initially I wouldn't get that pitch again, and my mind said, 'Yes, I will.' It's the truth."

ROY WHITE

"If there was one hit that was really extra-special, outside of my first Major League hit, it was a big game against the Red Sox in '77. I think it was the middle of June. . . ."

Roy White was back in the Bronx Zoo, in his mind. He was right in the middle of the zany atmosphere around the Yankees back then, and even if he sometimes wanted out, this hit shows why he never can truly leave it.

On June 17, White and the Yankees began a three-game weekend series at Boston, and they went there with a half-game lead over the Red Sox atop the AL East. Boston quickly captured that lead by opening the series with a 9–4 victory on that Friday night, crushing six home runs. The next day, the teams were in the spotlight for the "Game of the Week" national telecast, and the Red Sox came out slugging again, with Carl Yastrzemski hitting his third homer in two days.

In the top of the sixth inning, New York trailed, 7–3, and a national TV audience was seeing the very best of Boston. Billy Martin, the Yankees' manager, was uneasy with that. With one out, Reggie Jackson singled and then moved to third on a single by Graig Nettles. White doubled to left, scoring Jackson to cut the lead to 7–4, chasing starter Reggie Cleveland. Red Sox reliever Bill Campbell got out of the inning without further damage.

As it turned out, White would be one of *two* people who sent Jackson to the dugout in that sixth inning. In the bottom half, White was playing left field. At the other corner of the outfield was Jackson. With one out and Fred Lynn on first, young All-Star slugger Jim Rice stepped up and hit a pop fly. The ball dropped in, and Jackson trotted over to pick it up and casually threw it into second, turning a Rice single into a Rice double.

"Reggie hates to be embarrassed, especially in front of 50 million people," Sparky Lyle wrote in his subsequent book *The Bronx Zoo*. Lyle came out of the bullpen after that play, and he was not the only replacement. Martin also had Paul Blair go out to right field to replace Reggie. What happened next was baseball lore: a Billy-Reggie feud in the dugout, a war of words, a tabloid editor's dream. The Yankees lost that game, and then lost the Sunday finale as well when Boston hit yet another five homers, making it an unreal 16 bombs in the series. The Yankees' half-game lead had turned into a 2 1/2-game deficit.

This brings us back to Roy White, a veteran who was scrapping more than he'd like for playing time in 1977. The following weekend, the Red Sox and Yankees were at it again in another weekend series, only this time at Yankee Stadium. When that Friday night arrived, Boston's division lead was up to five games. New York had been swept by Johnny Bench and the Reds in the 1976 World Series, and now there was a real question whether they would even be in the running for another pennant.

"They had a five-game lead, and it was the first game of the series, and we were losing in the bottom of the ninth, 5–3," White remembered as we spoke before the Thurman Munson Awards Dinner in 2017, near the 40th anniversary. "Two outs, Willie Randolph gets a triple. Bill Campbell, their closer, was in. I was the next hitter, and I hit the first pitch out to tie the game. It was in Yankee Stadium and the crowd went nuts.

"We won the game in extra innings on a hit by Reggie. We swept them, and that started the momentum for us. Because if they would have won that game, we were going to be six behind, and things would have looked pretty bad for us. So we swept them in three games, they left with a two-game lead, and we ended up passing them and going on to win the pennant."

White won rings on those 1977–78 Yankees, playing a key role at the plate in the latter championship by going 8-for-24 with nine runs against the Dodgers for the repeat. He spent all 15 of his Major League years with the Yankees, finishing with 1,803 hits, as well as a few hundred more in Japan. I asked him what was going through his mind on that Friday night in the Bronx, with 54,940 fans on hand for an evolving rivalry.

"The funny thing—which was odd—it was one of the only times I felt like I was going to hit a home run," White said. "The prior time up, I had just missed one, but I had a really great swing, and I felt my timing was really at the point I wanted it to be. I said, 'Jeez, if I could just have one more time at bat, I think I could pop one.' All of a sudden, here I am with that one more time at bat. And it happened. Campbell had a great screwball type of pitch, forkball or something, deadly to left-handers. This one didn't really break sharply, kind of hung a little bit, and there it went."

There went the Yankees right along with it, on the way to two consecutive World Series championships. White focused on what he wanted, and so did a Yankees team that was so good at making headlines. He and his teammates overcame so much, including themselves.

"You're never out of the game, really," White said.

WILL CLARK

I have tried to ask good questions over a long sportswriting career, but like the athletes themselves, I have had better days than others. I realized that early on. While I was covering the Hoosiers basketball team for the *Indiana Daily Student* as a senior at Indiana University, Bobby Knight was talking fishing, one of his favorite subjects, at his usual postgame press conference inside Assembly Hall. He even made a casting motion. I, a free-spirited college student thinking the game story in my head and apparently having decided to steel myself against his famously hardened and abusive exterior, and well aware of his adversarial relationship with media ("Most of us learn to write in second grade and then move on to better things," he once said), for some reason decided to make a stand from a few rows back. Was I being brave or stupid? My grandmother had always told me about classrooms, "Don't be afraid to raise your hand."

"I appreciate your fishing advice, but can I ask a basketball question?" I asked.

"You mean you don't like to hear my fishing stories?" he replied.

Now I had the eyes of the veteran press corps on me, and I was abandoned.

"Some of us have deadlines," I said.

It was a Saturday afternoon, and the Indiana Daily Student's next edition was on Monday morning. I was digging deeper. At that moment, I was an intramural team playing his Hoosiers, who would win the NCAA championship that season. I couldn't tell you whatever happened after that, because I was busy repairing to my world as a college student, but I vaguely remember an *Indianapolis Star* writer saved me by changing the subject and asking about a key play, or maybe a fishing follow up.

I mention this story because the second-worst question I ever asked in my career was on August 15, 1990, in the visitor's clubhouse at Veterans Stadium in Philadelphia. I was the San Francisco Giants beat writer for the *San Jose Mercury News* my first year in the Baseball Writers' Association of America, and the team I was covering had just been no-hit by Terry Mulholland. Will Clark, who had just recently made his third of six All-Star appearances, had just gone 0-for-3, and it was not just the fact he made three outs, but that they were last outs of innings. He struck out looking to end the first, grounded out to end the fourth, and grounded out to end the seventh.

Sometimes when you are covering a beat, you become so familiar with the subjects with whom you hang around daily that you risk failing to remember that these are highly tuned professional athletes, in his case a superstar, who do not always handle failure so well. I had kept score of the game as usual and had Clark's at-bats right in front of me as I entered the Giants' clubhouse, but I should have paid more attention to the circumstances of his own outs. Being no-hit is bad enough, and making the last out all three times as the best player on the defending National League (NL) champions, who have just lost their fourth consecutive game, is grounds for major grumpiness. He had put this on himself as a leader. In those circumstances, you had better bring your A question-game. I brought no such thing as I spoke to him as he dressed. I mangled it.

"Hey, Will, what are your thoughts about being no-hit by Mulholland?"

"How the fuck do you think it feels to be no-hit by Mulholland?"

The sound waves of his Southern drawl ripped through the air, pierced my skin, and tore right through my body as teammates at neighboring lockers quietly dressed and winced at the fool from the press-box hill. It was not so much the words themselves, but in the case of Will Clark, it was the delivery of them, not far from the Bobby Knight delivery. Clark was known also for "The Nuschler." His middle name was the nickname used by the press corps to describe his devastating scowl, which you hated to see as an opposing pitcher. I got The Nuschler look and the F-bomb. It was the only no-hitter I ever covered to date, and I quickly moved on to the next day's game.

Fortunately in baseball, the story often is never over, only the last out of an inning, so to speak. Fast forward to more than two decades, after the same Giants franchise had just taken a 2–0 lead in the 2012 World Series against Detroit. I had done my interviews. There, sitting closest to the Giants clubhouse's main doorway at AT&T Park, was one the club's legendary Special Assistants, Will "The Thrill" Clark. We did a little catching up and we shared a good laugh together when I reminded him of what I had asked him after Mulholland's gem. "Oh, yeah, you don't ever want to ask someone how it felt to just get no-hit," he said. I thanked him for helping me become a more thoughtful journalist.

Now it was time for a much easier question.

"For me, there are two hits," he said.

"My first at-bat in the big leagues was a home run off Nolan Ryan, so needless to say that's getting your career started off on the right foot. I shoulda quit while I was ahead. The second one for me would be the base hit up the middle off Mitch Williams in 1989 in the NLCS. Put us into the World Series. And as a kid when you grow up playing Wiffle ball in the backyard—bottom of the eighth, bottom of the ninth, two outs, bases loaded—you always play that game, and I had a chance to win it.

"One that's more special? Probably my first because it's Nolan. First at-bat in the big leagues and you're facing The Express. You're three pitches into your first at-bat in the big leagues, all of a sudden you're trotting around to home plate, and it's like, 'Whoa.'
"It was a 1–1 fastball away. I got him out to center field. You touch home plate, and you go, 'Oh my god, did that just happen?' It was pretty unbelievable."

That happened at the Astrodome on April 2, 1986. Clark even waved at his family in attendance, something Ryan no doubt noticed.

"How did he respond?" I asked. Notice that I did not ask Ryan how it had felt to give up a home run to Will Clark on the rookie's first at-bat.

"Well, after everything settled down, I was sitting on the bench, sitting next to Chili Davis," Clark replied. "I looked over at him. All of a sudden it just hit me. I said, 'He's gonna hit me next at-bat, isn't he?' [Davis] goes, 'Oh yeah.' So [Ryan] was in the middle of his windup the next at-bat, and I was already falling on the ground.

"You know what, he blew out his elbow in 1993, and I was a free agent, so I went over and started my career with the Rangers in '94. He signed a 10-year personal services contract, so he would come around the clubhouse and stuff like that, but he didn't talk to me. He talked to a lot of other people, but he didn't talk to me. That's understandable. He's old-school." Clark had been so focused on what he wanted that he never thought about a consequence. I learned a similar result and it taught me to ask a better question, like "What hit meant the most to you and why?"

BRAD HAWPE

During the 2007 World Series in Boston, I was roaming the Fenway Park crowd and interviewing people about the meaning of having a World Series ticket. I interviewed Richard Gere as he walked through the turnstiles with his young son. I interview fans and player family members. One of those happened to be Paula Hawpe, mother of right fielder Brad Hawpe of the Rockies.

"It's the neatest feeling," Paula said as her son was out on the field. "That's why I came over. We're here from Fort Worth. There was this one time when I went to Denver to see Brad play, and I saw all of these people wearing Hawpe shirts. It was Brad Hawpe Shirt Night. I told my husband, 'All of these people are wearing Hawpe shirts,' and he said, 'Why should that surprise you?'"

Now it was two seasons later, and I was standing across from Brad Hawpe as he sat at a table during the National League interviews a day before the 80th All-Star Game in St. Louis. I told him about having met his Mom and I said I had a question that only he could answer. His parents might have an opinion, but I wanted to know what hit had meant the most to *him* at that point in his career, when he was in the midst of his fourth consecutive season of at least 20 homers.

"The hit I always remember is the first one," he told me. "That's one I know I won't ever forget. My first big-league hit. I remember the feeling

I had at the plate, I remember exactly where I hit it, the pitch, everything about it. It's just something that I dreamed about as a kid, playing in the Major Leagues, and hitting there. So getting that opportunity and getting that hit was a dream come true."

"Can you tell me what that feeling was and were there any specifics about the hit?" I asked?

"It's funny, I had a lot of confidence in that at-bat," he replied, letting the feeling wash over him again. "I don't know why. Whenever I walked up to the plate, and stepped in the batter's box, I really believed and felt that I should be in the batter's box at that moment. I remember stepping out of the batter's box at one time during that at-bat, and thinking about that. I'm thinking: 'Well, I'm not that nervous right now. I should be, but I'm not. I can do it! I can get a hit right here.'

"I hit a base hit up the middle off of Kevin Gryboski, with the Atlanta Braves. We had a doubleheader that day. I pinch-hit that first at-bat and got a hit. The next game, I was fortunate enough to start. I went three for four that game with a triple and a homer. So I was four for five on the day, with a home run and some RBIs and a triple. I thought: 'Well, you know what? I'm ready to be in the Hall of Fame right now, if this keeps up.' Three weeks later, I was sent back down to Triple A. So that was a pretty humbling experience. I was down there trying to find my way back to the big leagues. This game will humble you immediately."

DARE TO BE DIFFERENT

Rarely did any of the legends I interviewed want to echo the general public's most commonly told stories about their times at bat. Mike Piazza did not put his fabled post-9/11 homer at the top. Probably no sports highlight ever was replayed more than Carlton Fisk waving his 1975 World Series Game Six homer fair at Fenway Park, but that was not the one that mattered to him most. Joe Carter's 1993 World Series-winning walk-off homer landed right in front of me in Toronto, and we even spent time together at his home in Kansas City just weeks later to talk about it for a cover story, yet it was not his choice here. Luis Gonzalez, Aaron Boone: the same thing. A pattern emerged during my journey over the years to delve into the minds of the legends we loved, and it became clear to me why they see their swings in a different light later than the rest of us. To them, the answer is personal. In fact, the very act of being different is what separated them from everyone else in the first place.

MIKE PIAZZA

On a cold Cooperstown morning in the winter of 2016, I walked through the Hall of Fame with Mike Piazza. I had voted for him in each of his four years on the ballot, and now his moment was arriving. This day was his orientation tour, something the Hall had been doing for electees ever since Steve Carlton was inducted in '94. Piazza marveled at such artifacts as the bat that his boyhood idol, Mike Schmidt, had used to pass Mickey Mantle on the all-time home run list—and the bat that he himself had swung to pass Carlton Fisk for most ever by a catcher.

It was Piazza's first visit to the Hall since he was a Dodgers rookie nearly a quarter-century earlier. By the time we were finished that day, the passage of time between visits seemed apropos for this book. I had been interviewing legends for nearly a decade during a journey to find the most important hits through the eyes of the men who hit them, and one constant was the fact that the most iconic hits of all typically are not the ones that those men will count as their most memorable.

Take Piazza, for example. He was about to go into the Hall as a New York Met, and most people will immediately recall the home run he hit for the Mets against Atlanta in Major League Baseball's first game after the 9/11 terrorist attacks. As you will see later, even Terry Cashman, singer of the famous "Talkin' Baseball" anthem, cites that as "the one." Instead, Piazza went back to the start of his career.

"The one, of course, for me was, because of my journey more or less, my first hit off Mike Harkey," he said. "Because it was all the trials and tribulations and struggles of getting there. It was ironic because my first big-league at-bat, I said to myself, 'I'm going to take at least one strike,' and I ended up walking. So it was really sabermetrics before sabermetrics. It actually started me on realizing the importance of the strike zone."

That happened on the first day of September in 1992. Piazza, who had been an unlikely 62nd-round Draft pick in 1988, had blazed through the Dodgers' farm system that summer, batting .350 with 23 homers and 90 runs batted in (RBIs) at the Double A and Triple A levels combined. As MLB rosters expanded, Piazza got the start behind the plate for Los Angeles at Wrigley Field, batting sixth in manager Tommy Lasorda's order. On that Tuesday, a Dodgers club going nowhere (54–78 through that day) won in 13 innings as Cubs reliever Heathcliff Slocumb walked Mike Sharperson with the bases loaded, and no one could have known at the time that the real story was what the rookie catcher had done.

In his first four MLB plate appearances, Piazza walked, singled, singled and singled. Had Eric Young not pinch-run for him in the eighth, Piazza would have batted at least another two, maybe three times. Piazza might have gone 5-for-5 with a walk in his first Major League game. As it was, it was a day worthy of inclusion here.

Top of the fourth, first pitch from Harkey: A double roped to the ivy-covered wall in right-center. Piazza had thoughts but pulled up at second to stay there.

"It was the funniest thing, because I had actually hit a ball off the wall," he said. "After I walked, then the next at-bat was the first pitch that I saw, and I hit it off the wall. I could have almost got a triple, which was kind of interesting. It would have been weird for my first big-league hit to be a triple. That one's big."

Piazza would go on to win the National League Rookie of the Year award the following season. He would finish with more home runs than any catcher, using his Mizuno lumber to pass Fisk with number 352 on May 5, 2004, and so the conversation surrounding his most memorable highlights always has centered on balls knocked over walls. But for the purposes of this book, Piazza focused on a ball that hit the wall rather than going over it.

His memory here will not be the same one that most people will summon, especially around New York, where he lifted spirits after 9/11 with the homer against Atlanta. But that is consistent with so many of the greats I interviewed for this book. What you recall is not necessarily what was most important to them.

"I think the 9/11 one is so hard for me to put into perspective, in a way," Piazza said. "I don't mean this in a disrespectful way, but it's just so tough for me to—what's the word I'm looking for? From an emotional standpoint, it was huge. The only reason I don't personally like to put it up at the top is because that whole week there were so many things that kind of transcend the game that I can't really embrace as overtly more significant than anything else that happened in that week. I mean, that night I was just happy that we got through the game emotionally, because that was the hardest part."

In fact, there is another home run in a game against Atlanta that at least gets an honorable mention in his recollections here. It was the last day of June in 2000, the year he led the Mets to the Subway Series against the Yankees. The Mets entered the bottom of the eighth behind, 8–1, and early that inning, Piazza singled and then was driven in as the Mets mounted a rally. As the club batted around, Piazza came up against with the score tied at 8–8, and proceeded to yank a three-run, line-drive homer over the wall inside the left-field foul pole, giving the Mets what would be an 11–8 victory.

Bobby Cox's Braves were still the NL powerhouse of the time, going to three of the prior five World Series, so it was a key summertime win that continued to boost New York's confidence. You could see that much in watching Piazza's demeanor as he rounded the bases—pumping his fist just before he reached first, giddy as he came home.

"The eighth inning, that three-run home run, that was the one really where I've always tried to be very austere and stoic when I hit home runs," Piazza said. "I didn't really like to celebrate them. I just thought that was the old-school mentality I had. That was the only time really that I had some emotion that I couldn't contain."

On this day, Piazza would love even more to talk about the work that his hero Michael Jack Schmidt had done. After his tour and his press conference were through, when the Hall was silent, I told Piazza what Schmidt's answer was for this book. As you can see in the following pages, it took a while for Schmidt to settle on a choice, his decisive homer that gave Philadelphia the pennant over the Expos in 1980, en route to the World Series title.

"In Montreal?" Piazza asked. Then with a smile that put him back in his boyhood, he added, "Yeah. I remember that one."

TERRY CASHMAN

Piazza's post-9/11 homer might not have topped his own list, but here's someone who puts it at number one. Terry Cashman wrote his hit song "Talkin' Baseball" in 20 minutes one January morning in 1981 on his Petillo guitar in New York City. He had grown up there watching local teams always in the World Series and grown men arguing on the street corner about baseball as they waited for the early editions of the *Mirror* and *News*. For the next three decades, through good times and bad within the sport and society, the charm of that song grew and even helped keep the memories alive. "They knew 'em all from Boston to Dubuque / Especially Willie, Mickey and the Duke."

I talked to Cashman a few days after a member of that Hall of Fame triumvirate, Duke Snider, died in February of 2011, and the first thing Cashman asked me was: "This is a book about hit songs?" I told him it was about the hits with a bat, but it occurred to me at that moment that I was writing about both.

"My brothers Tom and Jack were both older and they were great influences in my love of baseball because they were big Giants fans," said Cashman, who grew up in the Washington Heights area of Manhattan, close to the Polo Grounds. "My whole family liked the Giants, except for my rotten sister, who was a Dodgers fan. She was a rebel. But she had a crush on the Duke, so it was OK. My brothers took me to the games."

So the logical hit of a lifetime for Cashman, other than the one he strummed, was the Giants hit made by the immortal in his refrain.

"The one that jumps into my head: I was at the game where Willie Mays hit his first home run off Warren Spahn," he said. "Unless I'm kidding myself so many years ago. This was 1951. I was with my brothers. We were sitting in the upper deck behind third base. Mays had gone 0-for-12. He hadn't had a hit in his career. He hit the home run off Warren Spahn and he wound up saying throughout his whole career that he always hit Spahn very well. He always hit *left-handers* well. I was 10 at the time. I remember that Leo Durocher had to encourage him to keep at it, the hits would come."

We talked for a while, and after the conversation I got to thinking that I should have asked Cashman for one hit from Mays, one from Mickey Mantle, and one from Snider. But then the singer-songwriter called me back, making that thought a moot point. He wanted to change his hit after further reflection. That was OK because that was why I decided to write the book in the first place: self-rediscovery. Once you start reaching back and trying to chase those memories in search of that one true hit, you begin recreating some otherwise dormant moments that helped make you who you are.

"Absolutely the most memorable hit ever is Mike Piazza's home run after 9/11," Cashman said after that self-rediscovery. "I was moved so much by that home run and the reaction of the fans' seeming release of sadness and tension that was there that night, I wrote a song called 'The Tattered Flag In The Breeze,' which is one of my favorite songs. That hit is absolutely one of the most important things I remember in baseball."

Cashman is a New Yorker through and through, and on September 11, 2001, he lost some good friends in the World Trade Center. His friend Rusty Staub—whom he had written into "Talkin' Baseball" and who had put Snider on the phone in Montreal one day to say thanks for also writing him into the song—was living right across the street from Cashman. Staub had been in Battery Park during the terrorist attack and had to walk up to 38th and Third in Murray Hill to stay at the Balladeer of Baseball's place while unable to get into his own apartment.

"I was home watching the game like everybody else, thinking how important is baseball in the midst of this other stuff," Cashman said. "The game went on, and when Piazza hit that home run for the Mets, it seemed to lift everybody's spirits and send a message that there is nothing we can do about what happened, but we have to go on from here. Baseball is something very comforting in those moments. Those were a couple days in your life where you'll never forget where you were and what was happening."

RUSTY STAUB

"One hit. Everybody reflects back on their first Major League hit. Just one hit, I don't know if I can come up with one," Rusty Staub began. "I had a doubleheader against the Dodgers when I was with the Expos, and I hit four home runs. That was a pretty big day. Four for four in the World Series with five RBIs, that wasn't all bad. That's when I had that bum shoulder—I don't know how the ball went out of the ballpark. Lot of wind blowing. But . . . to isolate on one. By the grace of God, I can't do that. I can't give you one."

We were talking by the clubhouse at Sleepy Hollow Country Club in Westchester County in New York, at a charity golf event for Joe Torre's

Safe at Home Foundation. I told Staub that I've found when I ask greats about one hit, there are many teaching moments and I began to list some of them. As so often has happened, my words created space for a legend to dive into the memory center of his brain and extract exactly what he wants most to find. I never get to finish my sentence, because as I am speaking, the story of one hit just suddenly flows out:

"I can tell you one that meant as much to me as anything. Teddy Ballgame, they had a day for him at the Dome when I was with the Astros. And I was playing pretty good then. I was starting to become a good player, good hitter. He and I had a background together. He came to my home when I was a kid. We talked a million times in different Spring Trainings and stuff, and there's nothing he ever wrote that I didn't read, and he knew it.

"In this game against the Giants, my first time up, they threw me a fastball out over the plate and I singled to left. I came around and scored. Ted says, 'That was great hitting—you went right with that ball. Now, you know they're not gonna give you that pitch again.' I said to him, 'Actually, Ted, they're going to do the same thing. They're going to pitch me hard away the whole time.'"

Dare to be different.

"The next time up, I hit a double to left-center on a fastball outside," Staub continued. "I didn't score that time, but I came in after the next inning. He had stayed and waited. And he walked up to me and he said, 'You're gonna be OK, kid.'

"I was as proud of that statement as anything I ever had. 'You're gonna be OK, kid.'" Staub was a six-time All-Star whose outstanding 23-year career began with Houston, from 1963–68. I checked his game logs, looking for any multi-hit games at home against San Francisco, and there was one on May 18, 1967, when Staub was 3-for-3 with a run scored in a 6–2 victory. Another search resulted in an article that said Ted "Teddy Ballgame" Williams was making his first appearance in the Astrodome on May 18, 1967—not as a player, but to present awards at a "Kid Benefit Night" program. So without question, that was the game to which Staub was referring. The books showed that Staub singled to center in the fourth inning off future Hall of Fame right-hander Gaylord Perry (who also turns up in Felix Millan's hit in this book), but without scoring a run. The following inning, Staub singled again (not a double) to center, driving in Sonny Jackson before scoring the eventual decisive run when another future Hall of Famer, Eddie Mathews, singled in the following at-bat. Either way, Williams was duly impressed. He had scouted Staub in high school for the

Red Sox, talked to him about hitting and fishing, and later would say Staub was one of the best young hitters he ever saw.

I thanked Staub for the story and told him I wish I could have asked Teddy Ballgame this question. I have a feeling Ted Williams would have made it a challenge rather than simply allowing one to probe his successes and win a single hit.

"I'm sure he would have said something irreverent," Staub said.

CARLTON FISK

When you think of Carlton Fisk, chances are good that you see him "waving" a ball fair with both arms as he hops sideways down the first-base line. The ball hits the screen on the left field foul pole at Fenway Park and he claps gleefully as he goes into his home run trot. That walk-off blast in the 12th inning finally ended one of the best games in Major League Baseball history, Game Six of the 1975 World Series for the Red Sox, a prelude to Cincinnati's eventual world championship. It was iconic, after all.

Ask Fisk to tell you about one hit that comes to mind first in his Hall of Fame career, however, and the home run he describes is not what you expect.

"I'm not sure it mattered the most, but my first hit in the Major Leagues," Fisk answered when we spoke during 2011 All-Star Week in Phoenix. "It was 1971, as a matter of fact. I get called up in September. I already had gone 0-for-4 against Mike Cuellar and had struck out in one at-bat against Mickey Lolich, back in 1969. So now in 1971, I play a game against the Yankees and Stan Bahnsen throws a shutout. Then I play the next game against the Yankees, and I face Mel Stottlemyre. Now I'm 0-for-12. *I'm 0 for 12.* We go to Detroit, and I didn't know whether I could play at this level. I hadn't gotten a hit yet. So we play Detroit, and the fella's name, he was a left-hander named Les Cain. And my first hit in the Major Leagues was a home run off him, in the third inning. So I said, 'Maybe I can be a big-league player.' That was a very satisfying hit for me."

Fisk was a tall, athletic catching prospect who once scored 40 points and grabbed 38 rebounds in a state-tournament basketball game for his hometown team, the Charlestown Forts in New Hampshire. He led them to a perfect season in 1963, and eventually went to the University of New Hampshire on a basketball scholarship. In the 1967 January Amateur Draft, after a year at college, Fisk was selected fourth overall by the Red Sox. He outmatched Class A Midwest League pitching with a 1.005 OPS for Waterloo in 1968, and Boston gave him a cup of coffee the next year—for those at-bats against Cuellar and Lolich—without a game in Triple A. After spending 1970 with Double A Pawtucket in the Eastern League, he caught in 94 games for Triple A Louisville in '71, learning how to handle pitchers, and came back up to appear in 14 games for a Red Sox team playing for next season.

His first two games of that '71 season were at Yankee Stadium, against a team that had a young catcher, Thurman Munson, who had won the American League Rookie of the Year Award in 1970. It was a doubleheader on September 6, 1971, and Bob Montgomery had caught the opener. Fisk started the nightcap, batting eighth, and in that Bahnsen shutout, he could only manage a 6–3 groundout, a strikeout and a pop fly to first. Next game: Fly to second, strikeout, 6–3 groundout, strikeout—0-for-4 as the Yankees won in 11. The Red Sox moved on to Detroit, and Fisk sat on the bench, waiting. He came in as a defensive replacement in the eighth inning on September 11, left in the hole in a 1–0 loss.

In the getaway-day game at Tiger Stadium, where one of the most famous All-Star Games in history had been played just two months earlier, Carlton Fisk properly introduced himself to Major League Baseball. It was quite by surprise, too. He was still on the bench for the start of this one, as Duane Josephson, a former All-Star with the White Sox whose durability became problematic, was hurt in the bottom of the first inning when Al Kaline laid down a bunt to third. Fisk put on his gear and went behind the plate, batting eighth. By the time he came up in the third inning, Les Cain, a wild left-hander who had come up with the Tigers on the 1968 title team, had retired the first seven Boston batters in order and was in control of the game.

So there was Fisk, in the same building where an astounding six future Hall of Famers had each just homered in the Midsummer Classic. Fisk teed off on Cain, giving the Red Sox a temporary 1–0 lead in a 3–2 loss. It was Bahnsen who again blanked Fisk and the Sox a day later at Fenway Park, but it was all downhill from there. Fisk hit in the next eight consecutive games, and finished 15-for-48 (.313) in that 1971 call-up. The only question to people in the Boston organization had been whether he could hit Major League pitching, and going forward, that would no longer be an issue.

Boston made Fisk its regular catcher the next year, and in 1972 he was named American League Rookie of the Year and was selected to his first of 11 All-Star Games. He went on to hit 355 more homers after the one against Cain, and while history will most vividly recall the home run he hit into the night to end arguably the greatest ball game ever, he looks back now and most immediately summons the memory of his first hit, the homer he did not have to wave fair.

"I don't know if I even remember half of them anyway," Fisk said. "There are game-winning hits, there are important home runs, there are important games won, but a lot of times I contributed in other ways to winning a game than with my bat. I always felt that my most important position on the field was behind the plate, not at the plate."

JOE CARTER

One of the most famous home runs in baseball history plopped down right in front of me in the fall of 1993, as I stood in the front of the left field auxiliary press seating at what was then called SkyDome in Toronto. Just like that, a World Series was over. Just days later, I was in Kansas City, where the author of that home run resided. Joe Carter drove me around the area where he was building a new home near Joe Montana's place. Carter drove through a fast-food restaurant to grab a burger and talked about what had just happened to him in the month before. Then we went to his home and he talked about it some more. I wrote a cover story for *The Sporting News* detailing everything about his "Touch 'Em All, Joe" homer off Mitch Williams that ended the World Series and gave Toronto a repeat title against Philadelphia.

Nearly two decades later, we met again and caught up on what that day was like, what those times were like.

I told him I was writing a book about one hit in your career, and I laughed because there was an obvious one at the top of my mind. "I'm not going to prejudice you with one," I told him, as he smiled, "I just want to know what you have to say." He was about to take his cuts in a batting cage beyond left field at Kauffman Stadium, preparing for the 2012 Taco Bell Legends & Celebrity Softball Game during All-Star Week, and his mind wandered back to what happened as a young man on August 12, 1984.

"Well, everybody's going to talk about The Home Run, and that was a great time," Carter said. "But I think one of the biggest hits I had was as a rookie. You know, as a rookie, you're always looking to solidify yourself, to show that you belong in the big leagues.

"We were playing the New York Yankees, who we had never beaten before, I'm in Cleveland, and I'm facing Louisiana Lightning, Ron Guidry. I had never hit a grand slam in my life, in the Minor Leagues, and I came up with the bases loaded and hit a grand slam off Ron Guidry. Not only that,

Joe Carter remembers a rookie grand slam
that solidified his place in the big leagues

Courtesy of Gage Skidmore

but I hit two home runs off him that day, six nothing. I had all six RBIs off Ron Guidry. And that grand slam was a big hit because it's something I'd never done before. As a rookie, to go out there and do that, that showed me that I belonged in the big leagues."

"Do you remember what he threw?" I asked him.

"Fastball. Oh yeah, he threw a fastball. When I hit it out, you know, I'm running the bases and looking back going like, 'Did that just happen?' Because I wanted to make sure no one took it away from me. That was a big moment for me."

In his previous start for the Yankees, Guidry had added to his legend by striking out three batters (Carlton Fisk, Tom Paciorek, and Greg Luzinski) on nine pitches in the ninth inning of a 7–0 win over the White Sox. Guidry became the eighth American League pitcher and the 20th pitcher in Major League history to accomplish the so-called "immaculate inning," and the first to do so in the ninth inning of a complete game. It was yet another reason Carter's big day was rich in meaning.

That was a big Sunday all around sports in America. The Summer Olympics closed in Los Angeles, and you can almost still hear Lionel Ritchie's "All Night Long" hit song playing over and over as the U.S. athletes celebrated their gold rush. The Braves beat the Padres that day in a game that featured two brawls and 19 ejections. Harmon Killebrew, Rick Ferrell, Don Drysdale, Pee Wee Reese, and Luis Aparicio were inducted into the Hall of Fame, which probably was the most important thing that happened that day, unless you were Joe Carter or one of the 17,143 fans at Cleveland Stadium who watched a rookie homer twice and drive in all six runs for a 48–68 team against the Yankees. Guidry, meanwhile, was promptly placed on the 15-day disabled list by the Yankees because of an inflamed rib cartilage, finishing with an uncharacteristic 10–11 record before bouncing back with 22 wins and a Cy Young runner-up season in 1985. Carter got Guidry at just the right time.

LUIS GONZALEZ

During the years of interviews for this book, I was talking to 19-year Major Leaguer Steve Finley one time about the hit by his Arizona teammate Luis Gonzalez off Mariano Rivera to win the 2001 World Series.

"It's funny about that," Finley told me at the 2016 All-Star Week in San Diego. "We used to always say a blooper in the game looks like a line drive in the book—it's a base hit. I told Gonzo, 'That will forever be a blooper because it's going to be shown over and over and over again. Everyone's going to rewind it. But it was the best blooper in the history of the game.'"

Ah, but it was not the hit of Luis Gonzalez's lifetime.

As we have seen so often in this book, responses to my question do not typically follow the news headlines and *ad nauseam* TV replays.

"Well, I know everybody would seem to think that it would be my game-winning hit in '01 against Mariano," Gonzalez said before the Baseball Assistance Team's annual fundraiser dinner in 2013. "But for me, when I reached the 500th double. I ended up with 596 in my career, and not a lot of guys have been able to reach that milestone. I know we embrace 500 homers and 3,000 hits and things like that, but to reach the 500-double mark and know that out of all the guys who have played the game, not many have done that, that's an accomplishment that guys who play every day can appreciate. If you can hit a double—just driving the ball—and there are a lot of singles hitters, there aren't a lot of home run hitters in the game and we know that, there are very few guys who get to 300 or 400 homers, but there are a lot of singles and doubles hitters, and then to know that all these guys have played and to reach 500 and know there weren't many guys who did it, to me that's one of my favorite accomplishments."

On April 18, 2006, Gonzalez was batting cleanup for Arizona at home against San Francisco. It was year 17 of 19 in Gonzo's career, and the five-time All-Star still had a lot of hit left in him. His own greatest hit would be the most important one of that game, perhaps making it even more memorable for him. The Giants had just taken a 3–2 lead, and Gonzalez came up with one out and Chad Tracy aboard in the bottom of the sixth. On an 0–1 count, Gonzalez drove a double to deep center, tying the score and then going on to score what would hold up as the decisive run in a young season.

"It was at home in Arizona. I remember it was a ball hit to left-center field, and it was hit off [Matt] Morris," Gonzalez remembered. "It was a pretty unique experience, just to go up there and be in the 300-homers, 500-doubles club. There's not a lot of guys, so for me, I quietly went about my business, and I went out there. I enjoy playing the game of baseball, just competing."

Yes, his most memorable hit had come off of Mo all right: Matty Mo, as Cardinals fans called their righty. The hit off the other Mo, Mo Rivera, was maybe a close second.

After the game, his uniform was sent to Cooperstown. He had done something that greats such as Babe Ruth, Hank Aaron, Willie Mays, Ted Williams, and Frank Robinson had done. Gonzalez showed up in a postgame news conference in a D-backs T-shirt instead. Gonzalez's wife Christine had attended each of the games on the homestand along with their seven-year-old triplets, and they had made posters to commemorate the event.

"It'll sink in probably later on," he said that night.

Indeed, it sunk in, and there we were nearly seven years later at a major event, and it had sunk in with such importance that it was the one hit he wanted to discuss when the hit off Rivera might have seemed so obvious to others.

"I remember that all the fans were waiting, because it was kind of a unique situation," Gonzalez said. "At the time, there were only 20 players who had had 300 or more home runs, and 14 of them were in the Hall of Fame, and I think our fans in Arizona were excited to be at the ballpark. I don't remember how many games it took me to get there, because we had a homestand and I wanted to do it at home before we got on the road—because it would have meant a lot more for me to do it at home—and I was able to do that."

I told Luis that he was one of many legends who had opted for a hit other than the one with which most people associated his career.

"Because I think it's the most *obvious* one, and everybody always assumes that it's the one," he replied. "I could tell you, too, my 30-game hitting streak, that was big for me because not many guys have done that. The national attention is always in the big games. I'm sure Carlton Fisk, everybody would have thought it was the home run he hit down the line where he was pointing fair and things like that."

AARON BOONE

It was a walk-off, but not the one most Yankees fans would think. There was no rivalry, no spellbound national TV audience, no World Series trip on the line, no legend that would be passed on to generations. Aaron Boone had Salt River Fields's main playing field behind him in Arizona as we talked at 2012 Spring Training about one hit that stood out most for him personally, and he summoned it so instantaneously that it was as if he had always *wanted* to say it whenever anyone asked him about what he had done in 2003 to the Red Sox. *But you should have seen this one...*

"In 1999, we won 96 games with the Reds, and we were kind of a young team," he said. "It was my first-ever walk-off hit, and it was against Vicente Padilla, who was with the Diamondbacks at the time. It was just something that made me feel I could really do this at a high level. It was a big win in a big game for a team that was really growing up on the spot."

It was June 29, 1999, at Cinergy Field in Cincinnati. With most of the 24,672 fans still watching, Padilla took the mound for the bottom of the ninth for Arizona. It was his Major League debut. Tony Womack had just hit a solo homer in the top of the inning to give Arizona a 4–2 lead, and Padilla was greeted rudely right away. Greg Vaughn grounded a single through the left side, and then moved to third when future Hall of Famer Barry Larkin doubled. Eddie Taubensee then tied the score with a double, and Chris Stynes came off the bench to run for him. Mike Cameron laid down a bunt and reached safely with a fielder's choice, so there were now men at the corners for Boone, the number 8 hitter who was seeing his first full season of playing time that year. He was carrying on a famous Boone family tradition of playing baseball started by his grandfather Ray, and carried on by his father Bob and his brother Bret. Now it was Aaron's turn.

On a 1–0 pitch, Boone singled sharply to left, and felt the rush of an important walk-off hit in the Majors. It gave the Reds a 5–4 victory and marked win number 8 in a 10-game winning streak. Those Reds would finish a game and a half behind Houston that season, and Boone would go on to be far more recognized for the iconic walk-off home run he hit off Tim Wakefield to clinch the 2003 American League pennant for the Yankees at home against the rival Red Sox. That one was more famous, more memorable to the public, and it matters a lot to Boone. But if you ask him for just one hit, you are going to hear about his swing against Padilla.

"If you ask players, different moments that don't mean a lot to other people mean a lot to us personally," Boone said. "That's certainly what people ask me about all the time, and I'm amazed by how many Red Sox and Yankees fans there are all across the country, that when I'm at an airport, out in public, they have a story in itself about that night, about that home run. It blows me away all the time."

CURTIS GRANDERSON

On the morning of 2016 World Series Game Four in Chicago, Curtis Granderson was giving a tour of the new University of Illinois-Chicago stadium he helped fund, and then donating his time to teach baseball fundamentals to hundreds of boys and girls. He was one of them once, a kid who made it from Chicago to the Major Leagues, and just one night earlier he had been presented the prestigious Roberto Clemente Award— given to the player who best represents the game of baseball through extraordinary character, community involvement, philanthropy and positive contributions, both on and off the field. Standing amid the sea of smiling faces that morning, Granderson said it was not really about how well the boys and girls could pick up the basics of the game.

"As long as they're having fun, yelling and screaming, that's all you want," he said. "I've had people ask me about different camps and clinics and asking, 'Did you see any talent, any prospects?' That was the furthest thing from my mind. I just wanted to see kids enjoying, having the competition side saying, 'OK, we lost this time, how do we get better?' Whatever the activity happens to be, if it's running, hitting, throwing, catching—I just want to see them having a good time at the end of the day. If the kid happens to go on to play in high school or college, great, but that's not the reason you are doing it. You just want to get kids activated, and they'll realize, 'This game is fun. I might also be good at it. And I get a chance to be with different friends and different people throughout the city that I never got a chance to meet before.'"

Granderson had reached a point where everyone was noticing things that he had done so naturally, year in and year out. "I wasn't expecting that award," he said, of the Clemente honor. "It's not the reason I do all of this stuff. I just enjoy helping out the community that made me and where I still call home."

That takes us to his hit of a lifetime.

"Probably the biggest one for me that I'll never forget would be my first Major League hit—partly because it happened here in Chicago, against the White Sox," Granderson said. "I had 60 friends and family in attendance, and they all got a chance to witness it. Freddy Garcia, who I got the hit off, he ever remembers it, which I find odd considering all the guys he's had a chance to play against. He and I got a chance to be teammates, and he came up and said, 'Hey, ask him who his first hit was off of.' I said, 'Hey, Freddy, you remember that?' He goes, 'Yeah, I remember that.' So all that combined in it, and friends and family being there to see it, made it so memorable."

Well, one reason Garcia probably so eagerly recalled it was the fact he still got the win, a 6–1 White Sox victory over the Tigers in front of 19,269 fans on a sunny Sunday afternoon, September 19, 2004, at Comiskey Park. Garcia was cruising with a 6–0 lead in the top of the eighth, and Granderson, a left-handed hitting center fielder, pinch hit for Nook Logan to start the inning. Granderson had gone 0-for-4 in his debut against Minnesota, and he had gone 0-for-2 in his second game earlier in this series. Now facing Garcia, he swung at the first pitch and reached on an infield single. Granderson moved to second and third on a pair of walks, and that was the end of Garcia's day. Dmitri Young's sacrifice fly scored Granderson with the only Detroit run, and the first of what would be more than a thousand for the kid from Chicago.

"I think going into it, the question was: 'Will I ever get a hit?'" Granderson said of that first single. "Because I was 0-for-6. 'Am I going to be the first Major League guy to never get a hit?' That was my mindset. And then I finally got one, and I go, 'OK, it's just like all the other hits I've had, get a pitch to hit, hit it. Eventually it's going to get through, sometimes it's going to go right at people.'

"And right after that, 'Don't put too much pressure on yourself.'"

3

PUT IT BEHIND YOU

There are times for atonement, like when Carl Yastrzemski and Mookie Wilson had to make up for errors, when Lou Brock got caught in a rundown, when A-Rod finally came through in the ultimate clutch, or when Bernie Williams forgot the count. There are times for retribution, like when Maury Wills became an All-Star hero after feeling he had been "blackballed" by some players who voted for the game's rosters in the 1960s. Or when you've been knocked down at the plate, like Carlos Baerga and Felix Millan were, with a chance to get back up and do something special—to exact revenge in a big way. Don Kessinger may not have been known for his bat, but there was one day when he was the best hitter you ever saw. Sometimes there is poetic justice, recalling the brimstone words of the minister in the 1941 movie *How Green Was My Valley*: "Fear has brought you here. Horrible, superstitious fear. Fear of divine retribution. A bolt of fire from the skies."

CARL YASTRZEMSKI

"Wendy, darling, love of my life . . .

"Put down the bat, Wendy . . .

"Wendy, put down the bat . . .

"Wendyyyyyyyyyy! . . . Put down the bat . . ."

Crack!

It is arguably the most impressive crack of a bat in Louisville Slugger history. Wendy swings her bat with full force and crashes it into the head of Jack Nicholson's psycho character in the classic movie *The Shining*, and he falls down the staircase of the Overlook Hotel, unconscious. She drags him to the kitchen and into the walk-in freezer. It was a baseball bat, and it was a big hit indeed.

"Wendy, baby, I think you hurt my head real bad," he moans. "I'm dizzy . . . I need a doctor."

That hit deserved a place somewhere in this book, and I thought I would include it here because the inscription on the barrel of the bat said it all: Carl Yastrzemski. Stephen King's beloved Red Sox would have to be represented in that classic thriller involving New Englanders, and not just any Red Sox, but the great Yaz, who played more games for Boston than anyone, an icon and staple in King's formative years.

Carl Yastrzemski stretches out of the Red Sox Dugout at Fenway Park

On the first night of the 2013 World Series at Fenway Park, I just happened to find my own Yaz story. He was asked to throw out the ceremonial first pitch at the start of the Red Sox-Cardinals series, ultimately clinched by the home team. Famously private, Yaz was not doing a pregame interview-room session or any kind of press gathering. He was going to be in-and-out, walk to the mound with a few distinguished U.S. military veterans before Game One, then meet him in the Red Sox player parking lot. After interviewing him for my MLB.com story, I asked him if he would share one hit, and he was happy to talk about a moment that stuck with him, before going home to watch this World Series opener on TV.

"Oh, boy. I would have to say, it wasn't a home run, I would have to say the last game of the season in '67 against Dean Chance with the bases loaded," Yaz began, flashing back to his Triple Crown season and the "Impossible Dream."

Boston and Minnesota went into that showdown on October 1 with identical 91-70 records, and Detroit was a half-game back at 90-70. The Tigers won the first game of a doubleheader against the Angels on the final day, but they lost the nightcap so the Twins-Red Sox winner was going to decide the World Series representative from the AL.

Chance already had reached 20 wins going into that game—four of which had come against the Red Sox—against one loss. In those five outings, Chance pitched all but one inning for the Twins, and Yaz was a combined 5-for-17 (.294) with no runs and no RBIs against him. That amounted to a nemesis when you consider that Yaz won the Triple Crown that season, so Boston had its hands full on that final day. But the Red Sox countered with Jim Lonborg, who won his 22nd game that day.

Yaz proceeded to go 4-for-4 with a double and two RBIs, and, as he remembers it, had to work for his pennant celebration. In the top of the third inning, Harmon Killebrew singled to left, and Cesar Tovar scored on the play due to the left fielder's error, giving Chance and the Twins a 2-0 lead at the time. But in the bottom of the sixth, Lonborg led off with a bunt single, and the bases were loaded after back-to-back singles by Jerry Adair and Dalton Jones. That brought up Yaz, who made things right by driving a two-run single to tie the score on the way to a World Series date with St. Louis.

"We were down two to nothing, and I had made an error which allowed one run to come in," Yaz said. "The base hit to center field tied the game up and put runners on first and third. That was probably my biggest hit, because we had turned the whole thing around. We had been losers; my first six years with the Red Sox, we finished in last place. Now all of a sudden, we won a pennant. I think it changed the whole organization."

I mentioned that he had enjoyed a "great year" and did not need to atone.

"Well, I atoned for the error," he replied, "but the big thing was it changed the whole Red Sox organization around. We became winners instead of losers." And his autograph would be everywhere, even a thriller movie prop.

LOU BROCK

Lou Brock finished his career with more than 3,000 hits, and—had he never been traded from the Chicago Cubs to the St. Louis Cardinals—he might have simply chosen to talk about the day he first stepped into a Major League batter's box and slapped a single to center off future Hall of Famer Robin Roberts to get the whole thing started.

Instead, the Cardinals Hall of Famer will tell you about the day he had five of those hits. It was September 9, 1964, at Connie Mack Stadium in

Philadelphia amid one of the all-time classic pennant race comebacks. Naturally, the player who dominated the basepaths in his era specially honed in on a hit that involved his swift and crafty base-running prowess, righting a wrong in his own mind.

"The most significant hit I ever got was in Philadelphia, in a situation that led us to one of the greatest comebacks in baseball history, back in 1964," Brock said. "We were down, 5–3, and I batted in the ninth inning and got a base hit. I tried to stretch it to a double, and the ball got to second base before I did. Now I'm in a rundown. How you get out of a rundown, I really don't know. But I did. First baseman didn't tag me at first, we went on to win, 10–5, and a few weeks later we win the National League pennant. I go back to that game, and it's only because I made a mistake, and then got out of the mistake. When I turn back the clock and look at what happened, and try to evaluate my own performance, that certainly comes to mind.

"I had been given a green light by the St. Louis Cardinals to steal bases whenever I wanted to. That's what happened. I got out of the rundown, stole the next base. The next hitter hit a one-hopper to second base, so instead of a double play, I was on third base with two out. Then Ken Boyer got the big hit and now we're tied. All because you avoid the double play, you avoid the rundown, you do all those things that play out on the big stage. You really can't write the script."

This was the 80th game he played with the Cardinals since his infamous trade from the Cubs. On June 15 of that season, he was traded along with Jack Spring and Paul Toth to St. Louis for Ernie Broglio, Doug Clemens, and Bobby Shantz. "Brock for Broglio" would become a baseball-household term for years to come, referring to a quintessential lopsided deal. If I may digress: it's not like Broglio never produced; he has always been able to look back on his eight-year Major League career and say, "I led the Majors with 21 wins in 1960." That's something to be proud of.

Brock established himself as a difference-maker in that fourth season of his 19-year career. He reached 200 (exactly) hits and 100 (111) runs for the first time, stealing 43 bases, and more importantly he represented the turning point for those Redbirds. In his book *October 1964*, David Halberstam notes that people in Chicago had given Brock a hard time, and no one harder on Brock than himself. One Chicago writer had chided him for pulling a Rock, as in Brock, after the player was thrown out once trying to take an extra base. "Some in the press and in the stands considered him too casual about his job, but that was a misperception," Halberstam wrote. "In fact, he was driven, not merely by a desire, but by a rage to succeed. He was determined to show the people who owned the Cubs, the sportswriters on the Chicago papers, and most of all, his fellow players in the National League that he would not be merely a good major-league player but a great one."

Brock was so driven to be a good Major Leaguer, he used to write down his goals before each road trip—how many hits or RBIs he expected of himself. He kept his own records of how he fared against certain pitchers and how they threw to him. Was it any surprise, then, that he would always internalize that one rundown and remember what he viewed as a teachable moment? He wanted to make things right, in his own mind and in the minds of fans who had seen the spark he provided after the trade.

There are some very important elements of that September 9 game at Philadelphia that make this story even better. It was the first game of a brutal road trip, one that would be unheard of for today's ballplayers. The trip was from September 9 through 27, 19 days and 18 games, including three doubleheaders, taking the Cardinals from Philadelphia to Chicago, Milwaukee, Cincinnati, New York, and Pittsburgh. That the Cardinals could make a big September comeback to win the pennant when faced with that demanding journey makes it even more remarkable in hindsight. Brock batted .363 on that trip, going 29-for-80, with 12 runs scored, five home runs, 11 RBIs and four steals.

In that first five-hit game of his career, Brock batted six times and scored four runs. As with his very first Major League at-bat, he was facing a future Hall of Fame starter, this time in Jim Bunning. Batting second in the lineup behind Curt Flood, Brock singled in the first, flied out to start the third, and led off the fifth with a homer. He led off the seventh with a single to center—all of that against Bunning. Brock led off the seventh against reliever Jack Baldschun and singled to center. Baldschun was still on the mount when Brock came up again in the ninth to record the single that he would remember for this personal recollection.

Flood was already on third when Brock stole second. Flood scored on Bill White's subsequent 4–3 groundout to cut the Phillies' lead to 5–4, and then Brock scored the tying run from third on a Boyer single. Of course, Brock was not done yet. The game went into extras, and in the 11th, St. Louis sent 10 men to the plate, with Brock delivering a single to make it 5-for-6 on the day. He scored behind Flood on White's double that drove in the decisive runs, and even though Chris Short shut down Brock (0-for-4) in a complete-game victory for the Phillies the following day, a statement had been made. The Cardinals were not going away. Anytime discussion about dramatic pennant chases is started, there still has to be a place for the one that took place in the NL in '64. Yes, the Phillies may have folded down the stretch, but much of the credit had to go to the Cardinals' relentless push—and to the relentless pursuit of learning by their new outfielder in the number 20 jersey.

CLINT HURDLE

"Mine is more of a description of the beauty of life and the beauty of sport," Clint Hurdle began one morning before managing a Pirates game. "I'm going to give you the bittersweet part of it, but the sweet part of it, my first hit, it was actually a home run in Royals Stadium on September 18, 1977, my first start. It was A&P Day. The local grocery store. A packed house."

Twenty-year-old Clint Hurdle was hungry that day. Whitey Herzog penciled him into the starting lineup of a playoff-bound Kansas City team.

"It was the third or fourth inning, and I hit a two-run homer off Glenn Abbott, who was pitching for the Seattle Mariners," Hurdle went on. "A two-run homer. At the time, my folks were in the stands. My mom and dad, and a close personal friend. It was a combination of a four-year-old kid playing ball in the backyard, and then just playing ball for sixteen more years. I was twenty years, one month, and nineteen days old when I hit the homer.

"It was surreal because when I hit the ball, it truly was one of the few times in my baseball career when I hit the ball, everything slowed down. It was like when the ball came out of his hands, it was just slowed down; I hit it, everything was slowed down. The trip around the bases, it didn't happen in the blink of an eye. It was something I was able to embrace. It gave me goosebumps.

"The weird part was, the ball hit on top of the waterfall. If you remember the Royals' old stadium, it's nothing like it is now. There was a fence, and then there was another area, and there was another waterfall on another level. The ball hit right on the backdrop in right-center field and took one bounce and went out of the stadium. It's the farthest ball I've maybe ever hit in my life. It was my first hit and the ball bounced out of the stadium.

"So on top of my mom and dad and sisters being there—which was as good as I could have ever dreamed of, because they all poured into me, from the time I started playing until that moment, and they still do—the ball left the stadium. I can remember somebody saying, 'That's really crazy, you're not even gonna get your first hit.' And I go, 'What?' They said, 'You bounced it out of the stadium.' I wasn't even aware of that. To this day, I've got a ball that somebody said they found in the parking lot. It had rolled and some guy picked it up and said, 'Where did this come from?' Is it the ball I hit? I don't even know. I have a ball that I think was the ball I hit.

"That's the story. That's the coolest hit I ever got. I've been to the World Series, but unlike these Hall of Fame guys, I don't have that story about a certain pitch. But the best part of the story is my first at-bat. This was my second Major League at-bat when I hit the homer. So I'm one of X amount of guys who hit a home run in his first game. I did not hit it in my first at-bat."

Hurdle's very first at-bat in the Majors has to be combined with his second at-bat to fully deliver one of my favorite motivational lessons I came across in talking to legends for this book.

"My first at-bat, I was one of the last guys that came up from our championship team in [Triple A] Omaha to play," he said. "U. L. Washington, Willie Wilson, myself. They had starts before I did. They'd get a hit, they'd get their first ball, they'd stop the game; all these wonderful things. I was starting to get some ribbing from my teammates about, 'Is he ever going to get to play?' I'm trying to keep my mouth shut, thinking, 'I'm sure I'll get to play some day . . . we'll figure it out.'

"Well, I got the start that day. When I saw my name in the lineup to start, I was blown away. My folks happened to come up that weekend, and it obviously worked out, because that's not when you go, 'Hey, Whitey, am I going to play this weekend? So I can call my mom and dad and have them come up.' You can't just do those things. I got the Sunday start, and I was nervous all day. I took batting practice. I can remember Charlie Lau come up right before the game saying, 'Son, your first at-bat, your knees are gonna be knocking. Relax. Take the first pitch.' "

Hurdle responded to him that day: "OK, I got it, Charlie, I got it. Yeah. I'm going to take the first pitch."

"So finally my turn comes up to hit. Glenn Abbott's on the mound. He throws the first pitch, and for me, I was thinking, 'Oh my gosh.' I'm thinking: 'BIG LEAGUES. PITCHING!' He throws something, and I'm saying, 'My God, I can whack this thing. This is my pitch!' Oh no, wait, I'm supposed to take it. Wait. Hit it. Wait. Take. Check swing. Ball off the barrel of the bat, one-hopper to third base. Billy Stein, who I had worked out with all winter long, is from Rockledge, Florida, and I grew up nearby. He was playing third base for the Mariners, he gets the ball on one hop. I get thrown out at first base by fifty feet. It's a check swing. I take an absolute beating in the dugout. 'That a boy, wait to take a big swing!' 'Nice memorable first at-bat!' I mean, I wore it. All I can think is, 'Oh my God, I hope I get to hit.' The last thing I'm thinking is getting a home run. I just want to get a full swing off. Because that's embarrassing.

"Of course, Charlie came over to me, the voice of reason, and he puts his hand on my shoulder and says softly, 'Now do you see why I wanted you to take a pitch?' I said, 'Yes, sir. I'm so sorry, sir. I'll try to do better the next time.' And of course the next time, I hit the home run."

It came in the fifth inning. John Mayberry had led off the inning with a double, breaking up Abbott's no-hitter. That brought up Hurdle for his second at-bat.

"There wasn't as much jabbing in the dugout when I got done with the trip around the bases," he says. "That pretty much put everything where I needed to be, for the time being."

The moral of the story? "Take the first pitch!" Hurdle bellows with a laugh. "But if I didn't take the first pitch, it might not have worked out the way it did, so who knows? You know, you think of those who come before you. There's something to be said for experience. And that wasn't the first time as a young player that I got in my own way."

Clint Hurdle found his way through personal adversity in life, by learning from a mistake, by learning to listen to those "who come before you." Today he is a guiding light of inspiration, and I consider myself lucky to be among those on the receiving end of his daily motivational emails, the ones he always signs, "Love, Clint." He is a national spokesperson for the Prader-Willi Syndrome Association, and the father of a girl who was born with the rare and complex genetic disorder. Donating to that cause would only take a few moments, well-deserved for a man who stayed to sign autographs for one and a half hours after that first Major League game when he hit a check-swing trickler and then a 450-foot monster blast.

ALEX RODRIGUEZ

As noted in the first entry of this book, 19-year-old Alex Rodriguez was one of nine overall respondents—a dream lineup—in uniform during that frozen moment of 1995 when Edgar Martinez hit The Double in Seattle. Making his postseason debut, the 1993 number one overall Draft pick from Miami entered the game in the eighth inning to pinch run for Tino Martinez and stayed in the game at shortstop. In the bottom of the ninth, with two on and the score tied at 4-4, Jack McDowell struck out Edgar. That brought up Rodriguez, who could have clinched the ALDS in his first at-bat and possibly conceived a hit that would be worth recounting here more than two decades later. Alas, Rodriguez grounded to short for a fielder's choice that forced out Griffey and ended the inning to send the game into extras.

In the bottom of the 11th, as we all know, there were two on again, and Edgar was facing McDowell again. Rodriguez stood on deck, watching Martinez take care of business himself, then leaping into Griffey's arms like Yogi Berra into Don Larsen's in 1956. What if McDowell had struck out Edgar again? What if Rodriguez would have hit The Double instead? Would that have been a hit worth recounting here more than two decades later?

I thought about that briefly as I waited with a few antsy photographers on a red carpet at the Sports Emmys in 2017 at the Jazz at Lincoln Center in New York. I thought about how, as managing editor of *The Sporting News'* digital operation in 1998, I was suddenly responsible for starting AROD.com in partnership with this emerging talent and relaying fans' questions so he could answer them in what was then a unique "mailbag" format. Now time and technology had flown by. Rodriguez was now a broadcaster in his first full season of retirement following an eventful, explosive, 22-year Major League career. His countdown to Cooperstown eligibility and passionate expostulation was officially under way. We would chat about the one hit that meant the most to him, during idle time after talking about broadcasting.

There were 3,115 regular season hits from which to choose, including 696 home runs, more than everyone except Barry Bonds, Henry Aaron, and Babe Ruth. There were another 72 postseason hits, including 13 homers and 16 doubles, from which to choose. Who knows, maybe if Edgar had given him that one extra opportunity, the kid who would be known as A-Rod might have found his answer right then. It came instead in 2009.

"The double in the World Series to score Johnny Damon in Game Four," Rodriguez told me without hesitation. "That got us one game away from winning the world championship."

This book includes 16 members of the 3,000-hit club, and his response sounded a lot like the one given by Dave Winfield. The sheer savagery of Winfield's powerful swing inclined me to list his hit in a different chapter about leaving an impression, but they both belong here as well amongst stories of redemption and perhaps exorcising demons. Both legends provided pivotal doubles that led to long-awaited titles and profound redemption. Both had 12 All-Star Game selections and well-known Yankee postseason frustration under their belts when that moment finally arrived. A-Rod had come to New York and the hated Red Sox won it all instead, even found himself dropped to the bottom of the lineup by manager Joe Torre amidst 2006 ALDS futility. Winfield had been dubbed "Mr. May" by George Steinbrenner as the supposed antithesis to Mr. October, Reggie Jackson. I was in the locker rooms to see Winfield and Rodriguez; the former after his Game Six double for Toronto to beat Atlanta at Turner Field in 1992, and the latter after the Yankees beat the Phillies in six in 2009. "Success is counted sweetest by those who ne'er succeed," Emily Dickinson wrote, and both hits were sweetest here.

A-Rod had batted .438 with five home runs against the Twins and Angels in the first two rounds of the 2009 playoffs, but on the biggest stage once again, he was struggling under familiar scrutiny. In Game One, he struck out three times and was 0-for-4 against Cliff Lee as the Phillies won at Yankee Stadium. In Game Two, the Yankees won despite Rodriguez, who again struck out three times and was 0-for-4. Cole Hamels of the Phillies made the mistake of waking up A-Rod in Game Three by plunking him on the arm. "That at-bat kind of woke me up a little bit and just reminded me, 'Hey, this is the World Series. Let's get it going a little bit,'" Rodriguez said after that game. "So it worked out."

Then came the decisive double off Phillies closer Brad Lidge in the ninth inning that scored Damon to make it 5–4 and ultimately give New York a 3–1 World Series lead on the way to its 27th world championship. It was a solid shot to the left-field corner at Citizens Bank Park. "There's no question—I have never had a bigger hit," Rodriguez said that night, and nearly a decade later, it had stayed firmly cemented as his own choice hit. Amid the various scandals and controversies that punctuated his long career, Rodriguez did just about everything a ballplayer could do. Ultimately, that included the ability to move on and be happy.

DON KESSINGER

"I wish I could tell you it was one that got us to the World Series, but I missed that one," mused the affable president of Don Kessinger Real Estate, from his office phone in Oxford, Miss. The first 11-plus seasons of his 16-year career were with the Chicago Cubs, from 1964–75, where he was part of the long-running "Million Dollar Infield"—Hall of Famers Ernie Banks [first] and Ron Santo [third] at the corners, and Glenn Beckert [second] and Kessinger [shortstop] up the middle. They never tasted a Fall Classic, not even in 1969, when the Miracle Mets somehow slipped past them, but at least Kessinger was able to rejoice when the 2016 Cubs ended the drought.

"I was so excited for the Cub fans," he said of that breakthrough. "I love the organization, I want all of them to win, but I was so excited for the Cubs fans. We always felt they were greatest fans. Our disappointment in my fifteen years of playing was that we were not able to bring that to the fans. We thought we were a decent club but were unable to get there."

He was a six-time All-Star, and it should be noted that those National League All-Star teams for which he played would have been a perfect 6–0 in his appearances if not for Harmon Killebrew's two-run blast in the homer-happy 1971 Midsummer Classic at Detroit. Kessinger was known for his glove, for the way he moved to his right in the hole, and for the bullets he fired across the diamond to Banks.

"I got a couple hits in All-Star Games. I guess you remember those things," he continued, the thought of a hit taking shape. "I always felt like I played in All-Star Games defensively, because I was supposed to be good in the field. I would always tell my wife I'd love to get a hit in an All-Star Game, but I don't want to miss a ball in those games.

"When I walked into that locker room in my first All-Star Game in '68, you look around and there was Hank Aaron and Willie Mays and Roberto Clemente and Bob Gibson. You'd look around and say, 'Oh my goodness, what am I doing here?' But I didn't run out of the locker room; I was glad to stay. I was fortunate to play in six of them, and I never got to where I wasn't in awe of those guys."

Kessinger was good for 150 to 160 hits a season in his prime, and that would help keep the runners moving around the bases. He finished his career with a respectable 1,931 hits to go along with all of that defense, and there was one day that rose above all the others and brought an invaluable lesson to this journey of discovery.

"Talking about life, you never know what's going to happen," he said at age 74, the memories starting to sizzle and snap. "I remember in 1971, I played every inning a lot of the way. In early June, for whatever reason, I was tired. I really felt tired. I remember when I left to go to the park that day, thinking that if we got rained out today it wouldn't be bad. That morning, I said to my wife Carolyn, 'Woo, I'm tired. But it'll be all right.' She said, 'Won't you tell 'em you're tired?' I said, 'Oh, sure, I'll tell [manager] Leo Durocher that. I might not just get a day off, but a career off.'"

It was June 17, 1971, the start of a series against the Cardinals at Wrigley Field.

"Of all the days, that particular day I went 6-for-6 against the Cardinals," Kessinger said. "Steve Carlton was the starting pitcher, and I had been 0-for-3 years against him anyways. When you think about one hit, that's just one of those where, by the third or fourth hit, I felt great, I wasn't tired at all. The lesson is, you don't always feel your best; you just do the best you can. It worked out for me."

This was a month before Kessinger would join Carlton for the third time as NL All-Star teammates. Carlton was 10–3 entering this game, coming off a beating by Manny Sanguillen and the Pirates, that year's World Series champion. There were 22,749 fans on hand at Wrigley that Thursday afternoon, and they saw Kessinger lead off with a single to left in the bottom of the first, eventually scoring as the Cubs took a 2–0 lead. They saw him do it again to right in the second inning, this time driving in Brock Davis from second to make it 3–0.

Burt Hooton was unable to make it out of the fourth inning for the Cubs, so both teams were in for a long afternoon. In bottom of the fourth inning, with the score tied at 3–3, Kessinger singled again to right, this one moving Ray Newman from first to third before the rally died. Then in the sixth, with the Cubs ahead, 4–3, Kessinger singled to left with one out; he was eventually stranded on first. At that point, he was an astounding 4-for-4 against Lefty, evenly distributing the ball to outfields as if he owned the future Hall of Famer that day.

It was the last time he would face Carlton that day.

"I remember when I came to the plate after those first four hits, it was obvious everybody in the park knew what was going on, because they had given me a great ovation," Kessinger recalled. "I was hitting right-handed off Carlton, obviously, then I turned around and hit from the left side. I believe it was against Moe Drabowsky."

That was the case for hit number five. Carlton had handed over a 6–5 St. Louis lead to Drabowsky, a right-handed, 16th-year journeyman reliever who made 51 appearances for the Cardinals that season. It set up a showdown between a pair of Arkansas natives. Kessinger led off the bottom of the eighth, turning around to the left side of the batter's box, and pelted a double off Drabowsky to right—his third opposite-field hit of the day. Two batters later, Santo drove him in with a single to tie the score at 6–6. In the bottom of the 10th, Kessinger led off an inning against a different pitcher for the third time, in this case another righty, Chris Zachary. It was a leadoff single to left, Kessinger's fourth opposite-field hit of the day. He was sacrificed to second by Beckert, and then, following an intentional walk to Billy Williams, Kessinger scored the winning run on a Santo walk-off single.

Kessinger's batting average jumped from .269 to .286 that day. Approaching midseason, that is a pretty big hike when one considers the volume of at-bats. Kessinger scored the first and last runs that day, and Durocher said afterward, "It was a week's work in one day." Kessinger told reporters after the game: "You just have to be lucky to have a day like this. I was just swinging the bat and the hits just kept falling in."

Close to a half-century later, Kessinger said, "I'm still at ballparks all the time. I've got grandkids playing, and we've had a great time." The Kessinger name lives on in baseball, with big possibilities; grandson Grae made an emotional Don proud by "wearing my number and playing shortstop at Wrigley Field." Grae opted to forego the MLB Draft in 2016 and chose instead to attend Don's alma mater, University of Mississippi. It is in that setting that a longtime Cubs shortstop spends his time these days: happy that his franchise finally tasted sweet success, and settled on one hit that meant the most to him. It could have been any of those six he stroked on that special day at the Friendly Confines, so we'll just go with the decisive sixth one.

It was fitting perhaps: 6-for-6 for a six-time All-Star and a 6 fixture on a scorecard.

I asked Don what Carolyn said to him at the end of that day.

"She gave me a hard time about that," he said, laughing. "She was so happy that it was OK. Everything was fine. Honestly, baseball is such a great game for teaching you lessons in life. You've got to deal with failure, you've got to be able to come back, all those things you hear us talking about all the time. When the greatest hitters fail seven out of ten times, you've got to put it behind you."

Like the World Series drought.

MAURY WILLS

Maury Wills spent his entire 14-year Major League career (1959–72) in the National League, mainly with the Dodgers as a shortstop who took the stolen base to a new level. I have to mention the stolen base here because it is related to what he considers his most memorable hit—or at least related in his own way of thinking.

Of all the current or former players who participated in this book, no one surprised me quite the way Maurice Morning Wills did on the day of the 2011 First-Year Player Draft. As we chatted in Greenwich Village, NY, I was not expecting to receive the pent-up thoughts of a man who contends only now that he had been essentially blocked from starting for All-Star teams by players who voted, and chiefly those being pitchers and catchers who could not keep him from running.

"The most memorable hit . . . I got 2,134 hits in my Major League career. Isn't it amazing how we can remember? People ask us how many? We say,

'Oh, I don't know how many, I don't keep up with that.' . . . Yes, we do. You ask me how many stolen bases I had. I can tell you 586, just like that.

"I played in seven All-Star Games. Two years, we had two games. In my day, the players did the voting for the teams. And being a base-stealer, I was not very popular with the opposing players. So many years, they didn't vote for me, the players. And that's why I'm glad—while I'm on that topic, I'm kind of sore about it, almost bitter—I was glad when baseball gave it to the fans, because it is the fans' game. Let the fans do the voting. But in my day, the players did the voting. Many times when I went to the All-Star Game, I was the backup shortstop. But I was there.

"In fact, I remember one year, in 1962, Dick Groat, who started, he was with the Pirates, and he came up to me before the game and apologized. He said he felt terrible going out there, and I'm sitting on the bench. I said, 'That's OK, Dick, go ahead. I understand. Thank you.' But I was bitter. I didn't want to show it.

"It just so happens that I ended up being MVP of that game. Dick Groat played the first three innings. Then Johnny Keane, the Cardinals' manager, put me in and I played the rest of the game. I was the MVP.

"But in 1966, the All-Star Game is in St. Louis. And unquestionably I am the shortstop for the National League. But again the opposing players picked someone else. My manager took me, Walter Alston, because we had just won the World Series the previous year. In fact, he had to ask me two or three or four times to go, because I refused to go. A couple of times I had turned him down, because I was going as a backup. But I went anyway. And I'm on the bench, and I'm walking down the bench like a cat on a hot tin roof. 'Come on, skipper, get me in there!' He said, 'Just a moment, you gotta find the right spot.' So he came down to the last inning. Mays, Mantle, Killebrew, Kaline, Frank Robinson . . . all these people popping it up. 'Come on, skipper, let me in there.' Well anyway, it got to the last inning. Gaylord Perry got the win for that game. That was his thrill. The greatest win he had, the most memorable win. I didn't realize that until he told me. But anyway we got a man on first base in the bottom of the 10th, Tim McCarver got on base, Ron Hunt bunted him over to second. Now McCarver's on second with one out. My manager came down and said, 'Come here. There's your spot.' Walter Alston said, 'Go in there and win this game for us.' I got me a bat, and I went in there and I got the base hit to win the game."

It was a single to right off Pete Richert, a left-hander for the Washington Senators. The National League was a 2–1 winner in front of the "home" crowd of 49,936 fans at brand-new Busch Stadium.

"I didn't even take the team bus back to the hotel," Wills said. "I walked to the player hotel, which was the Chase Park Plaza, and it took me about an hour and a half. And I laughed all the way, with joy. I took my time. I signed autographs, laughing.

"I was sore. I mean, such satisfaction. I'll always remember that hit."

Then he added: "Come to think of it, baseball has treated me like that for a long time. Now you're bringing it out. I've never mentioned it. I don't feel too good about it. It's the same with the Hall of Fame. For some reason they just won't put me in there. Why, I don't know. I'll live with it. But I won't live peacefully with it."

Why would players have blocked him from the starting lineup?

"Because I stole bases against them," he said. "See, nobody on your own team could vote. I know I didn't get any votes from any catcher nor any pitcher from the other teams in the league.

"They weren't used to somebody running. They wanted to govern when I should run and when I shouldn't run. And when I ran and stole a base, they took offense to it. I didn't care to be very popular, but I didn't think it was right to be disliked. So they never voted for me. The only time I went is when the manager took me. And I played in seven, including two years when we had two games."

As a Hall of Fame voter myself, I was startled by Wills's contention. Do I think he belongs in Cooperstown? Not based on the "benchmark standards" I've always known. But the more I listened to him, the more I questioned what logic has presided during and after his career. He was an impact player to be sure. You could ask every surviving opposing catcher and pitcher from that era and ask if Wills was right, and if all of them denied it, nothing would be proven by denial. Why else would he have revealed this at age 78, in a random and unexpected interview, unless there were truth to his belief? It began with the mere question of asking him about just one hit.

There I was, talking to him throughout the day of the 2011 First-Year Player Draft, as he, Perry and Trevor Hoffman were among legends "presented" by Major League Baseball as the faces of tradition for that day, to appear at a NASDAQ bell-ringing and then interviews. Wills was going to be a Dodgers representative later that night at a table on the main Draft floor. I asked him if he thought, in some small way, this was an example of how the game cares about him.

"I know what you mean," he said. "I have a great relationship with the players. This is after my playing days, when I would see them at various functions, and that includes pitchers. But it was then. We were all younger, and brasher, and egomaniacs. So we were more sensitive toward things then. But we've grown up. So we get along just great. Being the fact that I have grown up, I can't believe that I'm bringing this out right now. I've never talked about this before, all these years. God has been good to me. I've been blessed. I'm blessed today. I'm still in baseball, I'm with the Dodgers, they love me and I love them. I don't really need to express it, but since you asked me the question, I wanted to.

"I'm proud of my career."

TONY PEREZ

I found it amazing that two legendary players who had the game-winning hits in extra innings of back-to-back All-Star Games each told me that those moments were at the top of their list for this book. Maury Wills had told the story of his 1966 walk-off at St. Louis, such a source of pride and pent-up contemplation over the years for him. Then it turned out that the following Midsummer Classic was remembered in this way as well, as I talked with Tony Perez just before the 2014 MLB Draft, where he was working the Marlins table as a club representative. Perez was yet another Big Red Machine cog I had to include here, and he proceeded to tell me about that one hit that meant the most.

"I got a lot of big hits, especially with the Reds," Perez said. "But personal, it's the 1967 All-Star Game, when I hit that home run in the fifteenth inning to win for the National League, 2–1. That's the one I never forget."

That game was played in Anaheim. There were three runs and all were accounted for by solo homers from third basemen. How amazing is that in hindsight? Bookend blasts were hit by two National League third basemen, the first one leading off the second inning when starter Dick Allen from the Phillies connected against Dean Chance for the game's first run, and the second homer by an NL third baseman came more than three hours later as the benches were gradually being all used up. Brooks Robinson squeezed his solo shot in there for the AL off Fergie Jenkins in the sixth.

"It's special because I didn't start the game," Perez said. "The game went 15 innings and I didn't get into the game until the 10th. That means from the beginning through the bottom of the ninth, I never was in that game. But we played long enough for me to get in there and be the MVP. I hit the home run to win.

"We played a lot of innings, there were a lot of strikeouts, a lot of things that happened in that game. I never saw Roberto Clemente strike out four times in one game [he was one for six with a hit]. It was tough to see because it was twilight that day, and a lot of good pitchers pitched that day. For me, to come up in my situation with nobody on base, and I hit the home run.... That is number one to me."

I asked the legendary run-producer if there was one most important piece of advice he could give to aspiring players, like those prospects he had his mind on later that night. He said: "Play the game. Play the game like they know how to play. It's always to win, that's all you can do. Practice and practice and try to get better. Listen, that's the important thing. Listen to your coaches, be coachable."

CARLOS BAERGA

"The two home runs in 1993, in the same inning," Carlos Baerga said. "It was April 8, 1993, against the Yankees. Steve Howe first, and then Steve Farr. That's a record in Major League Baseball, the first one ever to do it, and I'm never going to forget about it.

"I didn't even know it was still the same inning because we hit so much, and we almost got into two fights that inning. It was a crazy inning. Twice, we almost fought. But before I hit the last one, Steve Farr threw at my head. I went down. I said, 'I'm going to swing as hard as I can. If I hit it, it's gonna go. I know it's gonna go.' That's what I did. I stepped up to the plate, and I hit it. It was a crazy night, but I finished with a record and I'm never gonna forget about it."

In the top of the seventh inning, Jim Leyritz hit a two-run single for the Yankees to cut Cleveland's lead to 6–5. The Indians would score nine runs in the bottom half, and Baerga's unprecedented feat was a highlight that remained with him all these years.

Steve Howe replaced Rich Monteleone on the mound to start the bottom of the seventh. Alfredo Espinoza singled, and then Howe thought he struck out Baerga with a 2–2 slider just off the outside corner. Baerga blasted the next pitch over a large sign on the wall in left-center that showed a rendering of Municipal Stadium and read: "Cleveland Indians: 1932–1993"—the tribute sign. It was in front of empty bleachers in the seventh inning of a blowout game, in the finale of a three-game series to begin that season. The Indians had drawn 73,290 for Opening Day three days earlier, and 13,834 for this one. The 1993 season would be the official end not only to that ballpark itself, but also, perhaps not coincidentally, to a long era of "Mistake By The Lake" futility in Cleveland. The Tribe would finish 76–86 and in sixth place that year, but they would wind up 19 games over .500 in a strike-shortened 1994 season that welcomed fans to Jacobs Field and signaled an age of competitiveness.

As Baerga circled the bases, Howe nodded his head in disgust and waved frantically at Leyritz, his catcher, to throw him the new ball. Leyritz waited until both runners reached home, further affecting the shaken pitcher. Howe kept yelling, and Yankees manager Buck Showalter ran out to the mound to try to calm his hurler.

After Baerga's first homer, the taciturn slugger Albert Belle stepped up to the plate and was summarily plunked. A possible brawl was averted. The Indians ripped Howe for three consecutive singles, and Showalter replaced his troubled pitcher with Farr. After the first six Indians of the inning had reached safely, Farr got two quick outs, but then Kenny Lofton tagged him for an RBI single, making it 11–5 as Cleveland batted around. Espinoza hit a three-run homer, so now it was 14–5 and Farr was pissed.

Baerga went down, avoiding the beanball.

That's when he told himself, "Swing as hard as I can."

Next pitch, boom—this time over the wall in right-center, again in front of empty rows of home runs seats. What was he thinking as he rounded the bases?

"I just said, 'You better get that one.'"

That was his hit of a lifetime, after all.

The record was not immediately apparent, though, as announcers were focused on the fact it was back-to-back jacks for Cleveland, and the second time Baerga homered in the inning. Then they started going back to the books in the press box, assuring themselves that not even Mickey Mantle ever had homered from both sides of the plate in the same inning. Baerga took a curtain call, before he fully knew what he had done.

"First, it was against the Yankees," he told me, "and then to get the record in that way, it was awesome."

When we spoke, it was in the heady days of late October 2016. The Indians were playing the Cubs in the impossible Longest Wait Series, and we talked the morning of Game Two, after he had appeared at a local children's medical facility for an MLB community event. Baerga had been part of that young nucleus that had paved the way for a sustained era— nearly a quarter century—of respectability for Cleveland's baseball ways. The image represented in the comic movie *Major League* was long since gone, thanks to guys like Baerga. Farr, who had thrown him the historic pitch, reportedly broke the glass door of a water cooler in the frustrating aftermath, and the lesson of retribution is as clearly visible here as it was for many others I interviewed.

That is the competitor inside them; what we pay to see.

There was one other hit that Baerga wanted to talk about, and while this one came at home three games into the 1993 season, the other one came in the third-to-last game at home. It was a dinky bunt single to third on his fourth trip up to the plate in a 4–2 loss, and at the time, it meant everything to the batter who dropped the ball with his bat.

"The last one was when I made the other record, the first second baseman in the American League to hit.300, get 200 hits, 100 RBIs, 100 runs, and over 20 home runs," Baerga said. "Rogers Hornsby did it in the National League, so in the American League I was the first one to do it.

"The last series, I needed one more hit. Before, I spent five days in the hospital because I had cellulitis bacteria in my leg. I asked the doctor to let me get out, get the base hit and I would come back to the hospital. And that's what I did. They let me get out; they put an air cast on my leg with special stuff; I get the base hit; I spent three more days in the hospital. So I'm never gonna forget about that. That was the last day of the season and the last day of Municipal Stadium. They let me get the base hit and I came back to the hospital."

Baerga struck out swinging twice and popped out once before recording his 200th hit of that season with a bunt off reliever Scott Radinsky in the bottom of the eighth. A rookie call-up named Manny Ramirez came in to pinch-run for Baerga, who left the game with a second entry in the record books all within the same 1993 farewell season at Municipal Stadium.

FELIX MILLAN

There is a great game photo from The Associated Press that circulated around the nation's newspapers after the games of April 8, 1969. Félix Millan is in the batter's box, and his bat is in mid-air drop while his left hand is rushing to the left side of his face, which has just been struck by a fastball from future Hall of Famer Gaylord Perry. Millan's face is anguished. Dick Dietz is reacting in the picture as Giants catcher.

"Before the Slam," read the headline of the paper I saw it in, the *Reading Eagle*.

The slam. Felix the Cat was never going to forget that. When we spoke, he was 69 recalling '69. He could still feel the burning, searing pain in his left cheek. The light-hitting second baseman from Puerto Rico still could feel the satisfaction of what happened later in that game when he faced Perry that night in Atlanta.

"I don't have too many hits," said Millan, who had 1,617 in the regular season. "But if there is *one* hit that stands out, there was one day that I was playing against the San Francisco Giants, and Gaylord Perry was pitching. The time before, he had hit me, and I had my cheek very, very swollen."

It was the second game of the season, and Perry was making his 1969 debut. He had won 21 games and earned his first All-Star selection in 1966 and was looking to gradually return to that form, having won 15 games in 1967 and 16 in '68. In fact, this was a pitching matchup of two future Cooperstown legends, as Phil Niekro would be floating his knuckleballs for Atlanta.

The Braves lineup began with Felipe Alou, then Millan in front of two future Hall of Famers: Hank Aaron in the three hole and Orlando Cepeda at cleanup.

Perry was staked to a quick 1–0 lead, but he started the bottom of the first by giving up a double to Alou. Millan was batting righty versus righty, and first there was a wild pitch. Alou took third. At that point, Perry was either fighting wildness or he was a little pissed off. The next pitch was to the jaw.

What did Gaylord do at that point? I asked.

"I don't know what he did, because being the kind of pitcher he was, I didn't even want to look at him," Millan said. "I just ran the bases and went to the dugout, as a quiet guy."

Millan was checked out, and he was allowed to stay on first base a runner.

"Our manager wanted to take me out," Millan said. "I said, 'No, why didn't you take me out after I got hit?' The sixth inning, two men on base— third and second—and Felipe Alou was coming to hit. They walk Felipe to pitch to me. And God was on my side that day, because the first pitch that Gaylord threw to me that inning, I hit a grand slam. It was a fastball."

Here's what happened between the fastball to the cheek and the fastball over the wall:

In that first inning, Aaron doubled to score Alou and move Millan to third. Then Cepeda hit a two-run single. Those three runs would prove decisive in a 10–2 rout.

Bottom of the second, the pitch Millan hit in his return trip to the plate was actually for a single, following an Alou steal during the at-bat. Then on to the fourth, and with two out and Alou on after a double, Millan stepped up again and this time Perry induced him to fly out to left.

In the sixth inning, they met again. The Giants had cut the lead to 3–2 on a Willie McCovey solo homer. Sonny Jackson led off against Perry and grounded out. Bob Didier and Ralph Garr produced back-to-back singles. Niekro advanced the runners with a groundout, leaving first base open with two out. Perry was not going to mess with Aaron on deck and Cepeda in the hole. He had planted one squarely in Millan's jaw and figured he had an edge, anyway. So he went after the Cat.

"I had a lot of fastballs back then," Millan said, "because, hitting in front of Hank Aaron, I had to be pitched to."

What happened next is something Millan never forgets. His grand slam made it 7–2, blowing the game open. When Aaron followed with a double, it marked the end of Perry's night. Sixteen days later, Perry won a complete-game decision against Atlanta, so he was back to normal As for the Cat, his grand slam gained immediate notice around the league and his consistent play at the plate and in the field made him an All-Star from 1969-71.

BERNIE WILLIAMS

Bernie Williams had so many big hits at Yankee Stadium, but when we talked during a cocktail hour before an ALS fundraiser event at New York's Marriott Marquis following the 2009 season, he immediately thought of one on the road.

"I do remember one," he said. "Playing in Oakland, bases loaded, Mike Oquist was pitching. Fighting off some tough pitches, and he threw me a forkball that I let go, down for ball three. And I started walking down to first base, thinking it was ball four. The place is packed at the stadium in Oakland. Obviously anti-Yankees fans. So I came back, all embarrassed, and John Shulock is the umpire, he's looking at me and shaking his head like, 'What are you doing?'

"The next pitch he throws, I hit it out for a grand slam."

It was August 9, 1999. That grand slam capped an eight-run rally, and the Yankees went on to win, 12–8, en route to the second of three straight World Series titles.

The greatest irony to me, with the benefit of a full decade of retrospect, is that his teammate, Jorge Posada, was quoted after the game saying in

Courtesy of Clare_and_Ben

Only Bernie could have called a grand slam after losing track of the count

amusement, "Only Bernie."[1] During the 2009 season, Yankees teammates got a good laugh when Posada forgot the count, started walking to the dugout thinking he had struck out, then returned to the plate after a back-and-forth two-step. Only Jorge. Eventually, the best of them lose track of the count.

---

1   Buster Olney, "Baseball: Yankees Notebook; Williams Forgets Count But Knows How to Hit," *New York Times*, August 11, 1999. http://www.nytimes.com/1999/08/11/sports/baseball-yankees-notebook-williams-forgets-count-but-knows-how-to-hit.html

MOOKIE WILSON

When you bump into Mookie Wilson, you have to remind yourself: that wasn't a hit. One of the most famous contact swings in World Series history resulted in a grounder that went through the legs of Boston first baseman Bill Buckner for an error and won Game Six of the 1986 World Series. The Mets clinched the title in the next game, and that famous Mookie grounder off Bob Stanley in the 10th inning at Shea Stadium will be replayed forever.

I talked to Mookie at length about that moment as we pondered it three decades later, on the morning of Game Four of the 2015 World Series. We were looking out over 300 young ballplayers at an event held by MLB on a youth field in the shadows of the place where he had once worked that magic. I told him that the Mets were showing a 1986 season review over at Citi Field on the big video board relentlessly for hours before each home game in the series, to fire up fans after the team had started in an 0–2 hole of that Fall Classic against Kansas City.

"It's amazing how that moment, everyone has their own view of what happened, and why it happened and how it happened," Mookie said. "But it's just one of those things that you don't forget. It's very difficult to explain because it was such an in-the-moment time. Everything happened in a matter of seconds. So you have to analyze all of that. I've had thirty years now to kind of"—he laughs loudly here—"figure it all out, and go back and figure out how it got to that point. That's what you have to remember: How did it get to that point? That's what makes it so special."

It was special, but it was moot for the purposes of this book. Of course, it would not have mattered anyway. We have already seen a number of times that players who produce iconic hits are unlikely to have them at the top of their own totem poles. Had it been a clean single past a diving Buckner, you probably would not have seen it listed here, anyway. Mookie explained why:

"When you play as long as I have, you have a lot of hits that mean a lot. But you always remember that first, big hit. Now people say, 'Well, it should have been '86.' No, that wasn't my best hit." Even he needs reminded it wasn't actually a hit. "That was probably my fondest memory, but as far as the hit that really set me apart, it was early '80s and we were playing the St. Louis Cardinals at Shea Stadium. I made an error in the ninth inning, Tito Landrum hit a ball to center field; I lost it, made an error. They got an inside-the-park homer, put them up by a run. We came up in the bottom of the ninth, facing Bruce Sutter, two outs, and I hit a two-run homer."

He was referring to what happened on Sunday, September 20, 1981. Wilson was a rookie, having been called up a while during the previous season. On that day in September of '81, the Mets were out of contention and the Cardinals were in first place. Wilson went 4-for-6 as the Mets' leadoff man and center fielder, leading New York to a three-game series sweep. In the top of the ninth, it was a 5–5 tie when Landrum hit a triple and Wilson actually made a one-base error that resulted in what he remembered as an inside-the-park homer. It was another case of an error and a hit kind of melting together with time.

What mattered the most was what happened in the bottom of that inning. Sutter had been an All-Star for the fifth year in a row that summer, and he immediately got two outs after coming on for the bottom of the ninth. Frank Taveras, who had entered the game as a pinch-runner and stayed in, doubled to start a rally. Then Mookie, a switch-hitter, batted from the left against the right-handed future Hall of Fame closer, crushing a walk-off homer deep into the right-field seats—Sutter's sixth blown save at that point in the season.

"What's so special about that," Mookie told me, "that was the moment I said to myself, 'You belong.'"

I told him that his story sounded similar to the stories related by Lou Brock and Carl Yastrzemski. Both of them had committed a key mistake earlier in the game before atoning.

"That's what it's all about. It's about recovery," Mookie said. "It's about the moment, not the past. I learned a lot from that. But to me, when people ask me about that, I always tell them, 'That was the hit.' That was the hit. No matter what I had done or what I'd do from that moment, it was all coming from that because that gave me the confidence that 'no, you belong here, you don't have to wonder anymore.'"

I asked Mookie whether he thought people would learn and find their own incomparable hits for life by reading stories from legends like him.

"I think everybody has their own different story," he said. "If you follow baseball, you understand how fragile the game can be, how fragile the mind can be when you're playing the game. So I think they'll learn a lot from them."

JOSH HAMILTON

Josh Hamilton was the American League's MVP award in 2010, leading the Texas Rangers to their first World Series. There were many hits during the course of that year, and especially that fall, that might have qualified as a personal highlight for him. Halfway through that campaign, we talked hitting, and he told me there was one hit in his life that mattered most to him. It was not one of those majestic blasts into the right-field seats at old Yankee Stadium during the 2008 All-Star Home Run Derby, either—it was something that happened a week earlier at home.

"Probably the walk-off against K-Rod in '08," Hamilton said. "Because I was in about a 1-for-16, 1-for-18 little slump there. Satan was all over me—telling me, maybe this was a fluke, maybe I can't do it, maybe I'm not good enough. I was 0-for-4 that day, and that was going around my head out there in the outfield. I quickly told myself that I am good, that I can do it. The Lord just helped me that at-bat to get through it. K-Rod threw me a lot of sliders and curveballs, a lot of off-speed. I hit that walk-off home run."

It happened on July 9, 2008. Hamilton had gone 70 consecutive at-bats without a home run. Michael Young had singled in a run to cut the Los Angeles Angels' lead to 4–3 in the bottom of the ninth, and Hamilton took Francisco Rodriguez deep on a 3–1 curve. That made it an incredible 89 first-half RBIs at that point for Hamilton.

"When something like that happens," Hamilton said, "it reminds you how much you love playing this game."

4

SET BIG GOALS AND HUSTLE

If Meryl Streep wants to talk about acting, then you let her just keep talking. If Eric Clapton wants to talk about guitars, then you let him just keep talking. If Pete Rose wants to talk about hitting, then you just start typing as fast as you can and let him keep talking in a stream of consciousness, and you give him a chapter all to himself.

That is what happened on the morning of Game Seven of the classic 2016 World Series between the Cubs and Indians. I was staying at the Renaissance Cleveland Hotel, an iconic landmark built a century earlier and host to so many baseball stars of decades past. There was much work to be done far after midnight in the ensuing hours, history to be made.

PETE ROSE

Pete Rose has the most hits of any current or former MLB player

My phone rang early in the morning and I was awakened by the Hit King.

Hall of Fame or not, he is obviously in this book. There are 4,256 reasons, plus another 86 in postseason play, not to mention seven more in his combined 17 All-Star Games, including the 12th-inning single at just-opened Riverfront Stadium in his hometown of Cincinnati, where he scored two batters later by famously bowling over American League catcher Ray Fosse to win the 1970 game for the National League, securing the official nickname of "Charlie Hustle."

"Out of all those hits, if it's at all possible, I'd like to ask you if there was one that meant the most to you and why," I said, clearing the sleep away.

Pete started talking hitting, and by the time he was done talking, he had given a clinic on how to set goals and gain business leverage.

Bram Stoker wrote in *The Mystery of the Sea*: "All right," I said, "we shall take them in proper season and deal with them seriatim." I was afraid that the hit king might do the same thing in dealing with all of his hits seriatim, because he seemed to recall every one. He began rattling off at-bats in no particular order. Each hit was good enough to be anyone else's greatest ever, but merely worth consideration in this case. Red-letter hits would be suddenly punctuated by knocks out of the blue.

"I have so many milestone hits that it's hard to separate them," Rose began. "Every player goes to their first hit. There are World Series hits, and playoff hits, things like that.

"Individually, when I got 4,192, in Cincinnati, it's hard to imagine but I got a nine-minute standing ovation. I mean, for your readers, tell them if you want to understand how long that is, if you're married and you go home tomorrow from work and your wife's home in the kitchen cooking, go in there and stand for nine minutes and clap, and you'll understand how long that is. It was amazing.

"In Cincinnati, I played in front of those fans for over twenty years, love-hate relationship with all of them, felt like I knew all of them." He was just warming up, like in the on-deck circle.

"Then you remember your last hit," he said. "Got it off Greg Minton, I believe."

That was on August 14, 1986, in Rose's final homestand. Minton was a reliever on that Giants team, Roger Craig's first as manager. Rose singled in the first inning off starter Kelly Downs and produced the only run that mattered with a single off Downs in the fifth, but, naturally, what mattered most in the long run was his leadoff single off Minton in the seventh. At the age of 45 and serving as player-manager, Rose would come to the plate in four remaining games against San Diego during that homestand, going hitless and finally reaching the end.

Then he thought of all the round numbers.

"I remember my 4,000th: Opening Day in Montreal in 1984, a double off Jerry Koosman," he said. "I remember my 3,000th, in Montreal."

He got two hits off Expos right-hander Steve Rogers that day, batting from the left side of the plate and slapping the second single to left for number 3,000. Just think today how much hullabaloo, merchandising, and glory comes with a 3,000th hit chase and the actual attainment. Pete Rose was just warming up that day at Olympic Stadium.

"My 2000th, I got against San Francisco and Ron Bryant." Well, Ron Bryant started that game and paved the way, but was not the actual milestone victim. That day at Candlestick Park, June 19, 1973, Bryant was a 24-game winner sitting on 11 wins, and Rose picked up three hits off him amid a four-hit day. Rose was enjoying the best season of his career, a career-high 230 hits, and his only NL Most Valuable Player award. That day, he actually reached number 2,000 with a double off reliever Charlie Williams in the seventh.

"So those are all important," he said. "My 3,631st was momentous because it broke Stan Musial's record. He was there that day, and it was the first day back from a 56-day strike." Rose was playing for the defending World Series champion Phillies in 1981. Just to show how eager he was to resume hitting, Rose singled off Jack Morris on the first pitch of the All-Star Game in Cleveland a night earlier, the first actual MLB game played after a two-month labor hiatus. Then in the Phillies' first game back on August 10, he started 0-for-3 against Cardinals starter Bob Forsch, and then, batting from the right side against the lefty reliever Mark Littell, Rose pulled a single to left to pass Musial for the most NL hits with 3,631.

"I hit so many milestones. When you're going to guys who can remember their 4,000th hit, and you can only talk to one of them. And there's only one guy that can talk about 4192, that's me. Ty Cobb is 4191. When you talk about all the momentous hits you talk to me or Ty Cobb, and he's not around so you talk to me."

Cobb died in 1961, the first year Rose ever hit .300-plus in the pros. That year, Rose played 130 games for Tampa in the Florida State League. He was 20 years old with a vintage Midwest buzz cut, not even close to the fastest on his team, but the one with the most hustle. In those 130 games, he had 160 hits—including an amazing 30 triples, nearly twice his total in any other season of his professional career—and batted .331 with a .911 OPS, scored 105 runs, drove in 77 and struck out only 33 times in 563 plate appearances. Imagine the hopes that the Reds' organization had for this local product. If you include his three Minor League seasons (1960–62), he has 4,683 hits, and that is indeed relevant, as Rose has said, for anyone lumping Ichiro Suzuki's Japanese hit total with his Major League total. Not to minimize Ichiro's remarkable career, but MLB has always been the undisputed pinnacle of professional baseball worldwide. In 2016, I read a headline that said: "Ichiro Suzuki passes Pete Rose in combined professional hits." That was incorrect. Minor League Baseball is professional baseball, thus Pete is Earth's Hit King. Nothing will ever change this.

"But I remember an important hit I got that most people wouldn't remember," Rose continued. "It was a hit up the middle off Roger Moret in Boston to tie Game Seven, and also before Joe Morgan got the hit to center to give us our first championship. That was '75."

Now Pete was on a tear as he spoke. It was like he had a bat in his hands again in the '70s.

He was the MVP of that fabled 1975 World Series, and the reason Rose doubts many people will remember that hit is because people primarily remember what had happened the night before in Game Six. In arguably the greatest baseball game ever played—or at least the best one that ever captured national prime-time TV attention—Boston had kept their cursed hopes alive thanks to Bernie Carbo's pinch-homer off Rawly Eastwick in the bottom of the eighth and Carlton Fisk's epic walk-off in the 12th, complete with the body language to wave it fair.

NBC, which had debuted *Saturday Night Live* just 11 days earlier, claimed a record for most-watched sporting event in history with its Game Seven broadcast. Going into the seventh inning, the Red Sox had a 3–2 lead and Boston fans were poised to let loose, not having seen a title celebration in 59 years. This was their chance again. With two out and Ken Griffey Sr. on first, Ed Armbrister came to the plate. He had been a key figure in the Game Six theatrics, reaching base by a controversial catcher's interference call. This time he walked, as Griffey stole second during the at-bat. That brought up the top of the Cincinnati order, and Red Sox fans had to face the reality of a Big Red Machine. It started with Rose, who hit from the right side and faced Moret, a lanky lefty from Puerto Rico who had been 14–3 that season (the top MLB winning percentage) but whose 1.434 WHIP (walks and hits allowed divided by total innings pitched) said "hit me." Rose, who led off and went 2-for-4 in the finale, rifled a 1–0 pitch up the middle to score Griffey and tie it at 3–3. It would stay that way until the top of the ninth, when Griffey and Rose were on the corners, and Morgan singled to provide the eventual game-winner—and an answer for this book. As for Rose, he was named 1975 World Series MVP, batting .370 (10-for-27). Rose won three batting titles, his second one in 1969 with a .348 average. That was his highest average of any of his full seasons, and his mind flashed back to that year.

"Or I remember a drag-bunt single I got in Atlanta in '69, the last game of the season," he said. "The only way I could lose the batting title is if I went 0-for-4 and Clemente went 4–4. He was in Pittsburgh, and he was 3-for-3. I was in Atlanta and I was 0-for-3, and I dropped the bunt down to win the title. They were going back and forth in the press box and dugout, so we knew." Rose was .0008 ahead of Clemente and locked up the title with a .348 average. "We weren't playing for anything, we already had fourth place all wrapped up, and they weren't going anywhere," Rose remembered, laughing. "In those days, it was important to win batting titles because it gave you ammo to go in and negotiate contracts.

"The year before that, day before the '68 season ended, I was neck-and-neck with Matty Alou for the batting title. I was batting against Gaylord Perry, and Alou was playing for the Pirates in Chicago. He went 4-for-4, and I went 5-for-5. Then I went 1-for-3 the next day, and he went 0-for-3, and I won the next batting title." Rose had five (two doubles, three singles) of the 16 hits that Perry, the Giants' future Hall of Famer, allowed in his complete-game effort for his 16th win in that second-to-last game of 1968. It was a pretty good example not only of Rose's makeup, but Perry's as well. The next day, Jim Maloney pitched a 3–0 shutout in the Reds' finale, and Rose scored two of the runs, ripping his 42nd and final double of the year, on the way to his first of three career batting championships.

"Those are pretty momentous situations that you remember," Rose said.

Then he resumed the hit parade.

"Seventy-eight, last week of April, I had an uncharacteristic game for me. I had a five-hit game and three homers against the Mets off three different pitchers: Nino Espinosa [fourth inning], Mardie Cornejo [fifth] and Butch Metzger [eighth]. I went to all three fields. And I struck out the first time up that game, off Nino. That's the day I started choking up on the bat. He blew my ass away, and I said, 'I better choke up.'" I asked Rose if that's where he got confident in swinging with authority choking up, typical of his career. "No, I had to create some bat speed," he said. "I don't know if I was out late the night before, or if it was him."

He returned to the night of number 4,192, when history was made. It was his 3,476th career game. Reds 2, Padres 0.

"That was September 11, by the way," he says.

The sellout crowd of 47,237 was tensed up, hoping history happened on their watch. In the crowd was Pete's mother, who said at her seat, "I hope he gets a hit the first time up, so he releases my tension." So it was written, so it was done. Right-hander Eric Show was the Padres' starting pitcher, so Rose batted lefty. With one out in the bottom of the first, he took a ball, fouled one back, and took another inside for 2–1. Flash bulbs went off *en masse* for 1985 cameras, a rarity then, as Show delivered.

Here was the call from Reds Hall of Fame broadcaster Marty Brennaman: "He levels the bat a couple times. Show kicks and he fires. Rose swings . . . Hit number 4,192! A line drive single into left-center field, a clean base hit, and it is pandemonium here at Riverfront Stadium! The fireworks exploding overhead. The Cincinnati dugout has emptied. The applause continues unabated. Rose completely encircled by his teammates at first base. . . . a kind of outpouring of adulation that I don't think you'll ever see an athlete get more of."

My favorite part of that call is the moment Brennaman got out the words "Rose swings..." His words were immediately drowned out by the purely excited and sweet reaction of his booth partner Joe Nuxhall, who was screaming: "There it is! There it is! Get down! Get down!"

Now we are back to our 2016 World Series Game Seven wakeup call stream of consciousness, and Rose was flashing back nearly three decades.

"I had a real good swing before that and fouled it back, had a real good batting practice before that. Eric Show was kind of the right guy for me to hit off of, because he's not a 98-99 pitcher, not gonna blow you away. I usually got contact against him. He threw me a fastball and I just hit a line drive to center, for a base hit. It bounced up, [Carmelo] Martinez jumped up and got it. If there had been two outs, I believe it would have been a double, but because it was like I was leading off the inning, you can't get out at second leading off the inning."

During that nine-minute ceremony, Reds owner Marge Schott came out and hugged Rose at first base. They gave him a new Corvette, with the license plate PR 4192. Soon enough, Rose became overcome with emotion, wiped away tears, and then his son Pete Jr. ran out of the dugout and hugged his father.

In 2008, as I was just undertaking this project, I worked an event in Lower Manhattan with Goose Gossage, a month after he had learned he would be enshrined that summer in Cooperstown. We walked through a museum and I asked him if there was one hit he remembered most in his lifetime to date. Out of all that he could have offered—surely one he might have surrendered as a fearsome reliever—Gossage cited Rose's record hit.

"I was there that night," he explained. "I was in the bullpen for San Diego at the time. What I remember most was our pitcher, Eric Show, sitting on the pitcher's mound during the celebration scene in Cincinnati."

I told Rose about what Gossage said.

"Which is fine," Rose replied, recalling the same Show who died in 1994, at the age of 37, due to substance abuse.

"My last at-bat, Goose struck me out," Rose continued. "My last at-bat ever."

On August 17, 1986, Rose pinch-hit in the bottom of the ninth against San Diego, and Gossage set him down to end a playing career.

All of those hits touched most people in some way. His gambling resulted in a lifetime ban by Major League Baseball, keeping him out of the Hall, at least through his mid-70s. He was 75 when we spoke. My very interest now in writing about baseball, spending most of my life doing this, was due in no small part to him.

I told Rose that I grew up with a Pete Rose Hitting Machine in my backyard in Evansville, Indiana, about three and a half hours down the Ohio River from the Reds' home. The term "machine" is used loosely, as it was a long, hard-plastic skinny pole that you jammed into the ground, and then it had a hard-plastic arm that coiled with a big rubber band, and on the end of that arm was basically a Wiffle ball. I would beat that plastic arm to smithereens, and then I would constantly tape up the frayed arm with packaging tape, whatever I could do to keep it firm. The goal was to learn how to switch-hit like Pete, because no matter which direction you hit, it would coil back and spring back at you in the opposite direction. Hearing all of this, he could relate.

"When I was a kid growing up, I was always playing stickball," he said. "I had a younger brother, six [or] seven years younger than me, we always played stickball. Had a restaurant right in front of where we lived. Had a big wall with a fish on it, because it was Schulte's Fish Garden, in front of my house. I let my brother, the closer he got to me, try to strike me out as we used a rubber ball and a broom handle. We did it endless hours. The farther away he did it, the closer I made him get. That was just our batting practice every day.

"The place is gone now. It's torn down. But I ride by there a lot when I go back to Cincinnati, because you can almost see downtown there. I have all the memories in the world. It's right across the river, a ferry boat goes across there, I took the money on the ferry boat there when I was 12 years old. I always parked on the Kentucky side, because the man who owned it, that's where he lived. Everybody in those days, Anderson Ferry, where he lived, anybody who lived in Indiana had to take the ferry to get to the airport. We got a lot of action on that ferry boat. It was fun growing up.

"The difference in my growing up and younger people today, we didn't have much more to do in the '40s and '50s than play softball, baseball, football, basketball. We didn't have computer, cell phones, so I grew up playing sports. Whatever season it was, that's what you played. And I was pretty lucky, too. Real lucky, actually, because I had a father who was an athlete, a tremendous athlete, probably the best football player to come out of Cincinnati, and I was the water boy on his basketball team, batboy on the baseball team, and whenever he had a game, I would be sitting in the car waiting to go.

"I was pretty fortunate. I guess the main reason was: we all have hand-eye coordination; you don't make it to the big leagues without it. I just had one of those bodies that, one: didn't get tired, and two: very seldom, the way I played, I didn't get hurt. And if I did get hurt, I didn't go to the trainer's room. I wouldn't laugh it off, but many a night I spent in contrast—hot, cold, hot, cold. When we played, you couldn't take off every day you had a headache. If you missed games, you didn't get stats. If you didn't get stats, you didn't get a raise."

After winning that aforementioned batting title in 1969, Rose's salary hit six figures. He had wanted to become the first "singles hitter" to get $100,000 a year, but Rose was more methodical than that. He had a purpose every season, to help win championships and to gain leverage.

"My goals were 200 hits, bat .300 or more, score 100 runs, 40 to 50 doubles. Those were my goals. Other guys who hit home runs and drove in runs, they needed me. You need teammates to get your statistics. You can be the best hitter in the world, but if there's no one behind you, you can't score any runs.

"I used to set goals every year. Two hundred hits, if I do that, I'll hit .300. If I hit .300, I'll score 100 runs or more. Because the guys batting after me, they all have statues at the ballpark. Not plaques, statues. Morgan, Bench, and Perez. If you're going to get 200 hits and score 100 runs, I would probably get anywhere from 40 to 50 doubles every year. I wasn't a home run hitter, but I'm eighth in the history of baseball in total bases. Seventh is Ruth, sixth is A-Rod. Then you've got guys like Bonds and Aaron and Musial ahead of you. So those are household names. You wouldn't think a guy with only 160 home runs would be in the top ten of total bases, but that's because of so many hits—and so many doubles and triples among them.

"The thing about hitters, a lot of them hit home runs, but there's not a lot of them that, in their careers, hit over 100 triples, 100 doubles, 100 home runs. Because the guys who got the triples didn't get the home runs, and the guys who hit the doubles didn't get the triples. A lot of the home run hitters, [Willie] McCovey and [Harmon] Killebrew, they're not going to get triples. Then the guys like Larry Bowa and people like that who weren't home run hitters, they're going to get the triples but not home runs. If you look up the great names of baseball and see how many got 100 triples and 100 or more home runs, it's a tough combination."

Sam Crawford is the all-time triples leader with 309, and he just missed that club with 97 homers, playing before Ruth made the home run vogue. Roger Connor had 233 triples and 138 homers. Honus Wagner had 252 triples and 101 homers. Tris Speaker, the all-time doubles leader with 792, had 222 triples and 117 homers. There were other examples if you start with the triples leaders and look at their homer totals. On the flip side, Ruth had 136 triples and 714 homers, while Aaron just missed with 98 triples and 755 homers. Willie Mays: 140/660.

Rose was right. It is a pretty small club. But not nearly as small as the Hit King Club. For the rest of his life, most likely, he will be able to claim that distinction and talk about it whenever he feels like it. This was one of those days, on one of the most important days in baseball history. That somehow seemed only appropriate.

"Yeah, it's got to be tough when you've got 4,000 hits," Yankees legend Roy White told me months later. He had been a switch-hitter like Rose, an American League All-Star who played opposite Rose's Reds in the 1976 World Series. White tried to imagine what it was like for the Hit King to contemplate such a question: "How are you going to narrow it down to one when you've got that many?"

5

GET ON BOARD

The moment when you know you belong is even more important than the moment you belong to the masses as their hero. Many of the greatest hitters will instinctively recall a "first" that put them on the map, so to speak. It was that "I can" moment experienced by Brooks Robinson, Frank Robinson, Don Mattingly, and Andre Dawson. That was a time of reassurance. They satisfied an early curiosity about whether they could ascend to the highest rung, and learned something about themselves as more than mere parvenu in the profession. This theme is shared by others such as the great Mike Schmidt, who cited one postseason hit that "defined" him to this day. The ability to shrug off the weight of the world at that moment—whether from the lofty expectations of others or of themselves—would make this the singular hit in their careers. It was the time they came face-to-face with a moment they had dreamed about and their confidence soared, in some cases maybe even a little too high at the time.

BROOKS ROBINSON

Brooks Robinson is the first great Major Leaguer I really remember being aware of during my own indoctrination into the national pastime, when he and the Orioles were on my little white transistor radio during grade school in the late 1960s. I don't remember his first big-league hit, and my lasting memory of him honestly is diving for balls at third base. But for him, there is a hit that stands out many years later.

For the record, he was the first one to contribute to this collection. This is what he mailed me back in a letter with his customary grace as a true legend:

"I think my most memorable hit was my first one in the major leagues. I got a hit in my second at-bat in the first game I ever played in as a Baltimore Oriole. I was only eighteen years old. I remember, after the game, going back to the Southern Hotel in Baltimore and calling my Mom and Dad in Little Rock, Arkansas and telling them I got a big league hit. I said 'Man, I don't know why I played at York, Pennsylvania. I should have been in the big leagues all year.' I then went 0–18 after that, and I learned a valuable lesson. But my first hit is my most memorable because I learned such a valuable lesson."

Brooksie was a September call-up in 1955, and in those days, Washington versus Baltimore was a normal interleague series. Entering the game of September 17, it also was meaningful because both teams were trying to stay out of the American League cellar. The Senators were 51–93 and the Orioles were 49–95. They were the worst teams in baseball. But a new era was on the horizon for the Orioles. They had signed Robinson out of Central High School in Little Rock, Ark., assuring him that he could soar through their system faster than with any other organization.

"Coming from Arkansas myself, I can tell you he was something, not just he thought he was, but he was something," said six-time All-Star shortstop and fellow Gold Glover Don Kessinger. "And one of the really good guys."

In that debut, Robinson faced Senators left-hander Chuck Stobbs and popped a foul to the catcher in his first big-league at-bat. In the fourth, Robinson led off and singled off Stobbs. Robinson was 2-for-4 that day, and indeed he would finish that first month in the bigs 2-for-22.

Sure, enough, he realized that more seasoning was required after that 0-for-18 finish to the 1955 season. The following year, he played 154 games for San Antonio of the Double A Texas League. He was a September call-up again in '56, starting out 0-for-4 to make it technically an 0-for-22 Major League drought since that big debut. He started the '56 call-up 2-for-17, so he was technically 2-for-35 after his debut. You can see why a player might be humble in a hurry, why he might really remember that first hit, out of the 2,848 he struck in regular seasons.

Brooksie's story does not quite end there. About five years later, I met up with the 15-time All-Star again at the Major League Baseball Players Alumni Association Dinner in New York. I reminded him what he told me to start this book, and he smiled. "I went 2-for-4 and knocked in a big run and then the next 18 times at bat, I went 0-for-18 and struck out 10 times, so that was a pretty big lesson. Wonderful, I'm glad to hear a lot of people have told their stories. What did Bobby Richardson say?"

BOBBY RICHARDSON

Well, since Brooksie asked . . .

"If I had to pick one hit out, it would be 1962, playing in Minneapolis," said Richardson, the longtime Yankees infielder. "We were going into the ninth inning. That would have been the top of the ninth because we were playing on the road, and the Yankees were losing by three runs [7–4]. I was batting on this day in front of Roger Maris [third] and Mickey Mantle [cleanup]. The bases were loaded, there were two out, then I came up to bat, three runs behind. Mantle came over from behind, while they were talking to the pitcher, and said, 'See if you can hit one out, I don't feel good.'"

New York Yankees (1963)

Bobby Richardson played second base for the New York Yankees

This was seven years into Richardson's career, and it was a year he would end by winning World Series MVP and snagging Willie McCovey's liner in the final game to seal the Yankees' title. But on this one day, even a veteran was reminded that he belonged, answering the call in a crucial situation—for a teammate.

"Third pitch, I hit it out of the ballpark for a grand slam," Richardson said. "I came across home plate, and [Mantle] was laughing. I said, 'Why are you laughing?' He said, 'I didn't think you could do it.'"

That was the fourth game of a series, part of a 17-game road trip spanning 14 days in which the Bombers went 6–11—at Minnesota, Kansas City, Los Angeles [against the second-year Angels], and Baltimore.

"It was short-lived," Richardson said of the lead he gave New York in this one, "because they tied it up in the bottom of the ninth. Rich Rollins tied it on a broken-bat single, and then the Twins won it in 10. Still, I can remember that the count went to two balls and no strikes in my at-bat. I said, 'Boy, this is a time to take a good swing.' And I did. I was surprised, too, when it went out of the park. I do remember that."

MIKE SCHMIDT

"If I could sort of define my career by one swing, it would probably be..."

And so Mike Schmidt began his rumination. Ozzie Smith was positioned 10 or 15 feet away, as he so often was when they were regulars on the left side of the National League infield at All-Star Games, and he had just rattled off his hit of a lifetime with the quick agility of his signature backflip, taking his old position. For Schmidt, it was not so easy.

"I had some neat ones. Everybody does. Maybe I shouldn't start telling you what I'm leaving out...

"The one that hit the speaker in the Astrodome, that's a swing. It ended up on the cover of *Sports Illustrated*. That's one swing.

"One night, I had one swing, it was my thirteenth swing of the game. A home run to win a game against Montreal in the bottom of the ninth, after striking out four times on twelve pitches."

I asked what he remembered about that game, and of course he replied: "The thirteenth swing."

That was on May 28, 1983. Schmidt was whiffed by a couple of big righties, the first three times by Charlie Lea and then once again in the seventh by Ray Burris. With Rob Dernier on second after pinch-running for Joe Morgan, Schmidt connected on lucky swing number 13 for the two-run homer and an end to a six-game Phillies losing streak.

Worth digressing: The top of the order in that ninth inning featured Pete Rose, Morgan, and then Schmidt after Gary Matthews. Granted, Morgan was a year away from his swan song and Pete was in the latter phase, but that was some hitting for reliever Jeff Reardon to get through. Those are three players who were definitely at top of mind when I started writing this book, players who helped define my own passage into the game. Alas, Reardon was unable to make a clean getaway through that group.

As we spoke, Schmidt was getting closer to a clear choice.

"To define my career . . . it would have been the 500th home run, things like that. You do pass a lot of important people on the way in a home run chase, so they're all memorable. I remember McCovey, Mantle—number 536. I remember those at-bats. . . ."

Now he was closing in, like he had done so many times at bat, fouling off breaking balls and taking waste pitches while sitting on the one he wanted. Here it came, finally, the one you put the barrel of the bat on and send into orbit. It was from the 1980 season, when he led the NL with 48 homers and 121 RBIs, led the Phillies to their first World Series title, and claimed his first of three NL MVP awards.

"The biggest one for me was Montreal in 1980. We went to Olympic Stadium and had to win two out of three to win the National League East, against some tough pitching."

Schmidt had opened the Friday-to-Sunday series by clubbing a solo homer off Scott Sanderson to provide the difference in a 2–1 victory at Montreal. On Saturday, the Phillies clinched the pennant with a 6–4 triumph, thanks to his blast off Stan Bahnsen, at the time Schmidt's fourth homer in his last four games.

Amazingly, Schmidt homered in each of the last four regular season games. Talk about a clutch superstar.

"I hit that two-run home run in the top of the 11th to win that game," Schmidt recalled. "Rose was on base and they pitched to me. Dick Williams did. I hit the home run to win the game, and that home run really defined me. I was sort of starving for a big hit in a key time, a prominent hit for the organization. That probably would have been it, because from that point on, I think my career started skyrocketing after I hit it."

FRANK ROBINSON

"How can you do that? Twenty-nine hundred hits and I have to decide on one?" Frank Robinson asked me. We were at the NASDAQ headquarters in Times Square the morning of the 2012 First-Year Player Draft, an event that was not around back when Robby entered the big leagues. On this morning, he was among a group of legends ringing the opening bell, and after ringing it, I asked him for one hit. He finally agreed.

"My first one. My first hit in the big leagues. Double off the center-field wall against the St. Louis Cardinals, playing against Stan Musial," he said. "It was exciting for me. Opening Day. Never forget the first one. You always remember the first one. You always hope a lot more are going to come after that, but you're not sure."

I asked who was pitching, and he said, "Vinegar Bend Mizell. Told you, you'll never forget it. He became a Congressman later."

It was April 17, 1956. Robinson was a 20-year-old left fielder who had gone to McClymonds High School in Oakland and had been signed by Cincinnati as an amateur free agent in 1953. It was still a time of turbulence for a black man going into professional baseball and pursuing the Majors, but by the time this Robinson got to the parent club, almost a decade had gone by since Jackie Robinson, no relation, had broken the color barrier.

Frank's first game for the Reds was at chilly Crosley Field, and he would go on to tie Wally Berger's 1930 National League rookie record of 38 homers. The first man Robinson faced, Mizell, was a 6–3 lefty who had won 10 games as a rookie in 1952 and then 13 more in 1953. Mizell missed the 1954–55 campaigns because of military service, so that 1956 Opening Day game not only represented Robinson's Major League debut, but also the return of the guy they called Vinegar Bend.

In the bottom of the second, with one out and the Cardinals up 1–0, Mizell gave up a solo homer to Ray Jablonski. That brought up Robinson. Given his trademark number 20 right off the bat, Robinson laced it for a ground-rule double. On that day, Musial broke a 2–2 tie with a two-run homer in the top of the ninth, and Mizell stuck around long enough to record the decision, one of 14 he won that season for St. Louis. Robinson, meanwhile, went on to lead the league in runs (122), be named NL Rookie of the Year, and receive the first of 12 All-Star selections. He would later become the first black manager (a player/manager with Cleveland), be inducted into the Hall of Fame in 1982, and serve as a special assistant to the Commissioner.

"He was a tough out from time to time," Hall of Fame pitcher Ferguson Jenkins said as he stood next to Robinson during our conversation. "In Cincinnati, and then he went over to Cleveland as a manager. It was a challenge to get certain people out."

"What made him so tough?" I asked.

"He was on top of the plate with his elbow in the strike zone, so I used to try to knock it off. We had a few battles. I didn't want to wake him up, but there were some times. He didn't hit a home run off of me until he was a designated manager/player. Other than that, he didn't hurt me, but that one particular time he pinch-hit as a manager, I was with the Rangers at the time, and he ended up hitting a two-run homer off of me. He may not remember it, but I do."

Robinson remembers just about everything in that glorious career, from that first hit to those at-bats against Fergie.

"I hated hitting against him," Robinson countered. "The real key to Fergie was great control, with his slider and fastball. Pitching in Wrigley Field and doing what he did, that was quite an accomplishment. When you faced him you just wanted to get out of there."

DON MATTINGLY

I have my own favorite Don Mattingly hit. It was one of five that he slashed against our team one chilly day as high schoolers in our mutual hometown of Evansville, Indiana. He was a year behind me, playing for state powerhouse Memorial High. I was playing for Central. While I take ever-increasing pride in having caught two of his fly balls to center one day on his home field, I have vivid memory of him being such a natural, stroking a hit really whenever he wanted, and being virtually impossible to strike out as well as hit against whenever he took the mound.

As a Major Leaguer, Donnie Baseball was the pride of our hometown, still is. In his first full season, he led the Majors with 207 hits and won the American League batting title with a .343 average. Then it was 211 hits, then 238. He led the Majors with 145 RBIs in 1985, and won the AL MVP award. He was an All-Star six years in a row, unquestionably the dominant player at his position in his time, with nine Gold Gloves. He amassed 2,153 hits over his 14 seasons, all with the Yankees, a certain Hall of Fame career cut short only because of ongoing back issues that stole his thunder.

"One hit?" he asked me after managing his first season with the Dodgers in 2011. "Oh, my first one, probably. It was the start. First one you ever get.

"That was at the end of '82, you come up out of Triple A and you get a chance. Just that first one, the realization you got a hit in the big leagues."

Mattingly came up for the final seven games of that 1982 regular season. Starting as an outfielder, he had appeared in his first four games without a hit. The first game he never came to the plate, and he was 0-for-1 as a replacement in each of the next three. In his fourth game, he did drive in his first career run, a sacrifice fly at Cleveland after replacing Dave Winfield during a Yankees rout. Then the breakthrough, fittingly, came when Mattingly saw his first action as a Major League first baseman.

It was October 1, 1982, and the Yankees and the rival Red Sox were clashing again at the very end of a season, this time at Fenway Park. Steve Balboni had given way to pinch-hitter Graig Nettles in the ninth, and then Mattingly was the new first baseman in the 10th. Going into the top of the 11th, it was still tied at 1–1. Steve Crawford replaced Mark Clear on the mound for Boston. Leading off was the rookie from Evansville with the cobra-crouching swing, weight back in his stance, then exploding into the ball.

"I remember I didn't hit it that good," Mattingly said. "Hit a little roller in the hole to the right side, but it was a hit. And that was the biggest thing."

For all of that statistical glory, none of it truly tells the story of Don Mattingly, though. He was the guy who faithfully signed autographs at the start of every homestand at Yankee Stadium, the superstar whose signature you knew you could get because he cared about people, the Captain who was a true leader. When he gave an acceptance speech for a Lifetime Achievement Award at the 2011 MLB Players Alumni Association Legends for Youth fundraising dinner, Donnie Baseball was talking about his Dodgers players (he subsequently became manager of the Marlins) and talking mainly for many former players in the crowd:

"I learned to play baseball the way it's supposed to be played from the guys you grew up with. The guys you watched play the game. It's the same thing I try to bring to our club . . . we play the game with respect. Not only for the fans who come to see you play, but also the people who played the game before you, and the way they played it."

Mattingly's fans wanted to see him play in a postseason, and it was a shame that it never happened until the very end of his career. He certainly made the most of that long-awaited opportunity, batting .417 (10-for-24) with five extra-base hits and six RBIs in that unforgettable five-game American League Division Series won by Seattle. This book begins with "The Double" by Edgar Martinez, and it was that hit that ended Donnie Baseball's days as a player. Had Mattingly played for the Yankees in a World Series, I think it is likely he would have responded with a hit from late autumn.

ANDRE DAWSON

In the 45th game of his Major League career, Andre Dawson did something that would stick with him until the moment we discussed his favorite hit.

"One hit had to be my first home run, because I was on the verge of being sent back down to the Minor Leagues," he said. "It happened during my rookie season, and I was platooned with another left-handed hitter, a veteran outfielder, and that hit kind of jump-started my season. It gave me an opportunity to start playing every day.

"It was off of Buzz Capra. It landed out on the teepee where Chief Noc-A-Homa was."

That was in Atlanta-Fulton County Stadium on May 18, 1977. The game itself was a slugfest, with Atlanta holding leads of 8–1 and 9–5 before Dawson would strike his leadoff blow against Capra in the top of the eighth, and the result was a 10–8 Braves victory. Most respondents to the question in this book evoked a game that ended with a victory for their teams, but it was not the final result that mattered even several decades later to the Hawk. The hit meant he belonged. He had been homerless with just one stolen base over 24 games as a call-up in 1976, and now, 21 games into his first full season, Dawson was on the board. He had the power Montreal hoped to see. And not just power, but speed—two tools that would carry him one day into the Hall of Fame. He was batting only .225 entering that game, but the home run made a difference—to him.

Dawson finished that 1977 season with 19 homers and 21 steals, winning National League Rookie of the Year. Then in 1978, it was 25 and 28, respectively. Then in '79, it was 25 and 35. When it was all over, Dawson had 438 homers and 314 steals, eight All-Star selections, eight Gold Gloves. He also had one of the best instant payoffs of any free agent in history, winning the NL MVP award in 1987 after signing with the Cubs, finishing with 49 homers, 137 RBIs, and 11 steals. His last season was 1996 with his hometown Marlins, and that is the club he was representing when we spoke at a Play Ball launch event next to Yankee Stadium in June of 2015, right on the site of the old House That Ruth Built. Dawson waited too long to enter Cooperstown, but he was finally inducted in 2010, as a new emphasis on comparative analytics helped his cause.

Once he was there, it was a beautiful moment. I never heard a better Hall of Fame speech than the one The Hawk gave, with all those Cubs fans in the crowd, people representing different stops in his career. The theme of his speech was: "If you love this game, it will love you back." If you respect the game and work your way up, with a positive attitude, finally hitting that first home run after a tough start and proving you belong, it will love you back. In that speech, he quoted his grandmother, Eunice Taylor, who played such a big role in his young life: "As my grandmother used to say, 'Take God with you. Get on your knees and believe it. Be thankful of the blessings before you receive them. You can get left behind or you can get on board.'"

That is exactly what a long home run off Buzz Capra symbolized on the path to baseball immortality. It was that moment you when you get on board.

ERIC DAVIS

"My first hit was a triple in St. Louis off of Dave LaPoint," Eric Davis said as the 2012 postseason was getting under way. He was the Reds' special assistant to the general manager when we spoke. "Because when you are in the Minor Leagues and you get hyped and you come up, there's a certain amount of pressure. You might not talk about it, but you never really know what you can do until you actually get out there and start to perform, and to start to play against guys who you dreamt about playing against, who you saw on TV."

For Davis, thoughts of one hit brought to mind an actual pair of bookends, because he really wanted to talk about his first one and his last one.

"My first hit was very important, and my last hit was a double off Chan Ho Park when I was in San Francisco, to signify the longevity of 18 years. I was able to set that apart. There were a lot of great things that transpired in between those two dates, but the first one and the last one were synonymous as bookends, because that's where it started and that's where it finished."

Davis came up to the parent Reds on May 19, 1984, the year their legend, Pete Rose, also became their player-manager. That day at St. Louis, Joaquin Andujar was on the mound for the Cardinals, hurling a complete game, and Davis pinch-hit to lead off the fifth inning and grounded out to short in his first big-league at-bat.

The next day, Davis was starting in center, batting second behind Gary Redus in the Cincinnati lineup. First inning, strikeout. Third inning, groundout to second. He was 0-for-3 in the bigs. Then came the top of the fifth, scoreless game, 29,646 fans at Busch Stadium, the 21-year-old phenom from Los Angeles up to bat against Dave LaPoint with that unique stance, hands at waist level in front of him instead of cocked back.

"You're trying to get that first hit," Davis remembers. "The anxiety, your legs are shaking, and things are bubbling. When you finally get it out of the way, it's like a big weight off your shoulders."

Where did it go? How did LaPoint react?

"It was down the right-field line for a triple. And he's still mad at me."

BRIAN MCCANN

Brian McCann's second inning home run off of Roger Clemens in the NLDS made a big impression

Courtesy of Dennis Adair

"For me, it happened my first year, in the postseason, hitting a homer off Roger Clemens in my first postseason at-bat."

There was no doubt about this one when I talked to McCann before the 2016 Thurman Munson Award Dinner at the Grand Hyatt in New York. He was a Yankees catcher at this point in his career, but in this setting, far removed from playing in the days before Spring Training, his mind flashed back to his earliest Atlanta days.

"I'm 21 years old, catching in a postseason game. I'm catching John Smoltz, and facing Roger Clemens. I grew up a huge fan of both of those guys," McCann said. "It was just a surreal moment. I was able to come up in a big spot and come through, so that sticks out the most to me."

It was 2005. The Braves were back in the National League Division Series for a record 14th and final consecutive year (labor-shortened 1994 season excluded). Houston finally had broken through against Atlanta the previous year in eliminating the Braves in five, and now McCann was on a new stage as Atlanta's rookie catcher.

After Houston won Game One at Turner Field, Smoltz started opposite Clemens and the Astros jumped ahead quickly with a run in the first. In the bottom of the second, Clemens gave up a leadoff single to Andruw Jones, who was sacrificed to second on an Adam LaRoche bunt. Jeff Francoeur walked, and that brought up McCann with men on first and second. Clemens threw him a 2–0 fastball and was unable to locate it, and the kid made the legend pay for the missed location by crushing it over the right-center wall. It was suddenly 3–1, on the way to a 7–1 victory to even the series.

Houston would take Game Three back home at Minute Maid Park, and then came the historic Game Four, which the Astros won in 18 innings as Clemens came out of the bullpen to pitch the 16th through 18th innings. McCann actually hit another key homer in that one, a solo shot that gave Atlanta a seemingly safe 6–1 lead in the eighth inning—before Lance Berkman's grand slam and Brad Ausmus's solo homer sent Game Four into extras.

This really was the end of the glory run for Bobby Cox's Braves, as this resulted in a fourth consecutive elimination in the NLDS for Atlanta. But for McCann, it was the start of a special career, requiring a curtain call that night and leaving a lasting impression not only on others but on himself as well.

"I learned from that moment to not get caught up in the moment," he told me. "There were 50,000 screaming fans there, and I was just trying to stay focused on what I had to do. Trying to execute and not get caught up in my surroundings, and focus on the game plan and get the win."

REGGIE SMITH

At the 2014 Baseball Assistance Team fundraiser dinner in Manhattan, I sat at a table with Reggie Smith and we started talking about hitting. He was curious how others had answered.

"I would be surprised if most Hall of Famers didn't say their first hit in the big leagues," he said, "because if anything, I'd like to think that proved that I could hit Major League pitching. I remember it was a single—the excitement and joy that I felt when I got it here in New York in Yankee

Stadium off Fritz Peterson. I had three hits in that game. Those are the ones you remember. It told me especially that doing it in Yankee Stadium against the Yankees, it meant a lot. It meant I had arrived."

Smith, an outfielder from Compton, California, was signed by the Twins as an amateur free agent in June of 1963, and then selected from the Twins that same December by the Red Sox in the First-Year Draft. Boston called him up from Triple A Toronto in September of 1966, after it already had replaced its manager, Billy Herman, with Pete Runnels amid a horrid 72–90 season. Smith was part of the shakeup, an intended sparkplug, and he went 0-for-5 in his debut at home against the Angels and then went 0-for-4 in his next game five days later at Yankee Stadium. Both times he was leading off and playing center field for Runnels.

Game number 157 of that Red Sox season was the breakthrough for their rookie call-up. Smith singled to left in the first at-bat of the game in New York, and then he doubled to center with two out in the third. Anything was possible now. He led off the sixth with a strikeout, and singled to the left side in the eighth. Alas, Smith was the only trouble that day for Peterson, who fired a six-hit (half to Smith) shutout. Smith would go on to finish as runner-up for the 1967 AL Rookie of the Year Award, helping Boston to the first of his four World Series appearances, the last of which would result in a 1981 ring with his hometown Dodgers. He finished with 2,020 hits (25 more in postseasons) and was selected to seven All-Star Games. He also finished with a 64.5 wins above replacement (WAR), and considering that almost every right fielder who ranked above him on the all-time list (16th as of 2017) was in the Hall of Fame, Smith stands as one of those players who gets even better when advanced metrics are contemplated long after his retirement.

6

COME HOME WITH JOY

It was 1744 in London when John Newberry penned a children's book, *A Little Pretty Pocket-Book*. It featured a poem that once was considered the earliest known reference to baseball.[2] One cannot cull from it specific evidence of a hit, but evidence nonetheless that hits were just as integral then. It went:

B is for Base-ball

The Ball once struck off,

Away flies the Boy

To the next destin'd Post,

And then Home with Joy.

If the Ball once struck off and the boy came home, then we are going to record a hit here, the first one we know about. And the best part of all is the mental picture of the boy running "Home with Joy," because that is the fun at the heart of baseball. Fortunately, we have seen this happen in the course of most memorable hits. Chipper Jones' helmet is still flying through the air as he receives a hero's welcome at home plate after a classic *mano a mano* triumph. George Brett hit two newsworthy home runs off the great Goose Gossage, one that they took away and one that is immortalized right here. Rickey Henderson and Wade Boggs came "Home with Joy" in their own unique and calculated ways, by slide and by smooch, respectively. Chris Chambliss found a little too much joy in rounding the bases one night. Dave Parker remembered walking to first on a big homer just because he was floored at doing something for the first time, and Jim Eisenreich thanked the Lord above as he rounded the bases. Mark McGwire savored a special birthday as he ran around the bases with the whole baseball world watching, and away flew my own boy with joy.

---

2   David Block, *Baseball Before We Knew It: A Search for the Roots of the Game* (Bison Books, 2006).

CHIPPER JONES

Courtesy of Darkensiva

Always a strong hitter, Chipper Jones cites a hit
in his last season as his most meaningful

This book is being released just before I receive a ballot in the mail that allows me to gratefully check a box next to the name of Chipper Jones as a presumed first-ballot Hall of Famer. Writing this, I am awash in memories of number 10. For a generation, he was the embodiment of reliability, competition, consistent clutch performance and postseason presence, along with Derek Jeter over in the American League.

We are happily brimming on these pages with some of history's finest third basemen: Brooks Robinson, Mike Schmidt, George Brett, and Wade Boggs among them. Jones will be remembered among that group. The question here is whether he would summon from those 12 years of postseason baseball, or perhaps go back to one of those hits at Shea Stadium that always infuriated rival Mets fans who, largely out of respect, so often taunted him with chants of "Larry, Larry" in reference to his given first name. Jones had 2,726 regular season hits in 19 years, plus 97 postseason hits, and add to that his collective 6-for-14 showings across eight Midsummer Classics.

"I was very fortunate to have stood in the batter's box in some really special moments against some guys for whom I have a tremendous amount of respect," Jones said. "Being with the Braves for so many years, I was also in some really big playoff games that meant a lot to our city and our fans. And I can never forget the All-Star Game experiences, facing some of the game's best arms, specifically the one in Atlanta.

"However, the hit that stands out the most for me was the walk-off home run I hit off of Jonathan Papelbon in 2012, the year I retired, in the last month of the season."

It was an unforgettable farewell season for Jones. I covered his final All-Star Game that summer as fans across baseball sent him out in style, and aside from his single off Chris Sale that night, I will never forget how he sat there in front of his locker as long as possible after that game. He packed his equipment, soaking in every last moment and that familiar feeling of being amongst the best in the business.

On September 2 of that season, the Phillies built an early 7–1 lead at Turner Field against a Braves team that was 14 games over .500 and headed for one last Chipper Jones postseason. A two-run single by Reed Johnson in the sixth cut it to 7–3, and that was the score entering the bottom of the ninth. Papelbon, in his first NL season after a long run with Boston, had been Jones' teammate in that aforementioned 2012 All-Star Game. Now Papelbon was on the mound, loading the bases with a two-out walk, and in a jam as Martin Prado reached on an error by the third baseman and two more runs scored to make it 7–5.

That brought up Jones, who had been hitless in his first four at-bats. Two out, two on. The great switch-hitter batted lefty against the right-hander, power versus power.

"This was one of the best closers the game had seen over the previous 10 years; a guy that I always enjoyed competing against; a guy that was going to come after you with his best stuff every night; a true power closer," Jones told me. "I took great pride in performing in the clutch and my team wanting me in the box with the game on the line. I cannot describe for you the feeling of getting a big hit late in the game or to walk off the field. This at-bat had all of those qualities. This moment also happened to be the last home run I ever hit, and it was to walk off against a guy who was a perennial All-Star and one of the game's best closers as I was getting ready to ride off into the sunset."

Papelbon's first two pitches were 94-mph four-seamers. The first one missed inside, and the second one was fouled off. The great hitters rarely get fooled twice, and Papelbon's third pitch was virtually identical (95 mph) to the second. Chipper unloaded, and the ballpark was bedlam. A longtime superstar and community icon came home with joy, flinging his helmet high into the night air as he was greeted by gleeful teammates at the plate. It was his 14th home run of the season and the 468th of his career.

Even after the standard five-year waiting period for Hall of Fame eligibility, Jones was going with one so fresh in the memory.

"It was the perfect ending to a game; it was the perfect ending to a career; all in a game I loved," he said.

GEORGE BRETT

I talked to many members of the elite 3,000 Hit Club for this book, and it was fascinating to see which men wanted to talk about that magical milestone or some other moment that was more treasured to them personally. In George Brett's case, it was both, based on two interviews I did with him in Kansas City spanning nearly a quarter-century, and you will gradually learn which hit meant the most to him and why.

For the first one, I dug through a box of old issues of *The Sporting News* in my basement to find the cover story I wrote about Brett for the February 1, 1993 issue. For that assignment, I drove with legendary baseball photographer Rich Pilling from the magazine's home in St. Louis across I-70 to Kansas City, where Brett had invited us to his favorite barbecue haunt. Brett was preparing for what would be his 21st and final season as a Royal and was in the midst of a temporary rift with his forever-love franchise, as then-owner Ewing Kauffman had regretfully suggested that it might be time for the local legend, nearing his 40th birthday, to step aside and make room for a rookie. That had only motivated Brett, and he would wind up with his usual number of at-bats in '93, but his third straight year batting under .300 (.266). It was time to go, and he knew it.

So Brett met us at the BBQ joint, and we talked over burnt ends and beans about what was still driving him to play. "I always played the game because I loved to play the game of baseball," he said then, explaining a host of reasons why he was still motivated. He even mentioned Dave Winfield, citing the double that his future fellow Hall of Famer had hit to lead Toronto to its first World Series title just three months earlier, an example of a great near the end of his career, savoring some twilight glory. It was the same double, in fact, that Winfield would recall for the purposes of this book, another example of a 3,000 Hit Club member choosing between that big milestone and one that meant something bigger personally.

After we finished our barbeque, we drove to his new English Normandy estate in the exclusive Mission Hills neighborhood on the Kansas side of the border and talked with him and his new wife Leslie. They were preparing at the time for the arrival of their firstborn, Jackson Brett, named for George's late father Jack. I will never forget the moment when Leslie tried to convince George that a tan carpet sample went with the teddy-bear border on their blue-striped wallpaper in that nursery, and George proceeded to spit a prodigious stream of tobacco juice smack-dab onto the center of the yet-uncovered floor. "He's done that in every room," Leslie said with a sigh. That was George Brett, all right, always leaving his mark.

And always hitting. Here he was, a new member of that 3,000 Hit Club, sitting on 3,005 at the time. The big one was still fresh in everyone's minds. Robin Yount, yet another 3,000 Hit Club member who chose a different hit for this book, had just reached the milestone weeks earlier in the 1992 season. Some had questioned whether Brett had enough gas left in his tank to get there, but he had summoned his old magic and made a big run, batting .308 in the second half and chipping away during the Royals' final road trip. It started with three games at Minnesota, where Brett was injured in the finale. The Royals flew to Anaheim to play the Angels, and Brett missed the first two games. Time running out; there were only five more games left in the season, the Royals were long out of contention, and the best player in franchise history was stuck on 2,996 hits. At that point, I figured that he would return for the 1993 season if he was unable to reach 3,000, but he would have no reason to come back if he made it.

On Wednesday, September 30, 1992, Brett went 4-for-5 to get there in style. The first three hits came off Angels starter Julio Valero, and history happened in the seventh when Brett stroked a one-hop single off reliever Tim Fortugno. While some people may remember that Brett was subsequently picked off first—making Brett shrug with an oh-well smile and causing Leslie to be captured laughing on camera—perhaps forgotten is the fact that Brett would reach base a fifth time, thanks to an error by the second baseman in the ninth.

"It was more of a relief," Brett said as we walked through the house. "I didn't want to go through a whole winter of thinking about it, but I knew it wasn't going to be easy. I had torn some muscles in my right arm. Swinging at a pitch on a Sunday in Minnesota, [John] Smiley threw me a ball that sort of sailed, and at the last second I had to reach out a little farther, and I felt my arm cramp up. I stayed in the game, and each time I swung it got sorer and sorer, and the next day I could hardly lift it. I got a cortisone shot that Monday, and we did treatments all day and then all night during the game Tuesday in Anaheim. On that Wednesday, I went out and I said, 'I can swing a bat off a tee and it hurts a little bit, but if I swing easy I think I can get through the night. I'm just going to try to get one hit tonight.' I knew time was running out. We had five games [to go], and I needed four hits.

"I got a little blooper my first at-bat, a little ground ball to right my second at-bat, then I hit a line drive to center my third at-bat. And the last one, I hit it harder than I hit all three of the others. But I just swung so easy and stayed within myself, I was the most surprised person in the ballpark, to go out and get four hits in a situation like that, where you actually needed to get some hits."

There was a lot you can learn from watching George Brett play baseball. He told me that day: "I get more comments on the way I play than the success that I've had hit-wise, average-wise and RBI-wise." He played hard and with bravado. Witness the famous 1983 Pine Tar Game at Yankee Stadium, when another hit he could have chosen—a two-run homer off fellow future Hall of Famer Goose Gossage, was erased after Yankees manager Billy Martin protested that the pine tar on Brett's bat was higher than allowed. Brett had come roaring and charting out of the dugout, replayed for time immemorial.

No, Brett did not choose the Pine Tar Game homer for this book. But he did choose a home run off Gossage at Yankee Stadium, another thing that amazes me about his glorious career. How many guys launched legendary homers off Gossage in the House That Ruth Built?

I had a chance to conduct a more recent interview with him in Kansas City. It was batting practice before Game Two of the 2015 World Series at Kauffman Stadium, named for that iconic owner who had shown the temerity to question whether his iconic franchise player might want to call it a career. It was a picturesque late-October night there, and the city's favorite son, as Vice President of Baseball Operations, was watching the Mets take batting practice and began to venture toward the Royals clubhouse. These were the kind of nights when he once thrived. On his way in, I asked him what, among all those hits, he deemed his favorite and why.

"Home run off [Goose] Gossage in 1980," Brett said, matter-of-factly. "We won the first two games in New York, and now we were in Kansas City. This was the third and final game of the playoffs. We were losing at the time, and the Yankees had beaten us in '76, '77, and '78. I came up and hit a three-run home run to win the ball game. Even though it was the seventh or eighth inning, but it was a big hit for us."

Many people remember that homer as one of the loudest cracks of a bat they ever heard. Gossage would talk about that often in later years, comparing it to the sound of a cannon blast. Al Michaels, who called that game, would say he never heard the sound of a crowd go so quickly from uproarious to silent. That was Game Three of the 1980 American League

Championship Series (ALCS), when it was still a best-of-five format, and after the Royals had won the first two games at home. The Yankees had finally come alive with back-to-back singles by Oscar Gamble and Rick Cerone off Royals reliever Dan Quisenberry in the sixth inning, bringing the crowd to life. With two out and two on in the seventh, Gossage uncorked a straight fastball that covered the plate and was absolutely crushed by Brett. The ball was hit with such torque that it flew high into the third deck in right field.

I had seen Brett "Home with Joy" once before, there in the tobacco-spit nursery room as he began a new chapter in life in 1993. But if you ever want to see the definition of "Home with Joy" in a baseball trot, then watch the replay of that home run off Gossage. It took Brett a good half a minute to round the bases, a clear definition of the word "trot" as he savored every prancing step in the ballpark where he loved to slug, where his competitive juices flowed like the juice on that nursery floor.

I did not ask this specific question that day at his home in 1993, so I cannot say for sure whether 3,000 would have been so fresh in his mind that he would have cited it, or this one, or perhaps something more unexpected. Sometimes it is important where you ask this question, as he was clearly caught up in the heat of a Royals World Series bid, one that would lead to a parade for the ages.

"You came up with that one so surely and quickly," I said of the 1980 hit off Gossage.

"That would be the one," he said. "Yes, that would be the one."

RICKEY HENDERSON AND BO JACKSON

You have to fast-forward 23 years into Rickey Henderson's remarkable 25-year Major League career to find his hit of a lifetime. The first thing he did in even contemplating this exercise was to laugh heartily. It was like a kid sticking a hand into a filled candy jar and knowing you would come out with something wonderful, and by the time Bo Jackson sidled up to both of us near a batting cage one summer afternoon, it was all getting out of hand in a delightful way that can only happen when those two get together.

"I think if I had to pick one of them," Rickey said, "I'd probably say that my most memorable hit, or my most favorite hit, was probably playing with the San Diego Padres. I hit a home run to break the run-scoring record, so I remember that more than anything."

That happened on October 4, 2001, in his final days with the Padres as part of a tour of clubs to play as long as humanly possible. Ty Cobb had set the career record in 1928, and Henderson finally broke it with run number 2,246. He had planned that he was going to slide into home no matter what, so nothing about that was going to change even after the inimitable leadoff hitter took Dodgers right-hander Luke Prokopec deep with one out in the third inning at Qualcomm Stadium. Padres teammates formed a welcome reception at home plate, but Rickey cleared out space in the crowd so that he could slide into home with the record run under the watchful eye of umpire Mike Everitt. Future Hall of Famer Tony Gwynn presented Henderson with a gold-plated home plate to commemorate the occasion.

Never mind that just three days later, on the final day of that season, Henderson stroked a leadoff double for his 3,000th hit. The record-run homer was his hit of a lifetime, on the record. At that point, Bo came over and stood next to him, leaning in to hear everything we were saying about the great subject of hits.

"What would Bo say?" I asked Rickey, figuring we should add him to this.

Rickey translates: "One hit in your career, what do you like?"

"One I hit?" Bo shoots back. "When I hit that guy and we had that bench-clearing scene and I hit him in the nose. That one."

Rickey laughs, machine-gun laughter.

Bo: "About knocked his ass out."

Rickey: "I know that one was good."

Me: "Was there one hit with a bat?"

Bo: "No, bench-clearing."

We were done. I would have really liked to have included Bo's 448-foot signature home run he pulverized in the 1989 All-Star Game at Anaheim, but if he wants to go with a blow to the face, documented or otherwise, then I am not going to protest.

WADE BOGGS

After 3,010 hits in 18 years, Wade Boggs was coaching high school baseball players in the Tampa Bay area when we spoke in 2014. "They're like little balls of clay," Boggs said of his kids. "You get to mold them your own way and teach them the game the right way. For some of these kids who may not know who we are, they can sort of Google us down the road and find out what it was like when we played."

Let's hope they read this book, because there will be plenty of insight into what it was like when he and many other great hitters played. In Boggs' case, they will understand why, out of all those hits over a Hall of Fame career, the one that mattered most to him was one of the very last.

"Number one is just as important as number 3,000," he began. "To get your first hit in the big leagues. But my number 3,000 was in grand fashion— the first guy to do it with a home run. So that has the most significance.

"There was a big buildup. We were at home. That Friday night I had gone 0-for-4, and we had a Saturday game and I needed three hits. I was facing Charlie Nagy at the time, and I didn't have too much success off of him. But I wound up getting a couple hits off of him. They brought in Chris Haney, a lefty, and I wound up hitting a home run for 3,000. So it was a fitting end for everything that led up to that."

It was August 7, 1999, a Saturday night game in front of 39,512 fans at Tropicana Field. The "Devil Rays" were still far from turning the corner as a competitive franchise then, and they were playing a powerhouse in Cleveland. The chance to see a 3,000-hit milestone was a magical time in St. Petersburg, Fla. Fortunately for Boggs, it was a slugfest. Everybody hit, and it was a great day for legends going deep. Manny Ramirez and Jim Thome homered for the visiting Tribe. The final score was 15–10, Cleveland.

Boggs had grounded out to second his first time up, so it was not looking likely that the milestone was going to happen on this night. But he had five plate appearances and reached base four of those times, as the bats thundered all night. Boggs delivered RBI singles off Nagy in the third and fourth innings, and history was made in the sixth. The reliever Haney threw a big hook, and Boggs turned on it, yanking it three rows deep into the right-field seats. He gave first-base coach Billy Hatcher high-fives, did a little Kirk Gibson pump, and then pointed up at the sky, even though it was covered with a roof. A fan tried to reach him just before he reached home plate, and security attendants tackled the man. Boggs, unfazed, got down on his knees and kissed home plate.

"It was a 1–2 count and he threw me a curveball," Boggs remembered. "MLB had exchanged the balls out with a hologram so that if it was a ground-rule double or a home run, they could authenticate it. It turned out it was a home run."

We talked at the 2014 MLBPAA Dinner, where he accepted the Lifetime Achievement Award along with Brooksie, the impetus for this book project and the man after whom Boggs said he patterned his game. I asked him to describe what it felt like to hit so successfully in his career, and Boggs replied, "It's a science. I think Ted Williams explained it very well. 'It's one of the most difficult things to do, hit a round ball with a round bat—and do it consistently.' For guys who can do it on a consistent basis, to hit .340, .350, or .360, then you're a little bit head and shoulders above everybody else."

CHRIS CHAMBLISS

"Pretty easy for me, because I hit the home run that put the Yankees into the World Series in '76 for the first time in twelve years. So that was obviously the biggest home run of my life," Chris Chambliss said, almost 40 years to the day since it happened.

"The only lesson is, I was just at the right place at the right time. It was just a great moment. The only lesson I got from it really was the fact that dreams come true. That's what that was, that was a dream."

It was October 14, 1976, the decisive Game Five of the ALCS between the Royals and Yankees, the year when America celebrated its bicentennial and Chambliss celebrated his finest season. He was selected to his only All-Star Game that summer, leading Billy Martin's Yankees to 97 wins, and he had been locked in at the plate during that playoff series, already singling and doubling before coming to the plate to face right-handed reliever Mark Littell to start the bottom of the ninth.

The World Series had been a fact of life for generations of Yankees fans, but they had gone a dozen years in a row without an appearance, their longest such drought since Babe Ruth came over from the Red Sox, dating back to the seven-game loss to the Cardinals in 1964. To say that their fans were hungry for a Fall Classic would be a great understatement. George Brett, who had so many candidates for his greatest hit, had temporarily disquieted the sellout crowd of 56,821 with a three-run homer off Ed Figueroa to tie the score at 6–6 in the top of the eighth. But Figeroa had answered right back by retiring three straight Royals, and now those fans were ready to explode onto the field, despite the readiness of New York's finest, who were poised in the bullpens and elsewhere. It was up to Chambliss, the first baseman who had slugged 17 homers during the season, who would go 11-for-21 in the ALCS.

There was a delay while Chambliss waited—and perhaps preventing Littell from getting adequately loose. Legendary Yankees P.A. announcer Bob Sheppard warned the crowd about throwing debris onto the playing field, but there already had been multiple delays caused by bottles, beer cans, firecrackers and toilet paper being thrown onto the field. It was sure to be a wild scene if the home team won.

Courtesy of Jim Accordino

Chris Chambliss put the Yankees into the 1976 World Series
with a home run

"It was just a tight moment, because it was a game that went back and forth," Chambliss continued during a cocktail reception at an MLB alumni event in Manhattan. "We had a three-run lead, and it was the eighth inning when George Brett hit a home run and tied the game. So we come into the last of the ninth, and I was the first hitter, so it was really a tense moment. I happened to hit the first pitch, high fastball, and hit it out. It was a great moment."

It was a high-and-tight fastball, and Chambliss, batting with a slightly closed stance, turned on it fast and tomahawked it high into the air. The ball came down toward the right-field fence, in front of those cops, and Hal McRae's attempt to leap and catch it fell just short. Chambliss had taken a moment on his swing to watch the ball's mighty arc, and it became clear soon that he would need to get a move on.

Fans poured onto the field, a scene so far from today's reality in sports. Rounding second, he was jostled and lost his balance for a moment, before regaining himself and trying to find any kind of path toward third base. In fact, second base was actually uprooted by a fan before he got to it, so he reached out and tagged it with his hand while trying to circle the bases. At that point, it became a matter of survival more than an effort to touch home plate. And so he never did, as police tried to help escort him through the chaos and finally into the dugout ahead of Willie Randolph.

"It was a little rough for me, because all of the fans came on the field right after I hit it," Chambliss said. "I had to make my way through a lot of fans and knock some people over and stuff. It was a wild run."

Teammate Graig Nettles coaxed Chambliss back out of the clubhouse to try to make it official and touch home plate. Chambliss was given an NYPD raincoat to throw on and escorted back out there to do just that, as home plate umpire Art Frantz was still waiting and had made no formal signal. Alas, there was no home plate. Fans had uprooted that, too. So Chambliss touched the hole where home plate once rested, and that was good enough for Frantz, making the Bronx Bombers' return to the biggest stage official.

I asked Chambliss, still burly and strong approaching his 68th birthday when we spoke, if he had played football back in the day.

"I did, I played in college," said Chambliss, who had attended MiraCosta College in Oceanside, Calif.; Montclair State; and then UCLA. "I played end at first, but then I became a halfback later on. I was OK, I was OK."

OK enough that he romped 65 yards for a touchdown on his first carry as a running back after moving to that position his senior year. He was a burly football player, and that is what Chambliss looked like on that glorious night for the Yankees.

"And then Home with Joy;" this one was a little different. It brought him joy, it brought his fans joy, but you could forgive him for not exactly smiling his way around the bases. He has said that he still has the bat and ball from that moment, courtesy of the NYPD. No one knows where the helmet went, because fans stole it during his journey home.

"That was just a culmination of a great year," Chambliss said. "We went into that year into the new Yankee Stadium, because they refurbished the ballpark. Seventy-six was a special year, and it ended with that home run. We played the Reds and they wiped us out in the World Series, but again, that home run was really the highlight of my career."

DAVE PARKER

The "Cobra" was on his home turf when we talked during 2015 All-Star Week in Cincinnati. Dave Parker had made two of his seven All-Star Games while representing his hometown Reds in 1985–86, and when MLB staged a Guinness World Records event involving 1,058 kids at the "Largest Game of Catch" during 2015 All-Star Week in Cincinnati, Parker was right there to help teach future ballplayers a thing or two.

He taught me something that I did not expect: sometimes the best moments are saved for last. The hit that had mattered most to him came toward the tail end of a formidable, 19-year career, and not in those formative years with Pittsburgh, where he had filled a void left by the incomparable Roberto Clemente and later helped the 1979 Pirates to the World Series title. Here was someone who had won batting titles, a Most Valuable Player award, was a regular All-Star, had the ring, had the contracts, and had the reputation as one of the game's best. He had batted .345 in that 1979 World Series, devastating Baltimore pitching. And yet he was holding onto something.

"It was my first postseason home run in Oakland," Parker said. "Because I had been in two World Series prior to that and never had hit a home run, or any other playoff round. So hitting that was like getting the monkey off my back."

Surprisingly, it had been there for nearly two decades. Few could have known it was so important to someone who had done so much. But playing for Tony La Russa's Athletics in the 1988–89 World Series, Parker was on a personal mission. The '88 Series was a shocking Dodgers sweep, and the '89 Series was the earthquake-marred Bay Bridge Series. When the Loma Prieta earthquake struck on October 17, just before Game Three was about to begin at Candlestick Park, it caused 63 deaths and more than six billion dollars' worth of damage.

Talking baseball was done in a measured tone, respectful with perspective of human life. To those who remembered it at the time, Parker already had made what would turn out to be his most treasured contribution. He had homered three times already for Oakland in that 1989 postseason, his first three postseason homers.

Two had come against Toronto in the ALCS, and one had come off Scott Garrelts of the Giants in Game One of the World Series. It was that first of those three postseason homers, in the bottom of the sixth as the A's were protecting a 2–1 lead in Game Two against Toronto, that Parker held onto dearly for the years to follow.

"It was off Mel Stottlemyre," he recalled. "Fastball down-and-in. I hit it to right-center, and I was so excited, I walked to first base. Not because I was showing off, but it's because I was so excited about hitting a home run. So that's the one."

JIM EISENREICH

"I hit two home runs in the World Series," Jim Eisenreich said, "but the one that I'm thinking of was my first Major League grand slam, off Randy Johnson. It was in Seattle in '89. Of course, Randy Johnson being a great big lefty, throws hard. I'm a lefty. I don't know why I was playing, but I was. The first inning, I got a single to left and drove in a run. The third inning came around and bases were loaded, and his ball hit my bat."

"Were you thinking grand slam when you walked up to the plate?" I asked, smiling sarcastically, as we walked around Kauffman Stadium one day, in his hometown of Kansas City. He had played there from 1987–92, and that included the year he did the apparent impossible against the Big Unit.

"Absolutely not," Eisenreich replied. "He was a guy you never really felt comfortable with—at least I didn't. But at the same time, I did OK. I got two hits that day including the grand slam, and I got a couple other hits, too. I'll never forget that. Number one, it was a home run, which is unique to me anyway. It's a grand slam, it was a first. Being off Randy Johnson, it was kind of special."

August 19, 1989, that grand slam put Kansas City ahead for good in an easy victory at Seattle. It affected Big Unit enough that he was removed after walking the next batter in the fourth inning. It's worth remembering that Johnson, who dropped to 5–8 that day amid a 7–13 campaign, had just recently been traded from Montreal to Seattle, so he was adjusting to the new league in his first full season. The Hall of Famer everyone would come to know was just getting loosened up.

Looking back at it years later, one thing that made it special was that jaunt around the bases, savoring the moment while at the same time being introspective and asking yourself quite honestly, "Did that just happen?"

"I didn't hit many home runs in my life," he said. "To hit one like that, I came around the bases and I'm thinking, 'Holy cow—thanks Lord—what did I do?"

I told Eisenreich that Dmitri Young also had claimed a home run off Johnson for inclusion in this book, a feat accomplished 10 years after Eisenreich's. He replied with a look as if to re-emphasize the story he had just told: "He was a switch-hitter, though."

JUSTIN UPTON

As the number one overall selection in the 2005 First-Year Player Draft, Justin Upton came to Arizona with big expectations. He had some for himself, too. Upton was called up by the Diamondbacks in August of 2007 at the age of 19. After four games in The Show on a trip to San Diego and Los Angeles, his debut came with a bang. On that August 17, in front of 25,340 fans, Upton hit a double, triple, and homer.

"I think my first home run was pretty significant for me," he remembered. "I met the team on the road, so I hadn't played in front of our home fans yet. We were in a pennant race that year, in '07, and we finally came home off a road trip. I hadn't gotten my first hit at Dodger Stadium, got my first RBI there, but I still didn't have a homer. We get home to Chase Field, it's a big crowd, we were playing Pittsburgh. I hit my first home run off of Tom Gorzelanny. When I hit it, I sprinted out of the box, because I had never hit at Chase Field before. Around second, it goes out, all the fans start cheering. For some reason, I couldn't slow down. Most guys slow down a lot when they get around first base and they know it's a homer. So I'm still moving at a pretty good pace, I get around the bases pretty quick. Chris comes up to me and he says, "Why'd you even run out of the box?' I was like, 'What? I didn't know, I thought it was a line drive off the wall.' He says, 'No, you done landed about ten rows up.' That was pretty funny. They were getting on me."

"Chris" is Chris Young, a practically inseparable friend, teammate, and fellow former All-Star when I talked to both of them in the first month of the 2011 season. The three of us were watching highlights of a Pirates game hours before those two headed over to Citi Field for the night's game against the Mets, and Young suddenly noticed that Pedro Alvarez was close to hitting for the cycle (a single, double, triple, and home run in the same game). I asked both of them to tell me the hardest thing about getting a cycle.

Young said, "For me, a double." On September 2, 2008, he started a game at Colorado single, home run, grounded into double play, and triple. Through five innings, you have to feel pretty good about the possibility. In the top of the seventh, reliever Luis Vizcaino walks him at leadoff. Then came one last chance in the top of the ninth, off Steven Register. Again leading off the inning, Young got a hack but it was a screaming liner to third and Jeff Baker reached up to snag it—robbing Young of what would have been a sure double. "If that gets over him I've got my cycle," he said.

I then asked J-Up for his toughest part of a cycle, and he told me, "Single." That's the amazing thing about how his first home game in the Majors began. He was just one single away from the cycle when he came to the plate to a standing ovation with two out in the bottom of the ninth that night in 2007. Upton hit a hard ground ball up the middle and it appeared destined to be a single, but Freddy Sanchez, then the Pirates' two-time All-Star second baseman, made a nice play to throw Upton out and end the game. Some people might have remembered it as falling a single short of a cycle, but Upton would remember the night for a hit of a lifetime.

MATTHEW NEWMAN

The 2006 season was a big one in St. Louis, as Cardinals fans celebrated a World Series championship in a brand-new ballpark. I was among them, clinging to my Cardinals loyalty because even people who work for Major League Baseball and its 30 clubs are entitled to have a favorite team. I remember the summer in St. Louis as even bigger than that, though. My oldest son Matthew was an All-State baseball player at Lafayette High School—alma mater of Ryan Howard and David Freese—in St. Louis that year. Matt filled the local parks with the kind of hits of joy in my life. I asked him to give his Dad "one hit" that he had to talk about. Here is what he emailed me:

"Marquette versus Lafayette, April 2006. Marquette was our rival. It was their best pitcher versus ours. Fourth inning, game tied at 2–2. First-pitch fastball low, golfed! I hit a grand slam over the left-center fence. When I hit it, I started walking, as did the person on first base; everyone else was at home waiting. I knew it was gone—it felt good.

"It was more of a laser rather than a long, high shot—but I hit it right off the middle of the bat. See ya! Turning third base, I looked over at Chad McCann, their right-handed pitcher, and he just smiled at me. It was our biggest audience of the year, everyone was there. Got to home plate and everyone jumped on me—we won the game. It was on the announcements at school the next day. I didn't get another ball to hit the rest of the game."

As a postscript, Matt had a chance to win a big game for his team in Lafayette's postseason tournament, but he fouled off the best pitch of his at-bat and then flied out with two out and the winning run left on base. I found him a bit later in the parking lot, standing there in tears after the year-end team meeting. I saw that and immediately felt bad for him, knowing how much he must have wanted at least one more big hit. But that wasn't it. "Dad," he said, hugging me, "it was such a great bunch of guys."

In those words, I felt the same love not only for my son but also for my sport, the national pastime, the game of boys and girls, of grownups, of generations. What had mattered to him most at that moment was simply the camaraderie, the unity of team, all those hits but also all those misses. They make the big hits feel good, the ones where you come home with joy and realize you truly love baseball.

MARK MCGWIRE

Now that I have just introduced you to my son Matt, let's go back to Sept. 8, 1998. *The Sporting News* had season tickets in the first row behind the Cardinals dugout in those days, and those treasured seats would rotate to employees during the course of a season. I lucked into two of them for Matt and I that day, as the Cardinals were hosting the Cubs. Mark McGwire and Sammy Sosa were the story of that season, and they were both there that day, each doing the impossible: trying to break Roger Maris's single-season record of 61 home runs. McGwire was already at 61, and Steve Trachsel was the Cubs' starting pitcher that day with history up for grabs.

The value of a milestone baseball in that era was almost priceless. I had no idea what I might do with it, but all I know is that I had to be in the expected landing vicinity of a 62nd home run. So I told Matt, then almost 11, to sit tight in our seats while Dad heads for the left-field bleachers during Big Mac at-bats. It was that significant. I patrolled an area in front behind the first section of left-field seats, in front of the old tunnel entrance to the concourse. If the ball got loose, it was going to be mine. Alas, McGwire lined his shortest home run of the 70 he would hit that season, a frozen rope that barely cleared the left-field wall so that a groundskeeper could come up with it and heroically present it to McGwire. I returned to our seats and joined Matt for an ongoing celebration, one in which Sosa (who had 58 homers at that point) hugged his adversary and friend, and we both reached over the backstop wall and scooped up the red-clay dirt to stuff into our pockets for posterity. We had just witnessed history.

I told Big Mac that story when we chatted recently before a game. I told him that I did not want to prejudice his pick, but that I had to know what one hit had meant the most over his 16 seasons, whether with Oakland or later with St. Louis, whether regular season or All-Star or postseason. Whether historic or otherwise.

"I'd have to say home run number sixty-one," McGwire said. "You're probably asking, 'Why sixty-one?' Well, it just happened to be on my dad's sixty-first birthday. So think about that, and what happened in '98—all these sort of mysterious things that happened. Like the ball I hit was marked number three—Babe Ruth. The inning I hit it was in the bottom of the fourth—the same inning that Roger Maris hit his. And then hitting the sixty-first home run on my dad's sixty-first birthday, of all things, and my dad being in the stands? That was pretty damn cool."

That happened the day before my son and I saw the 37-year-old record broken. On September 7, a day game at old Busch, McGwire faced Cubs right-hander Mike Morgan and in his first at-bat, crushed a 1-1 pitch into the left-field seats to match Maris at 61. McGwire hugged his own son Matt, who was a batboy during those glory days, and waved up at his father.

"As far as the at-bat, I remember right when I hit it, my God, I was with my dad prior to the game: happy birthday," McGwire said. "And then hitting that home run and having that feeling while running around the bases. Him being one of my Little League coaches. For him, not being able to play sports, because he was stricken by polio at seven years old, back in the day when they didn't have a vaccine. He couldn't play sports, because his right leg was a lot shorter than the other. For him to be such a great supporter . . . it meant a lot."

The McGwire-Sosa chase was pure joy while it lasted. McGwire would finish that season with 70 homers, Sosa 66. Barry Bonds later would pass them both, with 73 in 2001. Of course, the news to come would show that performance-enhancing drugs were prevalent during those big-power years, and in 2010, McGwire would admit that he juiced in that '98 chase. When we chatted in 2017, I told him that I had been one of his sparse Hall of Fame voters, before I finally had to give up a hopeless case as a ballot bottleneck soon appeared. He said he appreciated that, and we both agreed that it was a time before MLB and players developed an advanced drug and treatment program. The Summer of 1998 really happened, and I told him that he and Sosa had helped bring back the game. There is no question that they did.

"I do believe that, because I still get it today," McGwire said. "Some of the fans throughout the country, walking in the streets, being at the ballpark, and that's the first thing they say: 'Hey, you brought me back to the game, back in '98.' It's such a great feeling. Because the game was sour in a lot of people's minds, just because of what happened in '94, the strike. They took half of the season away. A lot of great things were happening in '94. People were sour about that. What happened in '98 brought people back, and I was one of the reasons, and it just makes me feel really good."

McGwire finished with 583 homers in his career, made 12 All-Star teams, led Oakland as part of the "Bash Brothers" to three consecutive World Series appearances from 1988-90, swept the Giants in '89. In 2017, fans voted him into the Cardinals Hall of Fame. His legend is secure, and I hope he will be added to Cooperstown one day.

I asked him what it was like to crush baseballs.

"When you're in a groove, it's really effortless; it's free-flowing," McGwire replied. "You're not thinking, even though you're doing a lot of processing, what is going on prior to the at-bat. It's like you don't think up there; it just sort of happens. It's a great feeling. I don't think there's a better feeling than squaring a ball up and hitting a home run. Right at contact, right when you hit it, you just go, 'That's a homer.'

"I've had a lot of people tell me that my swing, for how powerful it was, it was short, compact and effortless. And that's something I'm very proud of."

7

SEIZE THE MOMENT

The hit of a lifetime often was simply a matter of being in the right place at the right time. Robin Yount found one that was even more meaningful than his 3,000th hit. Ron Swoboda took advantage of the situation and rewarded his manager's confidence when conventional wisdom suggested that someone bat in his place. I saw Albert Pujols match Babe Ruth with three homers in a single World Series game, but the time he seized the moment in his first Fall Classic is the one treasured here. Bob Watson knew just what to do when he practically discovered a present all wrapped up with a ribbon the first time he stepped into a batter's box for a World Series game, and so did Joe Morgan in winning it all for the Big Red Machine. Tim Salmon lived out a childhood dream, even if others have a different memory, and he mattered to an entertainer of note because he made another childhood dream possible. His Angels teammate Jim Edmonds, meanwhile, made the most of an opportunity he was surprised to find.

ROBIN YOUNT

Robin Yount played his entire career with the Milwaukee Brewers, from 1974–1993, starting out with them as an 18-year-old shortstop and always remembered there as "The Kid." He mulled over his 3,164 hits, all but 22 of them struck during the regular season, and here came another example of a legend choosing one that might be surprising to his fans. Most of them might expect his 3,000th to rise above, but after reaching deep within to pull one out for this book, that is not the one that surfaced.

"Hitting a home run in the World Series," Yount said. "Obviously it isn't that memorable if I had to think about it, but I think I hit to right field in the bullpen. I know it was at County Stadium and, again, everyone probably thought it was the 3,000th hit. That was nice to get the monkey off my back so maybe we could go back to thinking about baseball again. That was probably more memorable, but the most important hit that I enjoyed the most was hitting a home run in the World Series. It actually meant something and felt like an important hit at the time."

106

Memorialized by a statue outside Miller Park,
Robin Yount is a Brewers icon

There were 56,562 fans at County Stadium on the night of October 17, 1982, a stadium record, and no one could have known that it would be the last World Series game in Milwaukee for at least the next three decades. That was Game Five against the Cardinals, a 6–4 Brewers victory that gave them a 3–2 series lead heading back to St. Louis.

In Game One at Busch Stadium, Yount had gone 4-for-6 and led Milwaukee to a 10–0 rout. In Game Five, he became the first player in Major League history to collect four hits twice in a Fall Classic. He wound up only a triple shy of hitting for the cycle in Game Five, where Yount produced his favorite hit.

As usual, Yount, the American League MVP that season, was batting second in a nonpareil batting order behind eventual fellow Hall of Famer Paul Molitor. On the mound for St. Louis was Bob Forsch, who had been lit up by Yount and the Brewers in that opener. Now it was the bottom of the seventh inning, and Milwaukee was protecting a 3–2 lead.

With two out and a 2–1 count, Forsch delivered and Yount smashed a solo shot far over the right-field wall. That and another pair of runs in the eighth would be important insurance for the Brew Crew, which would need them because of two Cardinals runs in the ninth.

"Any kid, from the day he picks up a baseball, dreams of playing in a World Series," Yount said back then. "Playing in the World Series is the ultimate in this game. This is better than I dreamed."

Few players ever had a better World Series than Yount did that year. He never had the chance to do it again, a demonstration of why to take advantage when an opportunity arises. The Cardinals would win those last two games at Busch, as John Stuper pitched a four-hit complete game to even the series, and Joaquin Andujar and Bruce Sutter combined to turn out the lights in the finale. Still, Yount and the Brewers were treated like heroes upon return to a celebration at County Stadium after the World Series, and The Kid raced his motorcycle around the track with a fist in the air.

Yount would go onto become the first player ever to win an MVP award at two different positions, including the outfield in 1989. He would go on to join the 3,000-hit club on September 9, 1992, an opposite-field single off Jose Mesa at home against Cleveland. "It was a bit of a distraction," Yount said years later. Forced to choose between a "monkey off my back" and something you "dream" about as a kid, Yount chose the World Series homer.

RON SWOBODA

"Well, I drove in the winning run in Game Five in the 1969 World Series. I guess if I didn't do it, though, somebody else could have done it," Swoboda bellowed.

Man, he bellows. When you are in a room with Ron Swoboda, you know it. And honestly, if I had stories to tell like Ron Swoboda, I would be loud and clear, too.

It was his first thought when the hit question was asked when he was at the Marriott Marquis in New York for a fundraiser that would honor his former Mets manager Yogi Berra and recognize the 40th anniversary of the Mets' 1973 pennant-winning club. What he really was thinking about was the 1969 Amazin' Mets, and what he had done to contribute to their miracle.

"I suppose it would be hard that year not to have a top two," Swoboda said. "I hit two home runs off of Steve Carlton in 1969. The second two-run home run beat him 4–3 while he was busily striking out 19 of us, and we win the ball game, and he just pitched the best he could pitch, and a guy who didn't hit him very well beat him.

"So those kinds of things, for a guy who ended up with a .240-something lifetime average, mean a little something."

Ron, if you had to choose one of those two . . .

"The World Series base hit, because Gil Hodges could have pinch-hit for me. And I was ready to go up there and hit against Eddie Watt. He was a little side-armin' right-hander out of the bullpen for the Baltimore

Orioles, and I wanted to be up there. I wanted it. You're not gonna beat anybody in the dugout."

Did you have to talk Gil into it?

"No, no, no, no. You didn't talk Gil into anything. I tried not to look at him. I tried to look like I was ready to go up there and hit."

Was there a 50-50 chance of Hodges hitting for you?

"Ah, he could have. We were a platoon team. He could have gone lefty. But it was just like he stopped pinch-hitting for me. Just like he stopped putting in a defensive replacement for me late in the year, because I worked my butt off becoming a better right fielder. I had swung the bat pretty good late in that World Series. I had five hits in the last two games. So I think he was going with a guy he thought might have been a little hot."

What do you remember about the situation and the count?

"I went up there and I hit pretty early in the count. He threw me a wide breaking ball away, and I stayed on the breaking ball. He was kind of a slider-sinker guy, Eddie Watt. He stayed with the breaking ball. I sort of hit it off the end of the bat down the left-field line and Don Buford, who I let get a ball over my head, the first hitter in the World Series, Don Buford had a chance to make a play and did not. It went for double and an RBI, the winning RBI in Game Five."

Can you recapture that excitement and energy of New York in October 1969, that day the Mets won and the fans poured out onto the field?

"I always felt like if you had a chance to win a game, and you had a chance to get up there with guys on base, you have a chance to do some damage. A pitcher's gotta pitch to you a little more. He's gotta throw you more strikes when there's guys all over the bases. I was a hitter who, the fewer strikes you could throw me, the less hitter I was. I was a scuffler, I was a hacker. I was up there hackin'. With guys on base, they were a little more cautious. And I might have been the guy they wanted to get, you know?"

ALBERT PUJOLS

The day I asked Albert Pujols about his one hit of a lifetime, he was surrounded by a crush of media in the National League interview room on the second floor of the Hyatt beside the Arch in St. Louis. This was his home turf for 2009 All-Star Week. It was his show. I had just bought his wife Deirdre's cookbook for a $10 charitable donation at FanFest two days earlier. I have great admiration for the positive impact he has on people's lives even moreso than what he had brought to the national pastime as a player. This is a man who missed the visit to the White House after the 2006 World Series title because he had a commitment for his annual visit to his Dominican Republic homeland to get medical care and assistance to his homeland—the second coming of Robert Clemente in my view, and every bit the Hall of Famer.

In that moment, I had to know. All players like to think about at-bat situations, the count, the locations, the focus, the guesswork, the sighting of the seams and the spin, the feel of the contact, the power, and the glory.

"A hit, one hit? I would say the World Series," Pujols responded. "The first home run in the World Series in 2006, because it's like, you're on the stage, with everybody's cameras all over. The World Series. I mean, that's what it's all about. That's what you play for. To be able to hit it—what was it, a two-run homer, a three-run homer?—against a great pitcher like [Justin] Verlander, it was unbelievable. So I would say that."

It was Game One of that Fall Classic at Comerica Park in Detroit. The score was 1–1 when Pujols came up in the top of the third inning against Verlander. Scott Rolen already had tagged Verlander for a solo homer in the previous inning. With two out in the third, Chris Duncan had doubled in Yadier Molina for the go-ahead run. That brought up Pujols, the cleanup hitter, and with first base open, manager Jim Leyland and the Tigers somehow decided to pitch to that season's MVP. That, to me, was the "unbelievable" part. Pujols saw it as a challenge, and he seized the moment, making them pay with opposite-field power that sent a two-run homer over the right-field wall. Now it was 4–1, St. Louis, and Cardinals' starter Anthony Reyes needed little help that night. He dominated the Tigers over eight innings, and that opening victory propelled St. Louis toward its world championship. Number five jerseys dominated new Busch Stadium.

In 2011, Pujols led the Cardinals to another World Series title. Would his response change? In Game Three of that Fall Classic at Texas, we saw him put on one of the greatest offensive exhibitions in postseason history. I sat in the left-field auxiliary press box seats, working on a helmet loaded with Texas-sized nachos, as he blasted two home runs in our direction, and then I was in the main press box later in the game when he made it a trio. That night, Pujols joined Babe Ruth as the only players to hit three homers in a World Series game. Albert compiled a record 14 total bases that game, going 5-for-6.

In a perfect world, Pujols never would have left St. Louis. He would have kept doing what he was doing, maybe even surpass Stan Musial as the greatest Cardinal ever. After all, no one in baseball history ever had a first decade like Pujols. Alas, professional sports are a mobile world for players today, and so Pujols would move on to the Angels after winning that second title. He was a work in progress as this book was produced, approaching more and more historic milestones, even a 3,000th hit. On June 3, 2017, at the age of 37, Pujols became the ninth player to reach the 600-homer mark, and the first to get there with a grand slam. That homer for the Angels off Minnesota's Ervin Santana was special to him because his family was there. But only time would tell where it ranked on his own list. It seemed like his homer off Verlander in 2006 would remain a strong candidate, because he associated it with winning his first title.

"Five hundred, six hundred, I don't think about numbers," Pujols said in a press conference after number 600. "We'll see how far I can get when I'm done playing. I'm being honest. I don't think about that. I come here every day, thinking about what I can do to help this ball club win. This game is already hard enough. If you bring stuff in from outside and start thinking about the guys you have to chase, it makes it even tougher."

JOE MORGAN

Joe Morgan had a big smile on his face as he arrived at MLB's "Wanna Play?" youth baseball clinic the morning of Game Four in the 2009 World Series. I told him that I don't ever remember seeing a smile on his face quite that impressive.

"I love the game and I remember when I was their age," he told me as he was surveying the swings of some of those wide-eyed inner-city kids who wielded Wiffle ball bats on that chilly November Saturday. "I loved being out on the baseball field. So it's great for me to see those kids doing the same thing."

I told him that I used to play Wiffle ball almost every day when I was their age. "Me, too," he replied. "I played Wiffle ball every single day in the summer."

The difference was that when I played, he was a leading force on Cincinnati's Big Red Machine, helping the Reds to back-to-back titles in 1975–76. We used ghost runners when we needed to back then, so that my buddy Jimmy and I could play Wiffle ball even if it was only a pitcher and a hitter. Jimmy's family was from Cincinnati, so he was a Reds fan and his "team" of ghost runners was always that Big Red Machine. Morgan would come up to bat, with Pete Rose on base, as I pitched to him. My team was always the Minnesota Twins, because my uncle played, coached, and later managed for them. Only my team was not really the Twins as a whole, but rather it was Rod Carew hitting in every lineup spot.

Carew was my idol, and if I may digress for a moment, it is just funny the way baseball and life work together, because in 1991, while covering the San Francisco Giants beat for the *San Jose Mercury News*, the Giants were one of the two teams in the then-annual Hall of Fame Game at Induction Weekend. By sheer coincidence, I just happened to be making my first visit to Cooperstown that summer when Rodney Cline Carew, swinger of the magic wand, was enshrined. I listened to him talk about hitting, captivated, thinking of my boyhood.

There I was decades later, asking a contemporary Hall of Famer, the great Joe Morgan, what one hit in his lifetime comes to mind first. My question was right there, grooved down the middle, like he was sitting dead-red on a fastball, and he blasted it.

"Probably a game-winning hit in the '75 World Series," Morgan said without a moment of hesitation, referring to his one-out single off Red Sox reliever Jim Burton to give Cincinnati a decisive 4–3 lead in the top of the ninth inning in Game Seven, a fact almost lost to many in history's constant replaying of that Game Six classic. "You only get one. And that one always stands out in my mind because it gave us a world championship. The Reds had not won a world championship in Cincinnati since 1940, so it was great for the city and it was great for me and my teammates.

"The winning run was at third base [Ken Griffey Sr.] and there were two outs in the ninth. That's what I remember most."

BOB WATSON

Game One of the 1981 World Series was Dodgers at Yankees, and Bob Watson liked what he saw out on the mound: his old friend and former teammate Jerry Reuss.

"I had very good years hitting Jerry," Watson recalled. "Back when he was with St. Louis [1969–71] and Pittsburgh [1974–78]. He came to Houston for a while [1972–73] and then went on to LA [1979–87]. He was one guy who I would send a limo to pick him up so I could get a hit. I knew I was going to get a hit off him. And then to have your first game you play in the World Series—to have your favorite pitcher on the mound—that made it good."

Watson batted fifth for the Bronx Bombers in the bottom of that first inning. Jerry Mumphrey had singled and moved over to third on Lou

Piniella's ground-rule double. There were two out. Watson smashed a 1–2 pitch deep over the wall in right-center.

"I hit a home run my first at-bat in the World Series in 1981. I hit a three-run homer and that actually led us to win that game. If I had to give you one hit besides my first, that would be it," Watson said 30 years later, appearing at New York's Marriott Marquis for a Baseball Assistance Team fundraising dinner. "That put us up 3–0, and we didn't look back."

The Yankees won that opener, 5–3, but in fairness to Reuss, the shoe was on the other foot in his next outing at Dodger Stadium. With the series tied at 2–2, he took the mound and threw a pivotal five-hitter in a 2–1 Dodgers victory. They would clinch in the next game back at Yankee Stadium. Watson was 0-for-3 with a walk in that Game Five against Reuss, but he was still probably the Yankees' best offensive performer in the series, batting .318 (7-for-22) with two homers and a team-best seven RBIs. The way that series started still means a lot to him.

I asked Watson what hitting meant to him in those days.

"I took it very seriously. Seriously enough where I didn't play golf or anything else, to interfere with my swing," he said. "I hit the inside half of the ball, all the time. If you really want somebody to get 'em fired up about me hitting, ask Tom Seaver. That'll get him fired up. He tried to throw it in there."

Watson was motioning across that meeting room where "The Franchise" was holding court with media, a center of attention at an event that would honor the 50th anniversary of the Mets. But just then, another Hall of Fame pitcher sidled over to us: Juan Marichal.

"Here's another guy who knows," Watson said.

"What a hitter, this guy, man," Marichal said, wrapping an arm playfully around Watson. "*Line drive, line drive.* Anybody that hits like that becomes a great hitter. When you can hit that ball here, inside-out, you're a good hitter. You're a good hitter."

"Juan, you didn't let too many guys do that," I reminded Marichal.

"Oh, no, no, because he changed speeds," Watson said.

"Sometimes," Marichal said with a modest smile. "Sometimes."

TIM SALMON

A number of baseball legends in this book have told me the same story from their boyhoods—that schematic image created on a ballfield or in a street, when they simulated a moment to come. They likely have talked about that simulated event for so long now that they are vaguely sure it really happened that way, but it is how they remember it now, the first glimpse of what could be.

That is what came to mind for Tim Salmon when we spoke in December of 2012.

"In Game Two of the 2002 World Series, I hit a home run off Felix Rodriguez of the Giants in the eighth inning to put us ahead, and it was the most memorable to me because it was the culmination of a lifetime of dreaming of that moment," he said. "To come through in that situation, it's not quite Kirk Gibson's game-winning home run in that dramatic of a fashion, but I was growing up watching those kinds of things. It was my own moment in the limelight with a chance to accomplish it myself.

"I can totally remember, as a kid I can remember Kirk's home run in 1988 and just dreaming about that, and then your whole life, bottom of the ninth. Actually I hit mine in the bottom of the eighth. Nonetheless, it was a game-winner. You dream of those situations: To be a hero on that stage."

Salmon was 21 when Gibson staged his miracle moment in Los Angeles, and the next spring he was drafted by the Angels. Fourteen years after Gibson's homer, the World Series returned to the Los Angeles area, in Anaheim, and once again it was an all-California affair. It was Athletics versus Dodgers in 1988 and now it was Giants versus Angels.

Here is how Salmon remembers his moment of glory, and as you can see, it unfolds over the years with a new twist, based on something that happened the inning *after* his game-deciding home run:

"First pitch fastball, hit a home run to left, put us up by two, crowd went berserk. We were down in the series, 1–0, so it cemented that first win for us. It really propelled our team. First pitch, 95 miles per hour out over the middle of the plate. Then Felix Rodriguez is removed and Todd Worrell comes in for the Giants. It becomes even more memorable because it gave us a two-run lead and what happens next.

"The next inning, Barry Bonds comes up and he hits a solo home run, a magnificent shot to right field, and unbeknownst to me, everyone is reading my lips. I had been pulled for defense, with Alex Ochoa going into right. I'm on the top step of the dugout and when Bonds hits it, they flash to me on the dugout. I was on the rail, and I was just saying to another teammate, 'That's the longest ball I've ever seen hit in this ballpark.' Because it went to a tunnel in right—off Troy Percival, our closer. Everybody saw that, and I didn't know that till afterwards.

"It seems like I've gotten more comments for those words than from hitting the home run. I imagine they put the camera on me because I'd just gotten done hitting the two-run homer. But it was funny, because instead of me being the hero of the game, it was me talking about Barry hitting a bomb off Percival, a home run that could have led to them winning instead of us. That was the story of my career."

That is not the story of Salmon's career to me. I worked the 2010 All-Star Week in Anaheim, where Salmon was a Player Ambassador, representing the host Angels. I will never forget the end of that week's Legends & Celebrities Softball Game, when U.S. softball legend Jennie Finch threw some home run derby-style tosses to Salmon as a full house at Angel Stadium watched their retired hero take his cuts. Salmon pounded longball after longball, delighting the crowd and allowing Angels fans another moment of nostalgia, rekindling their love for a King Fish. You knew from the passion in the crowd right there how they remembered Salmon. It was not for what he said about Bonds' homer, but it was for what he had brought them day-in and day-out, and especially with that perfect, fast swing, when the meat of the bat sent a Felix Rodriguez fastball out into the bleachers, allowing Salmon to pump his fist once going around first base, a little nod to a moment of yesteryear, as he once imagined it as a boy.

ARSENIO HALL

While Salmon's hit brought his own boyhood to mind, I encountered another unexpected story about him and baseball's rite of passage.

"It was a hit by Tim Salmon to keep the Angels in the 2002 World Series that they went on to win," comedian and former late-night talk show host Arsenio Hall told me in 2012. "It was against the Giants. I remember taking my kid to see his first World Series game, and mostly because Barry Bonds is a friend, and I knew my days were numbered as to how long I could take my kid to see a legend play. So I remember it was a hit by Tim Salmon. It was big, but it was more than baseball to me. It was personal. It was a special moment that I got to see with my son. I never went to a baseball game with my dad, so it was a cool, cool day at the park.

"And Scott Spiezio, I remember his big hit in that series because I interviewed him for my late show. At that time, his hair had colors and stuff. We talked about a garage band he had. He was a good musician. I remember listening to music he had done with his garage band. I remember his hit, but I remember this Tim Salmon hit more, because I actually have the *LA*

Times with a picture of him from that game. It was a big game, important game, but mostly because of personal stuff."

JIM EDMONDS

Salmon spent seven of his seasons playing the outfield alongside Jim Edmonds, whose contribution to this book goes back to their first days together.

On back-to-back nights in October of 2004, I was sitting in the auxiliary press seating out in right-center field behind the wall at new Busch Stadium in St. Louis, and I vividly recall what Edmonds did in that 24-hour span. At Game Six of the National League Championship Series (NCLS) against Houston, his walk-off home run in the 12th inning assured that the series would go the distance, resulting in fireworks and pandemonium all around me. Then I watched in disbelief as he turned from his position in center field and started running toward the wall, diving full-flight and somehow catching Brad Ausmus's smoked liner that threatened to blow the Game Seven open for Houston. It kept that game close, and the Cardinals wound up going to the Fall Classic.

One might think that the first of those highlights could qualify as the hit that number 15 remembered most when it was all said and done. That would not be the case, however. I spent time with Edmonds while the Cardinals were facing the Brewers in the 2011 NLCS, shortly before he would throw out the Game Four ceremonial first pitch back home in St. Louis. As with many other ballplayers, Edmonds spontaneously chose to talk about the first Major League hit he ever cracked.

"I think my first hit was obviously the most important. It means I finally arrived," he said. "It gave me a chance to play in the Major Leagues with some of the greatest players of all time. Just to be accepted and be able to be up there and make something out of it was definitely a treat and a pleasure, an awesome experience. Number one was to be able to get my career started with the first hit of my career."

Edmonds' Major League debut was on September 9, 1993, when he played left field and batted seventh for the Angels, going 0-for-4 with a pair of strikeouts in a 6–0 victory at Detroit. The next day was a one-game stopover in Toronto as a rain makeup, and the Angels lost, 10–4, to the team that would repeat as world champions one month later. In fact, Joe Carter homered in this game, something he would do again to end that year in baseball in that same SkyDome. Luis Polonia was back in left field for that game, but with one out and one on in the top of the ninth, and Halos trailing, 10–2, Blue Jays closer Duane Ward found himself pitching against an unfamiliar rookie pinch-hitter. Edmonds, with his big looping swing from the left side, blasted the right-hander's pitch to the gap in left-center, and it bounced over the wall. It would lead to two runs, and it would be the first of 1,949 regular season hits for Edmonds, not to mention 63 more in the postseason, including that legendary blast that forced a 2004 NLCS Game Seven and made fans giddy.

I asked him what he remembered about that first hit, and Edmonds said: "It was a blowout in Toronto. I hit a ground-rule double off their closer. I probably never should have been in the game, so it was a great surprise."

8

<u>OUTWORK EVERYONE</u>

Each subject interviewed for this book put in countless hours of hard work behind the scenes, honing a craft and attaining the highest levels. But some examples were especially exemplary, a reminder that nothing replaces this trait.

<u>JIM KAAT</u>

Every exploration that has ever happened was as much an adventurous journey of self-discovery as it was the physical realization of a quest to distant places in the imagination. This probe took me somewhere I had not expected, and that was to the beginning.

Born in Southern California and the nephew of a Major Leaguer, I moved with my parents to Evansville, Indiana, and a month shy of my third birthday, I attended my first Major League Baseball regular season game. This is where I stumbled upon my first hit, my first favorite team, and my first news story.

My uncle, Johnny Goryl, was a young infielder on the Minnesota Twins in the summer of 1962, recently traded by the Cubs, and married at the time to my mother's sister. The Twins were playing the Detroit Tigers at the end of a long homestand at Municipal Stadium, home to the second year of baseball there since the Washington Senators moved. Through conversations with my mother and researching that night game on July 24, I have pieced together the key details that a two-year-old would not recall.

Mom and I took a train from Evansville to Chicago and then to Bloomington, Minnesota. We were there two or three weeks, while the Twins were home, to be with Uncle Johnny, Aunt Sue and my cousins, Susan and Tammy. We stayed at an apartment where some of the other Twins players and their families lived, and they had a swimming pool as a nice summer respite. I sat with Harmon Killebrew's children in the Twins players' wives' section down close to home plate. A Hall of Famer, Jim

Bunning, got that win that night. The weather was a little wet, leaving the infield a bit slippery.

The game was mostly memorable to my mother because Jim Kaat's teeth were knocked out—on the same night that he had just received his first All-Star selection.

"His wife was hysterical," my mother remembers, and I guess you could say that Kaat and I both technically started at the Teeth Game.

In the top of the seventh, with the Twins ahead, 3–2, Bunning dropped a sacrifice bunt. Kaat, a gangly, 6-foot-4 left-hander on his way to a breakout season, fielded it cleanly and threw to first for the first out. Jake Wood singled to short and pinch-runner Bill Bruton stayed on second. Then with one out and Kaat pitching out of the stretch, he threw to Bubba Morton and finished off his usual delivery style, bounding toward the batter with a big squared-up position. The sharply hit ball skipped on the wet grass and hopped up to the top of Kaat's glove's webbing, smashing into his mouth. A UPI photo the next day in Kaat's hometown newspaper in Michigan showed him prone on the edge of the mound, "stunned" by what had happened. He lost two teeth and part of another.

Killebrew, the great third baseman, and Bernie Allen, the second baseman, approached the mound after the play and both saw blood on his hand. Killebrew noticed that part of a tooth was lodged in the game ball. Lee Stange came out of the bullpen to replace Kaat and got two fly balls to escape the inning, but Norm Cash would tie it with a homer in the eighth, and Rocky Colavito would single in the decisive run in the ninth, leaving Kaat with a no-decision and a 4-3 Tigers victory. This was significant on multiple accounts. The old Washington Senators—"First in war, first in peace, and last in the American League"—suddenly had new life in the Twin Cities. In 1962, they would finish 91–71 and second only to the vaunted Yankees, five back, so each of their games was big now. They would be 5 1/2 game out after this loss. Kaat would finish the season with 18 wins and finish his career with 283 overall, so anything getting him closer to 20 and 300, respectively, would have only helped his Hall of Fame chances many years later. Kaat would win his first of 16 Gold Gloves that same year and would say later that what happened to him on this day put attention on his fielding.

And, of course, there was the matter of me being there, close enough to hear the crack of enamel, if only as a tagging-along toddler, supposed witness to history unfolding, seemingly destined to be wherever significant baseball events were happening. My mom and Aunt Sue would have been worried about Kaat's wife reaction, and I would have reacted to my mom's reaction. *What the hell is going on? What's the fuss?* I guess you could say I was born with a nose for news, especially baseball news.

Here is more from Kaat's hometown newspaper, the *Holland Evening Sentinel*:

> Kaat Injured During Game
>
> MINNEAPOLIS—Zeeland left-hander Jim Kaat said today he was planning to make the road trip Thursday with the Minnesota Twins in spite of injuries suffered in Tuesday night's game when he was struck in the mouth by a drive off the bat of Detroit Tiger Bubba Morton.
>
> Kaat was scheduled to have a medical examination and x-rays today in Minneapolis. He had two teeth and a part of a third knocked out when he was hit by the ball. His lips were badly cut, but he said he didn't think he had any broken bones.
>
> Kaat called his parents in Zeeland after the game at 12:30 a.m. today. He said he would try to make the road trip with the Twins Thursday even if he had to go without his front teeth.
>
> Part of a tooth had embedded itself in the ball. Kaat said he told his parents he had been stunned by the drive but had not been knocked out. Kaat was struck during the seventh inning of the game while he was working on a 3–2 lead over the Tigers.
>
> Kaat did not say how the accident would affect his selection to appear with the American League All-Stars in their game at Chicago, July 30. He had been selected Tuesday to join the All-Star squad.

During the 2016 World Series, I was in a rental car driving from Cleveland to Chicago for Game Three. On the way, somewhere near South Bend, Jim called me, so I turned on my tape recorder and put my iPhone on speaker. I had known him for many years, and I had reached a point during my research that I felt OK asking pitchers the question. One proviso: They needed to be longtime hitters, pre-DH. When we spoke during that drive, I had not yet known that I had attended the Teeth Game.

Here was Jim's reply:

"August 1, 1962. I was twenty-three, trying for my twentieth career win [as a Minnesota pitcher]. Robin Roberts was thirty-six and he already had two hundred twenty-five wins and was headed to Cooperstown. I had many of his trading cards as a young boy. We were tied at 1–1 with one out in the top of the eleventh inning. One out, runner on first. He didn't know I was a decent hitter for a pitcher and thought I'd be bunting. I got a fastball to hit and hit it over Jackie Brandt's head in right field for a triple. I then scored on a squeeze bunt by Vic Power. We won, 3–1. I pitched all eleven. Robin went ten and one third.

"Fourteen years later, we met at a press conference in Philadelphia when I was traded to the Phillies. We had never met in person. As soon as he saw me, he said, 'You lucky S.O.B. If I thought you were hitting, I'd have thrown you a breaking ball.' He later signed a picture for me that said the same thing. I got to see Robby many times after that and we always talked about that hit. That was one of my favorite wins as a pitcher and to get a game-winning hit off a future Hall of Famer and a man who would become a good friend was a memorable experience. Surely my most memorable hit."

For a pitcher who hit 16 home runs himself, it was pretty amazing that he responded with one that stayed in the park.

Not long after that phone call, I researched Kaat's 1962 season. Only then did I learn about the Teeth Game. Was it possible that the game in which he had his most important hit was really just eight days after a comeback had knocked out two of his teeth and a part of a third?

Today, if that happened to a pitcher, there would be at least a normal stint on the disabled list, possible cosmetic surgery. Today, it would have been after the All-Star Game, and most people would have understood if the pitcher were gone for an extended period, hopefully back for the heat of the pennant race. For Jim Kaat, there was no work stoppage. It was just teeth. He was a horse. He made his next scheduled start on July 28 and threw a complete game for a 5–2 win at Cleveland to record his 10th victory of 1962. This was the final year in which MLB scheduled two All-Star Games instead of one, so two days later, Kaat even made it to Wrigley Field to attend his first Midsummer Classic. He did not appear, and neither did his smile when the American Leaguers posed for their team photo. Then came his next scheduled start on August 1, the one where he recorded the hit that belongs in this book.

After a call to my Uncle Johnny followed by texts with my mother, I concluded that my first MLB regular season game had been the Teeth Game. I studied up on it, and saw that Kaat still has the baseball with teeth marks in it, part of his memorabilia collection. This was completely coincidental to Kaat's response for this book. I have no idea what happened to me after that game—we made our way back to Evansville—but I can tell you that Jim Kaat never skipped a beat. It was so heroic. We traded emails.

"Lots of time in the dental chair," he told me. "Wore a boxer's mouthpiece to protect my teeth . . . Lived on milk shakes with raw eggs for a few weeks . . . couldn't chew . . . tough posing for pictures as I was selected for the second All-Star game that year.

"Other than that, I felt normal. It was a good thing that the first start after getting hit in the mouth, Willie Tasby hit a comebacker to me in the first inning and I snared it. That cured me of any fear of getting hit again. We were all aware of the Herb Score injury several years prior to that."

Even more unbelievable is Kaat's innings-pitched totals in those days soon after he was smashed in the mouth with a baseball. "The next half-dozen or so were complete games or extra-inning games," he remembered. Kaat won his next three starts after the Teeth Game, pitching nine, eleven, and ten innings in each. Then he threw 10 1/3 but lost a tough 1–0 duel to Dean Chance of the Angels, and then pitched nine innings in four of his next six starts.

What happened to Jim Kaat on July 24, 1962 was harrowing to everyone around him, including those in the stands that night. But to Kaat, it was a momentary distraction, maybe even one other element that should be considered as Hall of Fame committees continue to pore over his case.

HAROLD BAINES

Kaat memories extend to many players as well, including a special one for Harold Baines, the White Sox legend. He was the top pick of the 1977 MLB Draft, and was a club representative for the White Sox on the floor of the 2016 Draft, where he told me how much things had changed since he was selected. "They came to where I lived and did a little press conference deal, but it was nothing like this," he said then. "That shows the way the game has grown, for the better.

"I was naive back then. I didn't have an agent and all of that stuff until the night before I got drafted. Big difference. And I was number one in the country. The money's a big difference, too. Back in those days, whatever money you got was a blessing, but you just wanted to play baseball. And I was just fortunate enough to do that."

Maybe it was because of this setting, because Baines turned on the wayback machine to find the hit that had mattered the most to him. He went way back to the very start of a 22-year career, one he finished with six All-Star selections and 2,866 hits—numbers that probably should get him more Hall of Fame discussion.

"My first meant the most, because it was the hardest to get," he said.

On his 19th at-bat of his rookie year in 1980, Baines came through.

"As a kid, my father was a semipro player, so I just thought I was playing baseball for him, not for myself," Baines said. "So whenever I made it to the Major Leagues, my first hit was for him."

What did he learn from it?

"It's hard," he said. "It's a lot of work to get that first one, and it's a lot of work to stay in the Major Leagues. I was fortunate enough to be around some veteran players like Carlton Fisk, Greg Luzinski, and Jerry Koosman, who had worked hard off the field, just as hard as they played the game.

"The first one was off Jim Kaat. He was forty-one years old then, in 1980. I hit a double down the right field line. Actually I had four or five RBIs before I got a base hit in the Major Leagues—sac flies or ground balls. Every time I see him I say I got my first hit off him. He smiles. He was a great pitcher—it's sad he's not in the Hall of Fame."

Then Baines turned his attention back to the young men who were about to be drafted that night, many of them with riches already lined up and cameras ready to capture their reaction to the big moment—a lot different than 1977, when it was not exactly a sweeping media buzz right after the first draft pick was decided.

"It's got to be more pressure on them, to get this attention before they've ever done anything," Baines said. "Wherever they go, I hope they have much success."

JOHNNY GORYL

Origins, baseball origins.

We all think back to them, the earliest memories of the priceless imprint that someone left on us. It may have been a flicker at first, just some simple act that opened the Baseball Gate just ajar enough so we could get a foot inside and then enter a magical kingdom that smells like leather and sounds like popping gloves and cracking wood and freshly cut grass. It welcomes you and stirs every sense so that decades later you remember the textures and the shapes and the mythical gods that Homer would have included had he written a book like this.

I think back to my Uncle Johnny.

John Goryl, aka "Gentleman John," is one of those inexorable baseball infantry soldiers who just keep showing up, leave their mark, and then give way to the next solid line and the ones after that. If you

Courtesy of Mark Newman

Johnny Goryl remembers hitting a home run against the Yankees in 1963

did not see him play, then someone you know probably did, and in various ways, most recently as the Cleveland Indians' senior advisor to the player development program in the Orlando area, he probably has left a mark on the national pastime that you can appreciate. As I mentioned in a previous entry about Jim Kaat, I was a boy in Evansville, Indiana in the 1960s, and aware that my Uncle Johnny—then married to my mother's sister—had played for the Minnesota Twins. In the late '60s, he was coaching for them. There was a sudden interest on my part in following professional team sports—especially Minnesota sports—because of him. When Uncle Johnny coached in the Twins organization in the 1970s, there was one time when he brought me a box of official Carolina League baseballs, making me slightly popular among other kids in my neighborhood, always a good thing. He could never have known what impact that simple gesture would have, how it would stay with a boy through life. I can still smell those baseballs, still feel the seams as I and other players on my youth team gripped would-be curveballs or screwballs, finding the nearest field to use them in a game of 500 or just batting practice. It made everything feel a little more real, piquing my curiosity as I stepped inside the Baseball Gate. Along the way I was hooked, utterly, a decent player in my own right but destined to write about the sport.

Origins, baseball origins.

I picked up the phone one day recently and called Uncle Johnny. He lived in the Orlando area, and when we spoke, he had just completed his astounding 65th season in professional baseball. Sitting beside him while he talked was his mom, who was celebrating her 101st birthday and checking on the status of Hurricane Matthew, which was barreling toward their state. Uncle Johnny was about to turn 83 himself.

Waiting for him to answer, I was looking at the bulletin board on my cube at work, at the three John Goryl baseball cards and the black and white photo of him turning a double play at second in his glory days.

"Hey, Uncle Johnny, it's mullion," I said. That was his nickname for a lot of people over the years. I realized that when Charlie Manuel, while managing a Phillies world championship team in 2008, told me to come into his office and then proceeded to sit me across from his desk as he called his best friend, Uncle Johnny, whom he affectionately always called "Mullion." There I was, covering a World Series for MLB.com, and the Phillies manager was summoning me to a phone call just so he could shoot the breeze for a little bit and take a breather from the intensity.

As for my own call with Uncle Johnny for this book, we talked for a while and I asked him how many years this is in baseball now.

"Actually eighteen in the big leagues as a player, a coach, a manager for a little while," he said. "Altogether since I graduated from Cumberland High School, Mark, it's been sixty-five years. I just finished my sixty-fifth season. Can you believe that crap?"

He managed the Twins in 1981, replacing Gene Mauch. Uncle Johnny's portrait looms large on the dramatic hallway gallery of Twins managers if you tour the club suites of Target Field, which I got to do during the 2014 All-Star Game. He was Mike Hargrove's bench coach when the Cleveland Indians played the Florida Marlins in the 1997 World Series—his first Fall Classic. Heady days when he and Grover would search far and wide for Beanie Babies wherever the Indians traveled. He was among those responsible for the development of players like Jim Thome, Albert Belle, Carlos Baerga, and many more.

We talked for a long time. It is possible that we never fully established one solitary hit as the most earnest achievement of a career, but then again, we may have done just that. In any case, the journey of getting there is what this book is all about. Indeed, that is the whole reason for this undertaking, the years and years of going after the true loves in the minds of the hitters.

We should start at the beginning, a remarkable scene. On Friday, September 20, 1957, two years before I was born, 23-year-old right-handed-hitting third baseman John Goryl walked up to the plate at Wrigley Field in the bottom of the first as the leadoff hitter for a Chicago Cubs team that was 31 games out and looking at prospects. He squeezed his bat firmly and looked out at the mound.

There he saw Warren Spahn. The greatest lefty in Major League history at the time, and still the winningest lefty (363 wins) in MLB history, although Steve Carlton and Randy Johnson might be mentioned first among greatest all-time lefties these days. The same Warren Spahn who would earn his 20th win of the season for the Milwaukee Braves that day on the way to the NL Cy Young Award and the World Series title. The same Warren Spahn he had adored as a youth in New England, watching and learning in the old Boston Braves days of "Spahn and Sain and pray for rain."

"I couldn't believe I was facing him," Uncle Johnny said of the 14-time All-Star. "I remember that World Series that they played in, against Cleveland in 1948, and the pickoff play with Phil Masi on second base." Bob Feller tried to pick off Maci in Game One, and although Maci was ruled safe to touch off a big controversy, Cleveland still won it all and Maci's will specified posthumously that he should have been called out. "Now here I am walking up to the plate and facing a future Hall of Famer. This was in September. The thing that I feared the most was to get on base because he had such a good pickoff move. You couldn't take a secondary lead. He had your ass dead to rights. He was such a great pitcher."

That first at-bat was a quickie. Back to the dugout with a strikeout. Welcome to the big leagues.

"It was short and quick and overmatched," Uncle Johnny recalled. "I didn't even give it any thought. All I knew was, I had a lot of company. So it didn't bother me too much."

His following at-bats against Spahn were a 6–3 groundout, a walk, a strikeout by reliever Don McMahon, and then a single to bring in a run in the bottom of the ninth. First Major League hit.

I looked up Uncle Johnny's game log on Baseball Reference to find his next matchup with Spahn, and it resulted in a hit that qualified as number three on that website's list of "Top 5 Plays." It was April 29, 1958, Milwaukee at the Cubs again. Spahn improved to 3–0 that day with a complete game, 8–4 victory. Uncle Johnny's first at-bat would end familiarly, with a Spahn whiff. But in the fifth inning, Spahn had just lost his perfect game on a Bobby Thomson double. Dale Long followed with a strikeout and up stepped Goryl, the number seven hitter.

RBI single, and a 1–1 game. Never mind that Uncle Johnny ended the seventh with a 6–4 force out, or that Spahn finished off the game by getting Uncle Johnny to fly out to right. Never mind that the RBI single was a blooper that found some grass. "I got a knock off the sucker, too," he said.

"It meant quite a bit, because here I was, 23 or 24 years old, still wet behind the ears, and only playing for four or five years in the Minors, and to get a base hit off of Spahn was every young player's dream back then," Uncle Johnny said. "Shoot, it would be like somebody getting a hit off Madison Bumgarner today or Nolan Ryan years ago. Those are huge accomplishments. It was for me too. I realized, here I was, even if it was a blooper, it was still a line drive in the box score."

He remembered a hit for the Twins against the Yankees on July 26, 1963, because, well, it was against the Yankees. It was in the top of the ninth at Yankee Stadium, against the team that had won the previous two World Series and was on its way back to another Fall Classic, a team you rooted against if you grew up in New England. It was a two-run homer that cut the Bronx Bombers' lead to 6–5.

"That was important to me later, just because of what I heard from Uncle Paul and Aunt Stella," Uncle Johnny said, rattling off names of relatives I had not known. "They were visiting mom and dad up in Rhode Island, and they had the game on the radio. It was a home run off Jim Bouton. Dad was so excited, and he turned to Uncle Paul and Aunt Stella and he said, 'That's my boy!' He was so proud. Just because of that small incident, that was told to me the following winter, and that made me feel pretty good."

The hit off "Spahnie," the homer off Bouton: they would loom large for Uncle Johnny in the years to come, but as we kept talking, I thought the lasting legacy for this book may be found on April 29, 1962. He had been traded by the Cubs to the Dodgers after the 1959 season in the Don Zimmer-Ron Perranoski deal, and then the Twins had selected him from the Dodgers in the 1961 Rule 5 Draft. That was the same year that Minnesota entered the Majors, having been relocated as the Washington Senators.

Now with a fresh start, Uncle Johnny got his first Twins start for manager Sam Mele by playing second and batting eighth in the second half of a doubleheader at Cleveland Stadium. Gary Bell, a past and future All-Star right-hander for the Tribe, started and gave up five home runs. Two of them were crushed by Uncle Johnny, a game-tying solo shot in the second and another game-tying solo shot in the fourth.

"Gary Bell was a very good pitcher, an above average fastball, his out pitch was his curve, which was nasty," Uncle Johnny recalled. "He just threw too many fastballs to me and I hit a couple jacks off him, because I never would have been able to hit his curve. He was one of the budding stars for the Indians that day and pitched a lot of years in the big leagues."

Both home runs off Bell went into the bullpen in left-center, their location before being moved to the foul grounds years later.

"The best day I ever had was with the Twins that day," Uncle Johnny said. "There was a roster move being made, they were going to send someone out, and I suspected it was going to be me. I went in the second game of a doubleheader, and I hit two home runs in the second game, and that changed all that. That was probably my biggest day in baseball, keeping my job."

So the lesson he learned was . . . don't let someone else steal your job?

"I don't know if it was a lesson so much as it was something that I had to deal with my whole career," he says. "I wasn't blessed with a lot of talent. I'll outwork everybody else. That's usually what happens with young players like me who aren't so blessed with talent. They do make their mark in the game somewhere along the way. I got five years out of it so I'm pretty proud of that."

MARQUIS GRISSOM

The 1990 season was my first covering a Major League Baseball team, after five terrific seasons following the Dallas Mavericks around the NBA. Taking over the Giants beat for the *San Jose Mercury News*, there were going to be a lot of new names to learn with the much larger rosters in baseball and the expansive organizations that are nonexistent on the basketball beat. There were a lot of first impressions to be made on me and by me.

One of those first impressions was made by a 5-foot-11 sparkplug named Marquis Grissom. It was his first full year in MLB, a rookie outfielder for the Montreal Expos. His first impression was dazzling, leaving you wanting to see more. Our first trip to Olympic Stadium was that May 4–7, a four-game series, and he was on the bench the first two games; he batted second each of the last two games, starting in right in Game Three and center in Game Four. In the May 18–20 series at Candlestick Park in San Francisco, he started the first two games and came off the bench in the third. Then he kind of faded away, at least from my scorebook, that year. In the August 20–22 series at Candlestick Park, he never played. Back to Montreal on August 28–29, and this kid from Atlanta never played.

The next time I covered Marquis Grissom in an Expos uniform was a three-game series at Olympic Stadium on May 6–8 of the 1991 season. He was a full-fledged stud who destroyed your bullpen and your game plan. In the series opener, he was 2-for-5 with two runs and a stolen base, a key figure in an 11-batter, five-run third, and chasing Giants starter Don "Caveman" Robinson by hitting the back half of a back-to-back homer charge to start the bottom of the fourth for Montreal. In the second game, he hit a walk-off homer off Trevor Wilson in the 15th inning as 8,699 fans and Youppi!, the mascot, watched in the echoing dome. In the series finale, he walked and scored the first run as the Expos never trailed and won, 5–4. For the series, Grissom was 4-for-13 with three walks, four runs and four steals, leading the Expos to a sweep.

These days he mentors and coaches young ballplayers, including his son Marquis Jr., with his Marquis Grissom Baseball Association in Atlanta. Our conversation was a full quarter-century later, and without any kind of prompting whatsoever, Grissom told me that out of a wonderful 17-year career in which he made so much October magic happen—perhaps most notably as a fixture in three consecutive World Series from 1995–97— the hit that meant the most to him had happened in the Expos' road trip immediately before that very Giants series that he dominated in the spring of 1991.

"In 1990, my first full year in the big leagues, I was still platooning with Otis Nixon and Dave Martinez in center field," Grissom said. "Then early in the 1991 season, we were in St. Louis, and I was facing Juan Agosto, the lefty, who was like a guy that I watched growing up. I just loved the way he threw the ball from the left side to the plate, a great attitude. To be able to face him, and knowing at that time I wasn't a starter, I hit a grand slam to the upper deck, a pinch hit, and I think that got me that starting center field job the rest of that year. [He started 131 games in the outfield in 1991.] So the next thing I know, I'm a starter. It really launched my career."

Indeed, his breakthrough was during a Sunday day game at old Busch Stadium, against a Cardinals team managed by Joe Torre—that skipper's first full season managing the Cardinals before his tenure eventually led to pay dirt in New York. The Expos and Redbirds were tied, 5–5, in the top of the eighth, and Cardinals reliever Mike Perez walked Delino DeShields to load the bases with Grissom on deck. Torre summoned Agosto, a durable Puerto Rican veteran lefty who had led the Majors in appearances a year earlier with 82. On the second pitch from Agosto, Grissom's eyes lit up and he pulled it over the wall down the left-field line.

"It was a slider down and in, and he had an unbelievable slider, but coming from a lefty to a righty, you're just waiting on that as a right-handed batter," Grissom recalled. "You go down and in and just drop the head on it. But at that time, I was young. I didn't have a concept of the game. Give me something close to swing at and I'm swinging at it. I knew my speed, and if I hit it on the ground I figured I could keep the rally alive."

Including that grand slam, Grissom was 4-for-5 with five RBIs that day. He also had an RBI double and two singles. And he had the hit of his life.

The lesson that he learned in that at-bat stayed with him forever. In fact, the lesson became so ingrained that he says it twice in a row when mentioning it.

"You always have to be ready. You always have to be ready," he said. "Coming into the Majors as a 21-year-old, you want to be a starter. I thought I should have been out there playing, and then you're not a starter, so you still have to put that work in. Come in early, get your swings in, practice in the field. I started lifting, and I wasn't a big lift guy but I started lifting to stay in shape.

"It came all the way back around full-circle to when, at the end of my career, I became a fourth outfielder, and again after being a starter for 14 years, I had to go back to that similar situation. It was hard to swallow that pill, but I had to come off the bench and be ready. And two of the years in that situation I had unbelievable seasons, with 20 home runs coming off the bench. Then I became a starter part of that year. To come off the bench like that in my career in San Francisco, it was awesome. If I had bitched and moaned and complained because I wasn't playing, who knows where I would have been. That prepared me for baseball the rest of my career. It taught me that you always have to be prepared, never take a day off, don't make excuses to the game or about the game."

Like so many of the subjects I interviewed for this book, Grissom has instilled those same lessons that he learned in the batter's box into the lives of youth. He grew up with 14 brothers and sisters in Red Oak, just south of College Park, Georgia, and his association was created to promote life skills, get scholarships, and give a leg up for kids who are "willing to work hard." As you can see, those words have always permeated whatever he does. When we spoke, Grissom was at a Perfect Game showcase event in Fort Myers, Florida, a trip that was made possible through funding by USA Baseball in conjunction with MLB. I asked him what he saw in the impressionable pupils he had with him there that day.

"I see a bunch of enthusiastic kids," Grissom said. "The majority of them love the game of baseball but don't quite understand the effort you have to put in it. Hopefully we can narrow that gap between their baseball IQ and putting in the work you have to do to be fundamentally sound. Attitude is everything, but so is being fundamentally sound. You have to have that love and desire to play in that next level. Some of them may feel overmatched and go in another direction, some of them may work harder to catch up with kids in their age group. They'll get a chance to really see where they are at, because you're going to play against the best talent.

"Normally when you're at home you play against the same teams over and over in your home state, you know what to expect, you start taking things for granted. But you can't ever take anything for granted. You have to go out there and grind every day and be the best that you can be."

That is what led up to his grand slam off Agosto, his takeover series for Montreal in the next homestand against the Giants, his catching the final out for his hometown Braves to win the 1995 World Series, his career-high .308 average with 23 homers and 74 RBIs to help Atlanta back to the '96 World Series, his 1997 ALCS MVP award (he stole home to win Game Three) for a Cleveland team that lost the World Series to Florida on a Game Seven walk-off, his 52 postseason games, his 227 homers, his 429 steals, his 15-game World Series hitting streak and so much more. The flash of greatness that I just happened to notice in my first year on a baseball beat was fully realized, thanks to hard work, a great attitude, and being ready when your name is called.

DR. BOBBY BROWN

Standing on second base with a World Series in the balance, Dr. Bobby Brown looked for his father in the stands. It was the fall of 1947, the same year Jackie Robinson had integrated baseball at last, and Brown was playing for the Yankees against Robinson and the Dodgers. In that very moment, Brown knew it was all worth it—all of the hard work, the passion and drive that had dominated his life had resulted in the achievement of a goal, the pinnacle of his profession.

"I had some big hits in the World Series," Brown recalled during an interview in early 2013, when he was making an appearance to honor his former Yankees teammate Yogi Berra. "In the 1947 World Series, we were in Game Seven, and I had pinch-hit three times before that game. I had gotten a base on balls with the bases loaded. I had gotten a double and a single after that. So I was up three times with two hits and a walk. In the game against Brooklyn in the Stadium, we were down 2–1 in the fourth inning. We got two men on base, men on second and first, and our pitchers were in trouble. They had bad arms, and they had to take Bill Bevens out because his arm was bad. They put me in to hit, and I hit a double that scored the tying run and put the go-ahead run on third.

"I was on second, and I thought when I was on second base that all the work I had done as a ball player was worth this moment. That was really something. I could see my folks in the stands. I knew where they were sitting. I could see my dad throwing his hat up in the air and catching it. They were behind home plate. They had a certain section where all the families of the ballplayers sat. That was a tremendous moment for me. It was 1947 so I was going to be 23. I was 22 when it happened."

Brown's double scored Billy Johnson to tie it at 2–2 and moved Phil Rizzuto to third, chasing Dodgers starter Hal Gregg. Reliever Hank Behrman walked Snuffy Stirnweiss to load the bases, and Tommy Henrich's subsequent single to right brought home Rizzuto with what would hold up as the deciding run. It delivered the 11th World Series title in Yankees history.

CONFIDENCE
AND CONCENTRATION

In the beginning of the seminal movie *The Natural,* Roy Hobbs walks up to the old porch and is reminded of sage advice his father Ed once gave:

"If you rely on your gift, you're gonna fail. You've got to develop yourself. . . . The secret is confidence and concentration. If you've got them, you don't need much else. . . . Roy, just pick a spot and work at it. A clear mind and the ability to see with the heart—that's real strength. . . . It's your spot, Roy. Pay attention to it."

Hank Aaron exuded "confidence and concentration" throughout his career, and especially throughout his pursuit of the home run that finally passed Babe Ruth on the all-time list, but what hit was he truly proudest of over those 23 years? Ruth himself had picked a spot and worked at it for a Called Shot, something we channel in these pages, but do we remember it more adoringly than he ever did? The power of concentration enabled Dusty Baker to make history of his own against a "nasty" pitcher, and it led to the unexpected start of a modern culture phenomenon. Confidence and concentration was exhibited by a wood-splitting pioneer lawyer from Illinois who, according to legend, had to "make a base hit" before acknowledging a U.S. presidential nomination. Jim Thome and Reggie Sanders reached milestones that were magical to them, thanks to confidence and concentration, Evan Longoria cleared his mind and finished a regular season in epic fashion, and Mickey Mantle used his "real strength" to muscle out memories for millions.

HANK AARON

"I was just doing my job," Hank Aaron told Ross Rossin, an Atlanta-based artist who created the nine-foot-tall bronze statue that was unveiled the week before the Braves' SunTrust Park stadium opened in 2017. Rossin had asked Aaron what was going on inside his head as he faced Al Downing on April 8, 1974, the night he hit his 715th home run to pass Babe Ruth's all-time record. The statue, complete with the ball on the bat, depicts that frozen moment in time. Aaron's confidence and concentration were legendary traits, as he somehow withstood those endless death threats and hate mail spewed by racists that wanted Ruth's record to stand forever. Hammerin' Hank finished with 755, the record until Barry Bonds passed it in 2007, and as he admired Rossin's creation and clearly appreciated that tribute, one would think that his homer to left that night at old Atlanta-Fulton County Stadium would hold up easily as the hit that meant the most to him out of 3,771 total hits over 23 years. However . . .

"The thing I am most proud of, I was able to get as many hits as I did," Aaron told the *Cincinnati Enquirer* in 2015. Once again, a moment that is so iconic to the masses is not necessarily what hits home the most, personally, to a legend looking back. "The most important thing in my career out of the 23 years I played is I never struck out 100 times," he told the paper. "Getting the base hits was the greatest thrill of my life." Furthermore, Aaron told the Enquirer that he has "always said" that and thus this was no fleeting thought told to a paper from a city where he had done something big.

I have had the pleasure to cover Hank's appearances at various events, and while there never has been an opportunity for me to ask the nine-word question, one can see an affinity on his part for his 3,000th of those hits. Most members of that 3,000 Hit Club are included in this book. Aaron got there on May 17, 1970, the second game of a Sunday doubleheader in the final days for old Crosley Field in Cincinnati. There were 33,217 fans, the most there in 23 years, and Aaron received a standing ovation after he singled off Reds right-hander Wayne Simpson in the first inning for number 3,000. It was a fastball inside, and second baseman Woody Woodward knocked down the grounder up the middle near the outfield grass, unable to make the play. So after all those home runs, all those statues, all that glory, maybe it was an infield grounder that mattered the most. Aaron had been 0-for-4 in the first game, but the crowd got its money's worth watching him in the second game. He was 3-for-5 with a homer off Simpson in the third, even walked in the 14th as the Reds walked off in the 15th. That's 24 innings on a Sunday, another reason it might be so memorable to Aaron; he earned it!

"Stan Musial came out of the dugout to congratulate me," Aaron remembered. He was talking in 2009 at MLB's Civil Rights Game festivities right there in Cincinnati, recalling Crosley as he accepted a Beacon Award. I was covering the event for MLB.com. Musial had been the most recent 3,000 member, way back in 1958, and it so happened that Hank's good friend Willie Mays would get there about two months after the hit off Simpson.

At the Civil Right Game roundtable discussion, Aaron sat in the front row and enjoyed a discussion by dignitaries on race and sports. Barack Obama had just been inaugurated months before, and Hank delivered another heartfelt message to those in attendance. "In baseball—that's my little world—I would like for everyone to understand that we are still trying to get a piece of the pie," he said. "We are still trying to get where we were supposed to get when Jackie broke into baseball. I just don't want people to lose the focus on what this is all about. There's been a few of us [who] reached the top, but a lot of us [are] still trying to get to the top."

Aaron has been an annual fixture at the World Series ceremony where a top hitter from each league receives the Hank Aaron Award as outstanding offensive performer. His words have carried power, as his bat did. Unfortunately, there never has been an opportunity there to ask him about one hit that meant the most. During 2012 All-Star Week in Kansas City, I was covering a Habitat for Humanity event at which Hank made an appearance with his wife Billye, and I asked him about a knee replacement surgery he had just undergone. "My wife said if I'd have hit two or three more home runs I wouldn't have had to slide, so I wouldn't have had this problem," he joked. Indeed, one of his best memories of playing was simply his durability, avoiding injuries that shortened others' careers. That is also how you get to 755 home runs. "I was lucky," he said.

There is so much to be proud of when you have lived a life like Henry Aaron has lived. There is no pressing need to pin him down on one hit. You can piece together his thoughts over the years, and you will have a pretty good idea. Maybe it was that 3,000th hit, if you had to choose just one hit. In Atlanta, amidst his own towering statue, it would be hard to imagine him choosing anything but 715. Or maybe it was a hit with the Indianapolis Clowns in the Negro Leagues. Aaron dictated outcomes.

BUD SELIG

There is someone else very close to Aaron who does offer one other hit by number 44 that has lasted for generations. Now that he is in the Hall of Fame along with his good friend, it was only appropriate that former Commissioner Bud Selig told a story about an Aaron hit that mattered the most to him. After taping a *Center Stage* show as Commissioner for the YES Network during the dazzling postseason chases of September 2012, Selig obliged my request for one hit—that he had witnessed—and he made it a double: "Henry Aaron's hit in '57 and Cecil Cooper's hit that won the playoff game for us in '82."

"Henry's hit. Well, I was in with the Braves, it was baseball and it was Milwaukee, and it was dramatic," he said. "It was just a hit that really made an impression on me for many reasons."

Selig proceeded to let his mind wander to a more innocent and carefree time and he told this story from his youth, 55 years earlier, like it was yesterday:

"I was a kid in Milwaukee, had just been in the service, and on September 23, 1957, the Braves will play the St. Louis Cardinals and if they win, they win the pennant. It was a long summer. I was taking an accounting course, because my father had asked if I had taken accounting yet. I hated accounting, hate it to this day. I'm driving down, I had never skipped a class. I said to myself, I can't go to that class. So I drove off the ramp of the freeway and parked about three miles away, walked and came up to the ticket window, and, 'I need one.' It's way up in the upper deck behind a post. That night in the 11th inning, Hank Aaron hit a very dramatic home run, off of Billy Muffett of the Cardinals. I can remember sitting in my seat crying.

"Henry Aaron and I have been friends for a long, long time now, very close friends. What struck me about all that, all the excitement, is the next day in *The New York Times*, there's a wonderful picture of Hank Aaron carried off the field, and juxtaposed right alongside that is Governor Orval Faubus spraying kids trying to go to school in Arkansas. It's a picture that really made a very deep impression. So the night made an impression and the next day made an impression on me as well."

Selig was among 40,926 fans who packed Milwaukee's County Stadium that night. It was a game loaded with future Hall of Famers: Aaron; Stan Musial; Eddie Mathews; and Red Schoendienst, who had been a Cardinals star but then led off for Milwaukee. Just think, three of the first four hitters in the Braves lineup eventually off to Cooperstown. Mathews had doubled in Schoendienst in the seventh to tie the score at 2–2, and Muffett had worked out of a bases-loaded jam in the 10th.

Milwaukee had two out and Johnny Logan on first when Aaron stepped up to face Muffett. The Hammer sent one to deep center for the 4–2 victory. It was his 43rd homer of the season as he busted out in his fourth campaign, and he would add his 44th and final one of the season a day later, a grand slam. Number 43 clinched the city's first World Series appearance, and he would lead the Braves to a seven-game triumph over the mighty Yankees for the championship.

There was so much more to come, and getting past so many power-hitting immortals on the list required plenty of confidence and concentration.

Hank Aaron had it, along with quick wrists, and he just did his job—with a hammer.

DUSTY BAKER

When Aaron broke that all-time home run record in Atlanta, Dusty Baker was in the on-deck circle on the first-base side, on his right knee, watching the pitch. He had a perfect angle to view the full flight of the ball. As the ball left Aaron's bat, Bake sprang up at once and thrust his left hand high into the air, his own gleeful respect. You can find number 12 if you look back at the videos: a relatively thin, 24-year-old man from Southern California who was Atlanta's starting center fielder that night. Bake had doubled Aaron in with the game's first run that night, a fact lost in time, as was the walk that Bake drew immediately after Aaron's home run. Under normal circumstances, as the next batter after a teammate's homer, he would have been the single greeter at home plate. This time, Bake was part of a massive greeting committee at home, a huge smile on his face, as Aaron made his way over toward the dugout and was hugged by his mother among others. All the while, Bake had his helmet on, knowing it would be a long wait before he officially stepped into the batter's box. He was witness to history then, and he has witnessed big hit after big hit in a lifetime spent as a player, coach or manager. He was even on deck when Mike Schmidt hit the winning two-run homer for the National League in the 1981 All-Star Game at Cleveland, and there was something significant about that greeting at home plate as well, due to something Bake by all accounts co-invented.

I don't know him as anything other than "Bake" because that is what we all called him when I covered the San Francisco Giants at the *Mercury News* in the early '90s. All those afternoons at Candlestick Park, leaning against the batting cage, when Bake was the Giants' hitting coach and answering my questions about Kevin Mitchell this or Will Clark that, always so affable and happy to help educate someone on nuances of the game. As long as I have known him, he has been talking about what other people do with a bat, mixing in the occasional LA soul food restaurant recommendation. It was a joy to finally seize the opportunity to ask him about his own hitting prowess when we chatted one afternoon in the Washington Nationals' dugout, before a night game against the Mets at Citi Field. I told him it was his turn to talk about himself now, time to pick out something from those 1,981 regular season hits or perhaps the 42 more in postseason play, where he played in three World Series (1977–78 and '81), winning a ring in his last one and claiming the NLCS MVP Award in the '77 meeting with Philadelphia.

"Probably the home run of J. R. Richard because he was my nemesis," Bake replied after a brief consideration. "To go into the record books as four guys hitting 30 home runs, and then Reggie Smith had told him on that Thursday of a four-game series that I was going to hit it off him, and I'm like, 'Come on, Reggie!'"

I told him that Reggie Smith shared his hit for this book, the first hit of his career, and Bake nodded and said with a grin, "Reggie was the second-best hitter I've played with. Hank Aaron was the only one better."

In 1977, National League batters lived in utter fear of facing Richard, the Astros' 6-foot-8 right-hander with a blazing fastball—one that would put him in the 300-strikeout club the following year. On the final weekend of the 1977 regular season, the Dodgers were hosting the Astros for two games. Smith hit two homers on that Saturday, October 1, giving him 32 for the year. Steve Garvey and Ron Cey already had 33 and 30 respectively at that point. Bake had 29 going into that Sunday finale, and the Dodgers could become the first MLB team ever to have a quartet of 30-homer players . . . if only he could put one over the wall in Chavez Ravine with Richard in his way.

"J. R. was hard on us," Bake remembered. "J. R., he might have been the best pitcher in the game, before he got hurt. Right before he got hurt, he was finding his control. He was nasty, he was just wild enough to give you a very uncomfortable at-bat. He was my friend, and I didn't have a whole bunch of pitchers as friends."

Richard threw a complete-game victory on that Sunday, striking out 14 Dodgers and limiting them to a measly four hits and three earned runs. Remarkably three of those hits and all three runs came in the bottom of the sixth, in the form of three solo homers. The first was by 39-year-old Manny Mota, the last homer he ever would hit. The second was by Bake, on a 1–2 count, in the pavilion to make it a 4x30 milestone for the Dodgers. The third was by Glenn Burke—his only homer of the year and one of only two he hit in his career. I wanted to know what Bake learned in that hit of a lifetime.

"Concentration. Concentration and the power of belief," he said. "Because [Dodgers manager] Tommy Lasorda told me you've got to believe, and I use that now. You've got to believe it."

One thing that is hard to believe, but by all accounts true, is that the same Bake who greeted Hammerin' Hank in one of the most historic home runs proceeded to invent a piece of popular culture when he was greeted following his own history-making homer. Bake rounded the bases and Burke, a second-year player who had replaced Garvey in the lineup one inning earlier, was there to meet him as the next batter. There was sudden excitement in the ballpark as Richard had completely shut down the Dodgers most of the afternoon, taking a one-hit shutout into that sixth inning. Burke was caught up in the excitement, arching his back and extending his right hand high into the air. Bake was perhaps expecting a handshake and was a little confused, so he reached up and slapped Burke on that same hand up high. The high-five was born. Bowlers would high-five each other after a strike. Co-workers would high-five each other after a successful deal. In every sport and in every walk of life, people would high-five each other the way Dusty Baker did when he crossed home plate in 1977, and today there is even a National High Five Day.

Back to that aforementioned 1981 All-Star Game in Cleveland, Schmidt hit that eventual game-winning homer. Four years after the invention, Schmidt crossed home plate and gave a high-five to Pittsburgh's Mike Easler. Then he gave a high-five to Bake, who was the next batter. Bake promptly singled off future Hall of Famer Rollie Fingers, and then was removed for pinch-runner Tim Raines. It was just another day in the life of Bake, the man who has seen it all and done so much for so many.

JIM THOME

Maybe the hardest I had to work to get one hit out of someone was Jim Thome, the first active player interviewed for this book. Because he was one of my earliest respondents to the question, I did not have the luxury of mentioning a handful of his peers' responses—a technique that typically helps stars dig down and find a gem. But I got it. I was in the Los Angeles Dodgers clubhouse long after their Game One victory over the St. Louis Cardinals in the 2009 National League Division Series. Thome, a class guy who was in the final stages of a Hall of Fame career, now as a bench role player, was sitting in front of his locker. We chatted for a bit and then I asked him the question.

"That's hard. That's hard. It'd be taking away from some of the other ones," he said. "To pinpoint one of them is tough. It's unfair to you."

Right about then is where the average person changes the subject. I was writing a book on this subject, so I held my ground.

"I mean, maybe your first Major League hit, out of respect to that. Again, that's so tough. That's so tough. . . ."

I asked him again, told him how much I would like to include him in my book. I told him what Prince Fielder told me. I told him what Albert Pujols told me. I told him what his former Cleveland general manager, John Hart, told me. By telling him those, he was having more time for the wheels of time to turn, for thousands of hits to roll by again, one to pick out above all of them. Then, inevitably, the result I was looking for was there.

"I mean, walk-off homer, 500th homer," Thome said. "To have your teammates greet you at home plate on your 500th was pretty special.

"It was a Sunday afternoon. I don't remember the sequence of it, but I think it may have got to 2–2 or 3–2, and I got a fastball out over the plate. Mosely was pitching. A man on. That one was very special. Very. There's other ones that would be—again, to pick one, you're taking away from the others."

The hit he chose occurred on September 16, 2007. It was especially memorable to many who were in attendance, because it happened to take place on Jim Thome Bobblehead Day.

Thome took two or three steps down the first-base line before pumping his right fist in celebration as career home run number 500 landed in the left-center field bleachers at U.S. Cellular Field. You have to be a special person to make a 500th home run milestone mean this much. He became the 23rd member of the 500 Home Run Club—and the first to get there with a walk-off. The 426-foot clout completed a six-run White Sox comeback, but also capped off a magical ride to immortality.

"Just can't believe it, I really can't," Thome said on that milestone day. He had waded through three curtain calls from the 29,010 in attendance, who stayed until the very last pitch despite the Bears game taking place at the same time. "The crowd and just the way they hung in there all weekend long, kind of the downs, they had a lot of downs all weekend. I would never have imagined doing that as a walk-off. It's just amazing to see your teammates standing there. It's like a movie script. It really is."

In 2009, he stood in front of his locker. "It's a good question, but a difficult one, because you don't want to leave the other ones out," he said. "Out of respect to, say a World Series hit, or maybe a big hit like [in 2008], the home run in the tiebreaker game that got us into the postseason with Chicago. That's another big one. So it's hard."

Thome was referring there to the homer he hit that gave the White Sox the 1–0 victory over the Twins in that tiebreaker game. I have no doubt that had I stayed there all night, we would have documented a long line of big hits, ones that were talked about for days and even years. But out of all of them, the 500th was the prize, at least at that very moment. I knew that by the time he got to a Hall of Fame Induction speech, he probably would be recalling many more, maybe number 600. Sometimes it's not so easy to find just one hit. Sometimes I felt a little unfair even asking the question.

MICKEY MANTLE

New York Yankees (1951)

Mickey Mantle is one of the best known names in baseball, and his memorable ninth inning home run only made him more famous

The only time I ever met Mickey Mantle, it cost $50. It was a "sign" of the times. That was the going rate in 1991 for the Yankees legend's autograph at a major signing show. I was building a nice little memorabilia collection in those days, and I thought The Mick's signed ball would be worth it in value. So Nick Peters and I were in a rental car—him covering the San Francisco Giants for the *Sacramento Bee* and me for the *San Jose Mercury News*— stopping by Atlantic City during an East Coast road swing that summer. Nick, whom we affectionately called "Greek," was eventually inducted into the National Baseball Hall of Fame as the J.G. Taylor Spink Award winner before his sad passing. Many remember him as an astute memorabilia connoisseur who often eschewed flying and preferred to drive and see the sights on road trips—especially if there was a card show somewhere along the way. That is why we were together in the rental car that day, going to see the great Mantle. So there we were in a line, $50 lighter, each holding a clean baseball, about to get his familiar, looping autograph on the sweet spot of life. It was a cordial greeting and a signing, with that beautiful and familiar penmanship, and a move on down the road to our next press box.

Had I only known what the future held, I would have *really* gotten my money's worth out of those fifty bucks. I would have said, "Mickey, what hit meant the most to you and why?" I probably would have incorporated "please." Come on, it was Mickey Mantle. He would have had neither the time (this was business) nor inclination for a detailed self-analysis of his well-documented lore—First hit? Longest homer? Walk-off?—but I am guessing that the man who hit the most home runs in World Series history would have gone somewhere toward one of those shots if he thought about it.

It would have been a fast ask, and so it would have been a fast answer. Many times, those situations have produced "my first hit" as the response. In The Mick's case, I am guessing that a fast ask would have produced a fabled home run. That tended to cement and define his legend over his years in the Big Apple, those prodigious blows. They are so easy to find in a Google search, so many tomes devoted to the power and the glory. After all, he literally invented the "tape measure" term used to describe a homer of exceptional distance. As he signed my ball, Mickey might have just said "Griffith Stadium," leaving me to fill in the narrative details here.

That was a 565-foot homer, according to Yankees PR director Red Patterson, who raced out of the Washington ballpark's press box to measure the ball's apparent landing spot after it cleared the left-field bleachers—the first time it ever happened there. It came off left-hander Chuck Stobbs on April 17, 1953, and the greatest power-hitting switch-hitter of all time was hitting righty. It ranks as one of the most famous home runs in history. Mantle's teammate Billy Martin was a baserunner on third when the ball soared out, and as a gag he had stayed on third as long as possible, pretending that he was tagging up. Mantle, who almost ran into Martin on the trot, had not seen the gag, because, as he later said, "I used to keep my head down as I rounded the bases after a home run. I didn't want to show up the pitcher. I figured he felt bad enough already." He agreed to post for a picture after the game with Patterson, holding up a tape measure.

Yes, that might have been Mickey's top-of-the-head response. It might have been one of several he hit even farther than that. He might have flashed back to his 1956 Triple Crown season, perhaps to the ball he almost hit out of Yankee Stadium in a rematch with Washington's Pedro Ramos, his friend who had dutifully (and later apologetically) knocked Mantle down with a retaliation pitch. It might have been a longball from his great home run race with teammate Roger Maris in '61, when the M&M Boys were on fire. It might have been the homer in the 1964 World Series that broke Babe Ruth's Fall Classic homer record, the shot he had told teammate Elston Howard he was going to hit that day. "You might as well go in and start getting dressed," Mantle told him. "I'm going to hit his first pitch for a home run." Who knows what Mantle would have said?

Four years later, sadly, he was gone. He was only 63. At the risk of going down a rabbit hole here—What would Ty Cobb have said? What would Cap Anson have said? What would Josh Gibson have said?—I am turning to a couple of experts for unique perspectives on Mantle hits that mattered the most.

BOB COSTAS

Broadcaster Bob Costas, representing the millions of baseball-loving kids who grew up in the '50s and '60s and for whom Mickey Mantle was baseball, delivered a eulogy at Mantle's funeral. In doing so, he shared a story that Mantle had liked to tell on himself: "He pictured himself at the pearly gates, met by St. Peter, who shook his head and said, 'Mick, we checked the record, we know some of what went on. Sorry, we can't let you in. But before you go, God wants to know if you'd sign these six-dozen baseballs.'"

Indeed, it did not seem that farfetched. Again, I was one of those who had eagerly paid $50 just to get that signature, that tingly representation of an American hero. There have been times in this book project where a player passed away after I asked him, and times where I asked someone as a knowing surrogate to speak for a late legend. The latter was the case here. Costas, my friend from St. Louis, had been known to have carried Mantle's 1951 rookie card with him in his wallet. Mel Allen had been the broadcast voice of the Mantle days, but Costas still represented those legions of admirers who felt a void.

In 2011, as the Cardinals took batting practice before World Series Game Seven at Busch Stadium, I was chatting with Bob and asked him what Mantle hit had meant the most.

"Here is a quirky answer, but what gets to you as a kid stays with you longer," Costas began. "So Mickey Mantle's home run off Barney Schultz in the bottom of the ninth, Game Three, 1964. I was twelve years old, the game was tied, 1–1, the series was tied, 1–1, and Mantle was tied with Ruth on the all-time World Series home run list with fifteen. And the homer into the upper deck off Schultz at Yankee Stadium was not only a classic Mantle homer, but it won the game, and it put him ahead of Babe Ruth all-time in World Series home runs.

"One of the things that annoys me is when people say, 'Here's the list of *postseason* home run leaders,' or '*postseason* pitching victory leaders.' It's not that that isn't a fine achievement, but it lacks context. I think Joe Buck always does an excellent job on FOX of always pointing out that there are additional rounds of playoffs today. But every one of Mickey Mantle's homers was in the World Series. Every one of Babe Ruth's or Duke Snider's was in the World Series."

JAMES CAAN

"It was in a championship game and I hit a triple," the legendary actor of *Godfather* and *Brian's Song* fame was saying one day in 2013, recalling glory days while in New York to promote a new (and short-lived) baseball-themed TV show. "We were down two runs in the ninth and I hit a triple to win the championship. We scored three runs."

That was his best hit. And then he added with a boyish laugh: "The other one was the one I think I hit somebody across the back with."

Caan played some semipro in California for a little while when he first got out to Hollywood to start an acting career, "to supplement my huge income. I was a shortstop and then as I got a little older they moved me to third base. Al Rosen was an old third baseman. He used to catch everything off his hand or his chest and then pick it up. That's the way I started off."

Free agency "screwed up everything," Caan claimed. I share this *saudade* (see: Albert Pujols section), although it did work out well for the union workers in this case. "I watched guys forever. I get interested now at the end of the year. You don't know who's gonna get traded or leave. Years ago, before free agency started, when I was a kid, I would see guys staying for years. Moose Skowron, Billy Martin, Clete Boyer, Maris and Mantle—those were my guys. Now you've got guys who move through some uniforms in all the sports. I can't keep up with the trades." As he spoke, another hit came to his mind.

"Mickey Mantle was my guy," Caan said. "Mel Allen used to be the announcer, and a beer company sponsored the Yankees games. At the end of the game, he'd be drunk and would almost fall out of the press box, so they stopped that. I remember one year, one shot. Mickey twice, he hit two into the bleachers. Only like ten guys had ever hit into the bleachers, and Mickey went back-to-back into the bleachers. It was great, because the ball went straight up into the air, and the center fielder started running in, the second baseman started running back, and the thing dropped into the bleachers."

ABRAHAM LINCOLN

In May of 1860, depending on how much you believe the lore of ages, Abraham Lincoln was playing baseball on the common in Springfield, Illinois when he was told of the arrival of a delegation from the Republican Party's Convention in Chicago. They were going to nominate him for the Presidency. "Tell the gentleman that I am glad to know of their coming; but they'll have to wait a few minutes 'til I make another base hit." Abe then stepped back in against the pitcher and took another cut at the ball. That is how A.G. Spalding recorded it in his book *America's National Game*. Some historians insist that Lincoln was actually at the Springfield depot closely monitoring the telegraph, but this is how baseball legends are built, and we have heard too much about Abe's honesty to think he would let such a good story go naught. Moreover, we have to assume he actually did "make another base hit." What pitcher would have denied him such happiness in that lofty moment? Given his determination showed in later years, who in his or her right mind thinks Lincoln simply whiffed and then walked away? This story is widely doubted through recent decades by baseball scholars, but it is now as much a part of American baseball lore as Abner Doubleday being the father of baseball. Call it a base hit.

Lincoln had strong wood-making experience and instincts, and unquestionably would have known what to do with a good bat. He would go on to take his passion of baseball with him to Washington. During the Civil War, as the game was being spread from North to South, Lincoln and his son Tad often would watch baseball behind the White House.[3]

In 2009, I was researching the Civil War era inside the Baseball Hall of Fame Research Library. There is an entire folder of clips pertaining to Lincoln. One document was a copy of a cartoon, drawn by artist Louis Mauer: "1860, post-election." It was originally published by Currier & Ives, 152 Nassau St, NY. Pictured were, from left to right, presidential candidates John Bell, Stephen Douglas, John Breckinridge, and Lincoln. The headline on the cartoon read:

---

3   George Vecsey, *Baseball: A History Of America's Favorite Game* (Modern Library, 2008), 24.

—THE NATIONAL GAME. THREE "OUTS" AND ONE "RUN". ABRAHAM WINNING THE BALL.

THE NATIONAL GAME. THREE "OUTS" AND ONE "RUN".
ABRAHAM WINNING THE BALL.

Currier & Ives 1860

The caption in smaller type read: "Gentlemen, if any of you should ever take a hand in another match at this game, remember that you must have 'a good bat' and strike a 'fair ball' to make a 'clean score' & a 'home run.'"

EVAN LONGORIA

"Ha! I mean, there's really only one: the home run in game one hundred sixty-two, the second one. It was probably the biggest hit of my career, maybe one of the biggest hits I'll ever get. It was just an unbelievable memory, a great day overall, and something that's just hard to put into words."

Many experts considered the final day of the 2011 Major League Baseball regular season to be the greatest night of baseball they ever had seen. Multiple games converged with meaning, drama filled with heroes and goats, resulting in surprise postseason matchups. Longoria was the biggest hero.

Tampa Bay needed to beat the Yankees, and the Orioles to beat the Red Sox, in order to clinch an AL Wild Card berth. The Orioles took care of their end of the bargain, finalizing a renowned Boston collapse. The Yankees jumped out to a 7–0 lead, but Tampa Bay roared back, and Dan Johnson came off the bench to hit the home run that tied it at 7–7 in the ninth and forced extra innings.

In the 12th inning, Longoria hit his second homer of the game. It was a rope over the left field wall. He became the second player in Major League history to send his team into the playoffs with a walk-off homer on the final day. The other was Bobby Thomson's "Shot Heard 'Round the World" for the New York Giants in 1951.

Longoria was in New York for a big postseason-push series at Yankee Stadium in September 2012, and the memory of a year earlier was fresh in his mind when we chatted during the morning. But I asked him what element of that classic at-bat might be unknown to the average fan who saw it happen. His homer was just inside the foul pole and came off Scott Proctor, the 11th pitcher used by the Yankees that night. They had kept all-time saves leader Mariano Rivera in the bullpen.

"There were two strikes, which I didn't know until I went back and looked again," Longoria replied. "The day was so slow up until that point, and then after that it was so fast, that there were subtleties about that at-bat that I didn't remember, and that was one of them, that there were two strikes in the at-bat."

REGGIE SANDERS

Reggie Sanders was called up by the Cincinnati Reds in 1991, during my second year of covering the National League and the Giants for the *San Jose Mercury News*. He put together a 17-year career, and that included five postseasons during which he compiled 43 hits—four of them for Arizona in Game Six of the 2001 World Series. When I caught up with him in October of 2011, he told me that winning a World Series was his greatest thrill as a player. But in deciding on a hit that mattered most to him in his lifetime, he looked toward the end of his playing days.

"When I hit my three hundredth home run," he said. "For me, it was the culmination of all the years that I played and being the fifth player in Major League history to have gone 300–300—three hundred stolen bases, three hundred home runs. I was with Kansas City, and we were at home against Tampa Bay in 2006. I remember it going over the wall, but I think I ended up shedding a tear inside, because I knew it was a milestone for myself, but not only for me, also for my family and all the people who ever supported me. So I think when I crossed the plate all the guys were there to greet me in excitement, and for me it was a full-circle moment."

It was June 10 of that 2006 season, the bottom of the ninth, and Sanders's two-run homer off reliever Chad Harville came in a 9–5 loss at Kauffman Stadium. Sanders, who had stolen his 300th career base a month earlier, thus joined this quartet in the 300–300 Club at that point: Barry and Bobby Bonds, Willie Mays, and Andre Dawson.

BABE RUTH

I will take a little liberty here and speculate a bit. In early 1927, *The New York Sun* asked top athletes in their respective sports what promises they would make for the New Year. Babe Ruth responded this way: "I promise sixty homers for Jake."[4] That was an assurance to Yankees owner Col. Jacob Ruppert, who saw his famed slugger do exactly that.

National Photo Company Collection at the Library of Congress

Babe Ruth might have chosen a 60th homer or a Called Shot

---

4   Seth Swirsky, "*Tom Zachary's Letter About Babe Ruth's 60th Home Run*," http://www.seth.com/coll_letters_26.html.

Ruth had hit 54 out in his 1920 debut season with the Yankees, and then a record 59 in 1921. He reached 60 on the second to last day of that 1927 regular season, at home against Washington. "Sixty, count 'em, sixty! Let's see some son-of-a-bitch match that!" he said after hitting it off Washington pitcher Tom Zachary, who also had surrendered numbers 22 and 36 during the season. A fan named Joe Forner caught the baseball and won the reward of $100 that had been offered by a company called Truly Warner—"Headquarters for Hats."

The Bronx Bombers' victory that day put them 65 games over .500, and a week later they would be on their way to a World Series sweep of Pittsburgh. It was the crowning individual achievement on the greatest team in Major League history, it was Ruth at his peak, and contextually it was just mind-boggling then and even today. He defined the home run and hitting that milestone was just so far beyond what anyone ever imagined, it was like fanciful fiction. Ultimately the record was surpassed by Roger Maris, who hit 61 in a 1961 season that featured eight more games on the schedule than Ruth had been allowed, and then it was further surpassed decades later. Ruth's legend nevertheless survived the test of time, and to this day he remains by far the most hallowed treasure in baseball history. Just visit the Hall of Fame, where his statue is in the main lobby and his plaque is the most revered. If you have to pick just one Bambino hit, then go with the one that mattered most to him.

Here is how Zachary remembered it in a 1965 letter, showing how much it always stuck in his own craw:

"...Tied 2–2 in eighth. Two outs, one man on and a count of three and two strikes on Ruth. I threw him a curve, but I made a bad mistake. I should have thrown a fast one at his big fat head. Lost game, 4–2. It was a tremendous swat down right field foul line. At that time, there were just bleacher seats in right field with foul pole. But since [at first] it went so [illegible] and far up in bleachers that it would be difficult to judge it accurately. I hollered "foul ball" but I got no support, very little from my team mostly so it must have been a fair ball—but I always contended to Ruth that it was foul."

Mike Gibbons, Executive Director at the Babe Ruth Birthplace Foundation in Baltimore, was less sure that would have been The Bambino's choice if you could ask him now. "As for his most important hit, sixty was a big deal, for sure," Gibbons said, "but the Called Shot home run from the 1932 World Series might be even more impactful." Indeed, that fabled home run in the fifth inning of Game Three of the 1932 World Series against the Cubs is no doubt Ruth's most iconic hit. After all, it is dissected in rich detail at the National Baseball Hall of Fame and Museum, with old video and interviews, helping to ensure that the fun controversy—did he "call" it or didn't he?—would last forever. Ruth gestured in the direction of the Wrigley Field scoreboard during that at-bat, and he did in fact hit a towering home run over that very scoreboard. Ruth initially explained that he was simply gesturing with his hand as if to tell the players on the Cubs bench who had been riding him unmercifully that he still had one strike left. Whatever the case, Ruth let the matter carry on as a public debate, and it never stopped.

Who remembers Babe Ruth singles? Here is one, thanks to a story told in John Durant's 1947 book *The Story of Baseball*. It is presented to show the important of good tact among umpires, so there is no date or location, merely the anecdote. Ruth was trying to stretch a single one day, and the ball got there just as the slugger slid in with a cloud of dust. Umpire Clarence Rowland called him out, and Ruth sprung up livid and ready to rage. "What a shame I had to call you out, Babe, after such a beautiful slide. It was the best slide I ever saw." Ruth was fine with that and trotted to the dugout pleased.

Would he have just wanted to be different and chosen something like that? Would he have chosen the Called Shot, as Gibbons suspects? After interviewing more than 100 legends for this book, a common denominator emerged: Most greats choose not to respond with their most iconic, signature moment, going with something more personal to them. That is not always the case, so we cannot be sure, but based on the sheer volume of respondents in this book who opted not for the iconic, I will go with 60 here. Babe would have gone big and with a bang.

10

THINK OF OTHERS

Of all the motivational lessons that resulted from the hits that meant the most to baseball heroes, perhaps the one categorized in this chapter is the one most needed in our current times. Thinking of others is so simple, and it is how a society comes together through understanding. I suppose one could say that every respondent to my question belongs somehow here, because in some way they all think of others. They may have cleared their minds for the at-bat, but when they stepped up to the batter's box, they naturally have thought of their teammates, the game situation, the fans, their families, maybe their jobs. They were the center of everything in that moment, and with one swing they were in position to make at least someone feel special.

Some of the respondents shared exceptional stories of why their moment was about so much more than themselves. Ken Griffey Jr. lined a single right after his father did the same—adding to their own bond in a historic way. Cal Ripken Jr. rounded third base and felt a familiar hand. Alan Trammell reached the pinnacle of his career, and of course it had to happen in conjunction with his double-play partner in Detroit. John Mayberry and Miguel Tejada experienced the thrill of being amongst their idols at an All-Star Game and doing something positive for them. Ed Kranepool and Steve Garvey lifted up entire cities with a swing, and David Wright savored the thrill of doing something special for his country. Carlos Beltran, and Jake Peavy had family members in mind when they recorded their biggest hits, and for Carlos May, that person was his beloved grandma watching on TV down in Alabama. Fergie Jenkins wanted to impress his new club. They saw a bigger picture, a thought worth sharing now more than ever.

KEN GRIFFEY JR. AND SR.

On Father's Day of 2004—at the same Busch Stadium where months later I would cover an unthinkable World Series clincher by the Red Sox—I was in the right spot to cover Ken Griffey Jr.'s entry into the 500 Home Run Club. His father, Ken Griffey Sr., was watching in a box seat just behind the photographers' well next to the Cincinnati Reds dugout. "Happy Father's

Day. I love you," Junior told Senior as he reached over the camera well to hug his father on that perfect day in St. Louis. Griffey Jr. sent a Matt Morris fastball deep into the lower right-field seats for number 500. "Boy, what a Father's Day gift for Senior!" blared the legendary Reds broadcaster Marty Brennaman as he made the call that day. The headline on my MLB. com story read: "Griffey's Special Father's Day Gift." It all fit just right.

I spoke to Junior on the morning of Game Three of the 2016 World Series in Chicago, fittingly at an MLB community event focused on kids. The Kid was here, at a ballfield made possible by former Cubs pitcher Kerry Wood, just to stop by long enough to speak to a crowd of wide-eyed youth players and to answer their random questions. On his way out, before flying to Arizona to watch his son Trey play in a University of Arizona football game that night, he answered a question about his favorite hit. Of course, Ken Griffey Jr., who had delivered so many magical moments, whose bright smile had returned baseball trading cards to vogue, whom I had helped vote into the Hall of Fame just months earlier, was going to pick a hit involving his dad.

"Probably the back-to-back singles, the first at-bat," Junior told me, going back to the last day of August in 1990, Royals at Mariners. "Simply because my dad and I had a bet, whoever got the first hit, the other one had to pay for lunch. But the other one had a chance to tie.

"We're playing Kansas City. He batted second, I batted third, I'm on the on-deck circle and I go, 'Come on, Dad, get a hit!' And everybody [in the dugout] starts laughing at me. I turn around and I go, 'What's so funny?' They go, 'It's the first time we ever heard somebody say, 'Hey, Pops, get a hit' and actually mean it.' Usually you call somebody Pops, Greybeard, Old Guy, Fossil. But it was the first time and they said, 'That is his daddy, and he did say, 'Get a hit.' ' "

"So he gets a single, I get a single, and he's at second and he gives me the sign"—gesturing toward himself.

That happened on a Friday night inside Seattle's old Kingdome, and it just so happens that I was covering the San Francisco Giants game that night against the Mets across the country at Shea Stadium. It was a pretty quick game in New York, two hours and thirty minutes, and working in the press box some of us had one eye on what was happening three time zones to the West that night. A father and son were in the same lineup for the first time in MLB history.

Junior was just 20 and coming off his first All-Star appearance. Senior was 41 and in his second stint with the Reds, having been a key member of the Big Red Machine that won titles in 1975–76. Senior was still popular in Cincinnati, a "last link" who was playing for a 1990 team that would win it all (eventually meaning a third ring for Senior). The Griffeys wanted to seize a rare opportunity for this unlikely father-son combo on the field, but first the Reds had to figure out a way to make him available. On August 18, Reds general manager Bob Quinn gave Senior exactly 15 minutes to decide if he wanted to retire, accept his release, or go on the disabled list. The elder Griffey figured that retirement would allow him to go to the Seattle club, so he opted for that route. Then he learned there was a 60-day waiting period before a retired player could sign with another club. So Senior had to unretire, accept his release and then make it through the waiver wire process before the Mariners could acquire him. It all just happened to work out, and it meant Mariners manager Jim Lefebvre would have the opportunity to do something no other Major League manager ever had done.

On August 31, a Mariners team that was 63–68 and 18 1/2 games out in the American League West posted a lineup card that featured Harold Reynolds leading off, Ken Griffey Sr. batting second and playing left field, and Ken Griffey Jr. batting third and playing center. A father and son, both batting lefty, both wearing their outfield glove on the right hand. Right-hander Storm Davis was Kansas City's starter. In the bottom of the first, after Reynolds flied out to center, Senior lined a 1–0 pitch back through the box past Davis's head, into center for a single in his first Mariners at-bat. Then Junior, with that sweet looping swing, ripped a single to right. Senior scored on Alvin Davis's subsequent single, and Junior would make it 2–0 by scoring from third on a wild pitch. Seattle won, led by the Griffeys, who each went 1-for-4.

The following month, the Griffeys became the first father-son duo every to homer in the same game, with back-to-back jacks off Kirk McCaskill of the Angels. Being together through that October 2 seemed to energize Senior, who built a 12-game hitting streak at point, and who collected a combined 10 hits over a three-game span. Senior had found the fountain of youth—in his son. "This is the pinnacle for me, something I'm very proud of," Senior said back then. "You can talk about the '76 batting race, the two World Series I played in and the All-Star Games I played in. But this is number one. This is the best thing that's ever happened to me." And the son had found the inspiration to begin building a Cooperstown career. "I got to play with my dad," Junior said back then. "That's the biggest thing that's ever happened to me, other than the birth of my children. That's bigger than any record I'll ever set."

Now we were back in 2016, Junior remembering how much it had meant.

"I think watching him for those six weeks actually helped me over the course of my career, because it was somebody that, I looked like him, and the things that he did at the plate, I could finally really understand," Griffey Jr. told me. "Even though I lived in his house for seventeen years, I could finally understand what he was talking about. Dads will say something and you have your own interpretation of things. But I finally was looking at him and going, 'OK, I see what he means.'

"It basically helped me become a better hitter watching him for those six weeks, because as a kid, even though people think that we were in the clubhouse and we ran around, we were at the ballpark early four times. It was father-and-son game, husband-and-wife game, and probably two times when my mom was like, 'Uh, you better take these kids because I got something to do and I don't need them to be around.' What we'd do is go out and hang out, but for the most part during those other times we were at the ballpark, it was run in there, grab my dad's glove, and run back out. And play in the tunnel with all of the boys."

Junior smiled as he thought about what a high school coach had told him many years earlier, something he related to the young ballplayers assembled at Kerry Wood's field.

"My high school coach actually told my dad, 'Don't even show up, he can't play in front of you. Now he's a monster when you're away, but when you're here, he can't play,'" Griffey Jr. said.

"But to actually play with me—what's really scary is he hit .377 that six weeks that we played together. He led our team in hitting. I told him I protected him. I said, 'For seventeen years, you protected me. For the next six weeks, I get to protect you.'"

Junior got his pilot's license at age 36, about the same time his father had earned his. "It was like I've just done little things that mirrored my Dad his whole life," Junior said. Then he started imparting the same kind of wisdom to the kids that his father had imparted to him.

"I played football and basketball, I played soccer, I was the goalie—at that time I was the only kid who could catch—I played tennis, I do a lot of golf now," Junior said. "My dad was one of those guys who, his first love was football. He could have gone to Marshall. He didn't care what we did, as long as we were active and had fun. The only thing he cared about is, once you start something, you can't quit until the end of the year, you have to play it. You can't just say, 'Coaches don't like me, I'm done.' Doesn't matter. You're going to have to deal with it the whole year, then you make a decision.

"It's important that you make the right decisions now, because later on somebody can come back and find you. Just try to make the right decisions all the time. It's going to be tough. I've got a fourteen-year-old, and he came home—and this happened three days ago—'Because they're talking about me.'

"I said, 'What are they saying? Don't worry about it.'

"He said, 'Yeah, but somebody else jumped in and ganged up on me.'"

He also told them this about being around people who have things in common with your interests, whether that includes a parent or not.

"Most of the people you know now, they're going to change. And they're not going to be the same people you want them to be. You've got to be able to let them go and be the people who [say], 'Hey, this is what we want to do. We want to go to college, we want to play pro ball, we want to do these things. We want to be a leader, on and off the field.' And that's important. All this stuff, you've got to put in the work. You've got to be around people who have the same common goals."

CAL RIPKEN JR.

Baltimore Orioles (1982)

Cal Ripken Jr.'s most memorable hit had less to do with the hit than the fact that he got to share it with his dad

Some of my own most memorable moments being around baseball are being around Cal Ripken Jr., one of the best people I have ever known. I was in the press box at Camden Yards in September of 1995 when he helped bring back the sport by playing in his 2,131st consecutive game, breaking Lou Gehrig's "unbreakable" record. I grabbed everything that wasn't bolted down that night as memorabilia, although the Orioles were exceptional in equipping fans with beautiful number 8 keepsakes that night. I was standing with Ripken on the main street in front of the National Baseball Hall of Fame and Museum in Cooperstown at about 1:30 a.m. on a Sunday in 2007, as he spectacularly obliged every last autograph request into the wee hours, knowing his own induction speech was just hours away. He has been a delight to work with over the years as he moved into his analyst role.

During the 2012 All-Star Week in Kansas City, we chatted at FanFest about a number of subjects, and I told the Iron Man that I was curious which of his 3,184 Major League hits had been the most important to him.

"My first big-league home run," he said, those blue eyes flashing. "It wasn't because it was a home run, it was because it was my first home run. I got a chance to run around the bases, and the first person that I shook hands with was my dad. He was the third-base coach, and it was ceremonial to shake hands. It was a flood of meaning that came through that embrace, that little handshake, so I will always remember my first big-league home run."

There were 51,958 fans in the stands at old Memorial Stadium in Baltimore on April 5, 1982. It was Opening Day, and the first such event for Ripken. He had been called up as a rookie the previous August, appearing in 23 games and struggling to adapt. Ripken was 5-for-39 (.128) during that call-up, and he had not homered. But now it was a new season, the possibility for a first full season, and Kansas City was in town.

It was the second inning, the first time up in 1982.

"Dennis Leonard was pitching, it was my first at-bat of the season, Ken Singleton was on first base," Ripken remembered, like it was yesterday. "He threw me a fastball, which I took for a strike—I was just nervous, didn't want to swing at the first pitch. Then he hung a slider that I hit over in the bullpen in left-center field for a two-run homer. Ken Singleton ran around the bases sort of slow, and I was all pumped-up, so I ran pretty fast. I caught him before he got to home plate. Even with the handshake from my dad."

It was the first of 431 home runs Ripken would hit over a 21-year career.

FERGUSON JENKINS

My first trip to the National Baseball Hall of Fame and Museum was in July of 1991, because the San Francisco Giants team that I covered was playing in the Hall of Fame game that they used to hold in conjunction with the inductions. It was a big deal to me then because that induction class featured Rod Carew, my boyhood idol, so in my eyes he overshadowed everything at the time. But it was a large class, one that also featured Gaylord Perry, and posthumously Tony Lazzeri and Bill Veeck. There was one other key member of that year's group, and if you go back through all of the available Hall induction speeches, I think you will find that his was one of the most moving. Ferguson Jenkins thanked his late mother, noting that she had been blind and never could actually see him play baseball. Then he thanked his father, former Negro League outfielder Ferguson "Hershey" Jenkins Sr., telling him that he was unofficially going into the Hall with his son.

"On this day, I am not only being inducted alone, I am being inducted on July 21, 1991, with my father, Fergie Jenkins Sr., Hershey," the younger Fergie told the crowd. I learned later that it was very typical of Jenkins, the only Canadian in the Hall as a player. Gracious and endearing, Fergie had a unique way of touching people, making those happy around him.

I met Jenkins during the Cubs' historic title chase in late October of 2016, and he was generously putting smiles on the faces of children who were going through rehabilitation for various disabilities in downtown Chicago, the site of a long-awaited World Series. Amid everyone's focus on the Cubs' history at that time, it just happened to be the 50th anniversary season of the greatest hit for this Hall of Famer, who made a living with his right arm but had 1,010 plate appearances in 19 seasons. Jenkins came up with the Phillies as a 1965 call-up, but the Cubs traded for him on April 21 of the next season, and his first outing for them came two days later in hopes of changing a 1–8 Cubs start. Bob Hendley started on the mound for the Cubs at home against the Dodgers, but after 2 2/3 innings, he already had walked four and thrown a wild pitch, so the Cubs brought their new 6-foot-5 right-hander out of the Wrigley Field home-side bullpen and he immediately ended the inning.

It soon became clear that his desire for making others happy was the lasting lesson imparted from this hit response. Here was his reply:

"My first at-bat with the Chicago Cubs in the fifth inning, I hit a home run against Don Sutton. My second at-bat in the seventh, I hit a single, drove in Randy Hundley. So I drove in both runs as we won 2–0, beating the Dodgers. That was just something you don't forget. I'm twenty-two years old; I'm happy to be here in the big leagues; Leo Durocher was the manager; I got a chance to come in for relief in the second inning; I pitched six innings of relief; and I drove in two runs.

"I think both pitches were fastballs, up in the strike zone. The first one I hit in the bleachers, and the next one I hit up the middle. I was always told to hit the ball where it came from. And then in batting practice, try to hit the ball up the middle. But in that situation, the first one I hit a home run. You know what, those are fun to do. The article in the paper the next day, they said, 'Well, I think the Cubs found someone.'" He laughed.

"I just tried to perform as well as I could, and Durocher was the type of manager that, if he thought you were in a winning situation, he never took you out of it. To me, he was a great manager. And I was able to win a lot of twenty-game seasons."

Jenkins had 148 hits in his career, including six home runs and a .243 average during his National League Cy Young season of 1971. Six homers and a .243 average would be a *cause célèbre* for a pitcher today. The bat was taken out of his hands for a long while after the Cubs traded him to Texas following the 1973 season—the first year of the designated hitter in the American League—so he went from '74 through '81 effectively without batting, for the Rangers and the Red Sox and then the Rangers again. Fergie wound up his career back with the Cubs in '82–83.

You have to go back to the end of that Hall of Fame speech in 1991 to really understand the man and what made him tick as a ballplayer.

"It was my father," he said, as that emotional father sat in the front row and pulled out a handkerchief, "who taught me to be conscientious and responsible." A quarter century later, the seven-time 20-game winner told me about his lesson here.

"You hope you win, as a performer," he said. "I got traded, I won my first game when traded to the Texas Rangers; I beat Oakland, 2–0. When I got traded to Boston, I beat the Yankees, 1–0. You remember these things because they're significant in your career, but you always want to do your best to show that the trade was significant. I've been very fortunate in that respect. And I was able to stay healthy."

ALAN TRAMMELL

Most baseball fans who followed the career of Alan Trammell know that he not only spent his entire career as the Detroit Tigers' shortstop, but that he also spent it almost exclusively with one person as part of a beloved combination up the middle over two full decades. Trammell was a call-up in 1977, and he finished his career with 66 games in the '96 season. Lou Whitaker, the second baseman, played 19 games as a call-up in 1977 and '95 was the bookend as his final season. Whitaker was number one, Trammell number three. Together it was "Trammaker." They are inseparable in the minds of fans and in their career stats, turning double plays into eternity as Ernie Harwell called the action. If I were king of the world, they would be inducted jointly and soon into the Hall of Fame.

Part of an inseparable pair, Alan Trammell includes
Lou Whitaker in even his most memorable hit

Advanced statistical analysis makes it glaringly clear that they both belong, based on WAR and other metrics that show most players who ranked above them at their positions are already in the Hall. It should be noted that this analytics availability was lacking when they were on the ballot. This is the reason I overhauled my own Hall of Fame voting process in 2016, a subject that drew widespread support when my column was shared across Twitter. It is time for the Hall to look at everything differently—even if it is just for one calendar year—and re-evaluate all former players and do justice where men no doubt belong. It is not just a matter of special committees to look at individual eras, but rather a need to go back to the full Hall of Fame voting body and offer a special ballot—with no limit on checks—so that players like this Detroit double-play combination are justly rewarded at last.

I was not surprised when Trammell volunteered a response to our question that had everything to do with his longtime companion.

"Actually two of them come to mind, and both would go back to 1984 and the World Series," Trammell said. We spoke at a luncheon during the day of the 2015 MLB Draft as he represented his former club. "Two two-run homers the first two times up, and we end up winning the game, 4–2. So in a World Series environment, those home runs meant something, and that stands out at the top. I don't separate them.

"The whole year, the Dream Year of '84 for the Tigers, we often started off early. It was Game Four against San Diego and starter Eric Show. Lou Whitaker led off with a hit, I hit a home run. Third inning, Lou gets on with a base hit again, I hit another home run. So we were linked together obviously, as we should be, but it seemed like that particular year we got off to a good start, and that was certainly a game that we did as an example."

The Tigers won that day, 4–1, and those two players scored all the runs for Detroit. It was the ultimate example of their bond.

"Heading into the playoffs, I was swinging a bat well," Trammell said. "In the playoffs, the first at-bat, I got a hit. In the first at-bat in the World Series, I got a hit. That's the kind of stuff that can lead to some success; obviously it gives you some confidence. It was just one of those times that I was swinging the bat very, very well, and I happened to get some hits in the World Series."

Trammell was not done talking about Whitaker, though.

"The other one that comes to mind, my first Major League hit, in Fenway Park off of Reggie Cleveland in 1977," he said. "I'll go back to my partner, Lou Whitaker. He hit second in the lineup, and I hit ninth that day, and we both got hits our first time up, off of Reggie Cleveland in Fenway Park. I will never forget the first hit. It's only fitting, too, again, but we're linked together as we should be, and I'm proud of it."

STEVE GARVEY

Trammell chose a 1984 postseason home run, and so did Steve Garvey. A 10-time All-Star, Garvey is primarily remembered as the durable first baseman of those Dodgers clubs that always contended in the 1970s and then into the 1980s. But the last quarter of his two-decade career was spent a little farther south in Southern California, and he told me during the 2012 All-Star Week in Kansas City that his greatest hit was during those days with the Padres.

"The one for me that affected the most people was the walk-off home run against Lee Smith in Game Four of the '84 playoffs," he said, "because the people realized what a champion looked like. The Padres had never won a game like that. It was voted the greatest sports moment in San Diego history, which measures how it affected people. People come up and tell me where they were when I hit the home run. They were on a boat in Mission Bay, or at a dinner in Beverly Hills, or in New York at something, so I measure it by how it affected people, and that was probably the biggest one."

It was a unique National League Championship Series: Cubs versus Padres. The Cubs had taken the first two games of the best-of-five series at Wrigley Field, and the Padres had won Game Three as the series shifted to San Diego. Now it was the bottom of the ninth, tied at 5–5, following a pair of Cubs runs in the eighth to build the suspense. Would the Cubs clinch and go to their first Fall Classic since the 1940s? Would the Padres go to their first World Series—Garvey's fifth?

He was up.

"I do remember that Tony Gwynn had gotten a single first, the score was tied," Garvey recalled. "Lee Smith had owned me that year. I think I faced him six times, he struck me out five of them in the shadows of Wrigley Field. And then he probably wasn't going to fool around with me, he was going to come after me with 94–95 fastball. The first pitch was up-away, the second pitch he threw over to first. I said, 'Well, I'm just going to rev up and see if I can get a fastball over the plate and hit it to right center', where probably the ten biggest hits of my life were. There was a standing ovation for fifteen minutes, and it got us to the next day, and we won it and went to the World Series."

CARLOS MAY

It was the summer of 1969, and the world was changing rapidly: Flower power, Vietnam, a man about to land on the moon, Rowan & Martin's *Laugh-In*, and four new expansion clubs in Major League Baseball: Kansas City, Milwaukee, San Diego, and Seattle. Color television and improving TV reception transformed the American living room as "prime time" gradually became important in society.

"It was my rookie year," Carlos May said in 2014, looking back at his beginnings with the Chicago White Sox. "Monday Night Game of the Week, in Boston, I hit a grand slam. My grandmother and mother were watching back in Birmingham."

Birmingham. Just think what his hometown had been through in those tumultuous '60s, where rioting and civil unrest was so prevalent. Now it was the night of June 2, and May was up the East Coast at Fenway Park. Ernestine, his grandmother, was back down there in Alabama. The Red Sox led most of the game, staked to a 4–0 lead by a Carl Yastrzemski two-run homer and an RBI double, and a solo shot by Rico Petrocelli. Then Chicago scratched out a couple of runs in the top of the eighth, loading the bases on Luis Aparicio's RBI single that made it 4–2 with two out. In from the Boston bullpen came a young left-hander who finished 44 games that season.

"Sparky Lyle was pitching, he threw me a slider, I hit it out," May remembers. "I don't know, chills just shot through. I knew my grandmother and stuff was watching. [Ernestine] called that morning and said she'd be watching. Rounding the bases, I knew that and thought about it. That brings back memories."

May was working for the White Sox when I chatted with him, representing the club at its Draft table in 2014. He tells kids today that "there's only one place to play, and that's the big leagues. You gotta do what you gotta do to get there." Getting there, for him, was "hard work."

"You've got to stay focused," he said. "I tried to stay focused. I played ten years. It's hard—hitting a round ball with a round bat. Hardest thing to do in sports. But I had that hand-eye; I guess I was good. I came up since I was five years old playing ball, hitting rocks, cans, whatever I could do. It paid off in the end."

JAKE PEAVY

"The one hit that means the most to me would have—to me, it would have to be the first homer that I hit in the Major Leagues," the former NL Cy Young Award winner told me before a start at Citi Field in 2013, when he was into his second decade on Major League mounds. He had spent most of his career to date in San Diego, where it started, so batting was standard and something he relished before moving to the AL, home of the designated hitter.

"Not because it was special or a game-winner or anything to that effect, but because my little boys were in the stands in Philadelphia," he continued. "It was around the Fourth of July, because we went and watched the fireworks show. I had my oldest boy, Jacob, and Wyatt there in the stands when I hit my first home run. Your little boys, when I would leave, when I played in the National League, they would always say, 'Daddy, hit me a home run!' That was obviously hard for a pitcher to do. So to do that and them to actually be able to be there was probably the most special hit that I've ever had."

That game was played in front of 40,000 at Citizens Bank Park on July 5, with many of them there to see the annual fireworks blast after the game. Peavy came up to face opposing hurler Scott Mathieson in the top of the fifth that day. Khalil Greene had led off with a single, and after fly outs by Vinny Castilla and Josh Barfield, Peavy ripped the first pitch from Mathieson to break a 1–1 tie and give himself a 3–1 lead. Peavy finished the game with a no-decision as San Diego won. Right after the game he said, "Sooner or later you're bound to run into one, I guess." At the time, he was just happy to get to the All-Star break while dealing with tendinitis in his shoulder. It was an off-year for him, squeezed between two All-Star seasons and preceding his Cy Young year of 2007, but looking back now, July 5, 2006, means something else. It was the first of three career homers, two of them struck in that 2006 season, and the next one a long nine years later.

His boys saw this one go out, and that meant the most. *Daddy, hit me a home run!* You perform for so many people: Teammates, ownership, fans, yourself and your career. But in that moment as a parent, the ultimate audience is the one you created.

DAVID WRIGHT

They say that young baseball players dream of getting the winning hit in Game Seven of the World Series in some autumn many years away. David Wright might have had the same thoughts as a boy, but his favorite hit came in March.

Yes, March. It was at the 2009 World Baseball Classic, Major League Baseball's international tournament held amidst that year's Spring Training.

"It's tough to go against, I had a walk-off single in the World Baseball Classic to send our team to the final round in Florida against Puerto Rico," he said. "Being tackled on the field by Derek Jeter, Kevin Youkilis, Dustin Pedroia, you get tackled on the field by some of the best players in the game. I still have pictures in my office of the USA team and everybody piled up on me, that's got to be one of the coolest things."

Puerto Rico had crushed the U.S.A. when they met three days earlier, 11–1, winning by the 10-run mercy rule. That was humbling for the Americans. These were rosters filled with active Major League stars, and there was something even more on the line, pride, because the U.S.A. had flopped in the original World Baseball Classic a few years earlier. Nationalism and pageantry had become a sensation at this tournament, played at various venues, and more than 13,000 fans were at the Miami ballpark, then home to the Marlins and Dolphins. Fernando Cabrera had just relieved J.C. Romero and walked Youkilis with the bases loaded to tie that game at 5–5.

The crowd chanted "U-S-A! U-S-A!" as Wright stepped in on a 2–1 pitch. He completed a 3-for-4 night by driving a liner to the opposite field, and as he kept running gleefully toward second, an atypical March moment, his teammates caught up with him around the bag. They were like kids, or like members of their own Major League teams in an autumn situation. Wright said immediately after the game, "The celebration was pretty wild. I never thought that we'd be dogpiling in March, but it was pretty special and something I'll always remember."

Nearly three years later, he was true to his word, remembering that one hit as he thought about this during an offseason. When he gave me that hit as his own personal choice, I was interviewing him before an offseason dinner at the Marriott Marquis, following the 2011 season. If there was any doubt about its impact over time, that was cleared up when the subject came back up on May 29, 2013. I was covering a New Era event promoting the company's newest line of baseball caps. Wright was one of the speakers, having just ruined a historic save opportunity for Mariano Rivera hours earlier at Citi Field in the Subway Series. Eric Strohl, senior director of exhibitions and collections at the Baseball Hall of Fame, had come from Cooperstown with a collection of historic ball caps to show their evolution. As a surprise to Wright, he also had brought along that same bat that Wright had used to beat Puerto Rico.

It was the first time Wright had seen it since being asked to donate it to the Hall.

"It was a special moment," Wright said again, this time recalling it for a larger audience, myself included, and this time with an added element of satisfaction. "Runner on first base. My [Mets] teammate, Carlos Delgado, was playing first base. All game, we had been talking trash back and forth. So to see the look on his face . . . I was yelling at him, 'Enjoy Port St. Lucie!' He was going back to camp and we were moving on. To see the look on his face was priceless."

ED KRANEPOOL

He was there in 1962 as a rookie at Shea Stadium when the Mets suffered the indignity of 120 losses, the most in Major League history. He was there in 1969 hitting that Game Three home run, helping the Amazin' Mets beat Baltimore for the world championship. Ed Kranepool experienced the highest of highs and the lowest of lows with the "Metsies," and his most memorable hit came straight out of that decade as well.

"A hit that comes to mind for myself is the opening game against the Chicago Cubs in July of 1969," he said. "We had been trailing them all year. They came into New York for a four-game series. We beat them in the bottom in the ninth, I did, with a base hit to left off Ferguson Jenkins. It's probably the biggest hit of my career, because it started them on a skid where we swept them in New York, continued to sweep them, and wound up winning the pennant by ten games."

Fergie, a respondent in this book, was cruising with a 3–1 lead heading into the bottom of the ninth inning at Shea Stadium on July 8, 1969. It was a pitcher's duel with Jerry Koosman, both going the distance. Kranepool had hit a solo homer in the fifth inning, the only damage off Jenkins at that point in the game. Cleon Jones's two-run double tied the score in the ninth, and after an intentional walk to Art Shamsky and then a 4–3 groundout by Wayne Garrett, Kranepool stepped up with two outs and delivered the big knock against the Cubs that would serve as a statement.

I told him that it may have been the most instantaneous answer to my question that any former player had offered. He replied: "The Mets had never celebrated anything but rainouts. When you finally get into first place, that's very important for us."

JOHN MAYBERRY

When we talked at the 2012 All-Star Week in Kansas City, walking through a children's hospital where he was helping to brighten spirits of kids, Mayberry was harkening back to the previous Midsummer Classic there, the one he participated in on the same field in 1973. Opposing pitchers did not throw to Mayberry that often—he led the American League in walks with 122 and intentional walks with 17—but when he saw pitches to hit, he did plenty of damage. It was his first of consecutive All-Star selections, and being part of the '73 game for the host club made this a natural choice.

"It was an experience that you really can't put into words," he recalled. "It was my first All-Star Game, right here in Kansas City, in front of my hometown fans, and just to be around great players who I've admired all of my life . . . now I'm on the same field with them, taking batting practice with them. I'm talking about Hank Aaron and Willie Mays and Johnny Bench and [Pete] Rose. On my team, we had Nolan Ryan and Reggie Jackson and just so much excitement in the air. A lot of trash-talking. We just had a lot of fun and I was watching every step those guys made.

"I couldn't compare myself with Hank Aaron and Willie Mays and those guys. But I could say I was having a good year. What shocked me was, when I went to the clubhouse that day, I'm looking for Amos Otis and Freddie Patek, and all of a sudden here comes Catfish Hunter; here comes Nolan Ryan; here comes Kenny Holtzman and all those guys. Brooks Robinson. I say, 'This is for *real*!' They had everything set up all nice and pretty in the clubhouse, the Commissioner came in; it was a real experience, something I will never forget."

Mayberry was the American League's starting first baseman, batting third in the order. It was a 1-2-3 bottom of the first for National League starter Rick Wise, who got Mayberry to ground into a 3–1 force. In the bottom of the third, Mayberry again came up with two out, but this time was walked by reliever Claude Osteen. By the time Mayberry got up for a third at-bat, it was the sixth inning and the always-powerful NL was sailing with a 7–1 lead. He led off that time, and then came his hit of a lifetime.

"I guess the All-Star double that I hit, really," he said. "I had been wanting to play in the All-Star Game my whole life. I dreamed of it. I got in the game, and played the whole game, actually. I got me a nice double off a guy I played with in the minors named Wayne Twitchell, with the Phillies. We came up the Minor Leagues together in the Phillies organization before we got traded to different teams. I got a double in front of the hometown fans, and stood at second base, and I got an ovation. That was a pretty good feeling."

Mayberry would be stranded on second as Twitchell proceeded to retire the side in order, and the eighth-inning reliever, Tom Seaver, got him to ground out to second in his fourth plate appearance of the game. That 7–1 score would hold up, but it could not spoil the feeling for a hometown first baseman on the big stage.

CARLOS BELTRAN

It was a cloudy summer day in September 1998 at Kansas City, and Oakland reliever Buddy Groom had come on in the seventh inning for mop-up duty of what would be a 16–6 Royals win over Oakland. After he retired one blossoming young outfielder named Johnny Damon for the first out, another kid came up to bat: Carlos Beltran, making his Major League debut.

Beltran lined to left field for a single in his first plate appearance. He would score that inning, and then walk and score the next inning—the start of a great career. We talked about that at a Baseball Assistance Team fundraising dinner in New York in 2011, because for all 11 of those home runs he pounded over the course of just two postseasons with the Astros and then the Mets, nothing could compare to that first feeling of reaching base on a hit in the Majors.

"You have to say my first hit in the big leagues. It was a good feeling," Beltran said. "In '98, I started playing baseball in Single A. I got called up in the middle of the season to Double A, and I ended up finishing the season in the big leagues that year. It was meaningful for me because I always told my parents that when I got to the big leagues, I wanted them to be there. So it worked out that they were at my last game in Double A. When I got that call to play in the big leagues, they were there with me, so I got the opportunity to have an at-bat. My first at-bat I got a hit, and they were there. It was very emotional for me, because sometimes you dream about something and it doesn't come true. For me, this was something I was dreaming about. And it came true."

MIGUEL TEJADA

Miguel Tejada was sitting in a corner of the National League clubhouse the night of July 13, 2009, dressing after watching Prince Fielder win the Home Run Derby. Back in 2004, Tejada had won that same event at Houston, which ironically was the club he now was representing at this All-Star Game. I asked Tejada for his hit of a lifetime, and he said it was not a Home Run Derby shot, nor a regular season or postseason hit. It was one while he was representing the Orioles.

"It was my home run in the 2005 All-Star Game," Tejada said, referring to his big hit at Detroit's Comerica Park. "I hit it off John Smoltz, and that made me the MVP of that game. It meant more to me than the Home Run

Derby. The Derby was all for me. The All-Star Game was for my team. That is why it meant the most to me."

11

DO SOMETHING MEMORABLE

Every once in a while, there is a booming sense of awe that stays with you. It is not cockiness, but rather a feeling that you just did something that warrants a moment of appreciation—or in some cases, a lifetime of appreciation. As Ralph Waldo Emerson wrote, "Do something memorable."

FRANK THOMAS

Before Game Three of the 2011 World Series at the Rangers' ballpark, I was chatting with Frank Thomas next to the visitor's dugout. There was a pretty good likelihood that I was going to be checking his name on a Hall of Fame ballot when 2014 eligibility came up—and indeed I did, and he was a first-ballot inductee. Thomas hit 521 homers and was an on-base machine before on-base percentage was cool. For now, I was wondering which hit in his prodigious career meant the most. He looked out toward left field—*way out* to left, high up at a luxury box.

"The one that put me on the map, so to speak, was here in Texas, actually. The 1995 All-Star Game," he said, his mind doing a happy dance back into glory days. "I hit a two-run homer down the line here, actually right into that executive suite up there, by the foul pole. That was my coming-out party as a player. I just felt like I was in a groove. I saw it well and hit it well."

That was so worth reliving, we arranged for Thomas to accompany me and a pair of our MLB.com multimedia staffers up the next day to that very seat where his home run had thudded way back then. Thomas tried his best to remember exactly which seat it was, and we settled on the "Fort Worth Suite." I threw out the questions and the Big Hurt answered them on-camera, sitting in the seat and breathing in the moment in rich detail.

Carlos Baerga, one of our respondents here, was on base with two out that day. John Smiley, the National League left-hander from the Pirates, cut him a fastball middle-in. Thomas pulled it to left, against the glass.

"I crushed it," Thomas said, looking out over the field. "The first thing I can look down and see is how far home plate is from here. When you're there, it really doesn't look this far away. But I guess, retired now, you finally realize how far you hit the baseball.

"It was the new Mall Ball here in Arlington, Texas. Everyone was talking about this stadium. It was constantly filled, 50,000 people, great fans, always loud and energetic. At the time, it was probably the nicest ballpark in the Major Leagues.

"Coming to the ball game, you just felt very dangerous. I know I felt very dangerous after winning the Home Run Derby. In that at-bat, I really wanted to make something happen.

"The first at-bat, I just barely missed it. The second at-bat, I came up and I said, 'You really gotta lock in here and make something special happen.' Carlos Baerga had just got a single in front of me. I didn't think about hitting a home run, I just wanted to hit the ball hard.

"[Smiley] threw a cut-fastball in on my hands. I recognized it early when he released it. Just dropped that [bat] head there and hit one of the most beautiful home runs in my life."

I will always be thankful to the Big Hurt for something else he did the previous spring. Your curious correspondent was one of more than 300 print media members who descended on Sarasota, Florida, to cover Michael Jordan's first game with the White Sox after he decided to give baseball a try in 1994. Jordan struggled in that exhibition game, and I went out to the White Sox dressing room beyond the outfield fence in hopes of talking to him about it. As a Chicago Bulls great, Jordan had once given me a 15-minute interview in the Bulls locker room despite battling the flu (nevertheless scoring more than 40 points that day). Would he speak on this day? Understandably no. But there was one commanding presence in the White Sox locker room who was happy to take his place and serve as the surrogate: Frank Thomas.

DAVE WINFIELD

Growing up in St. Paul, Minnesota, Dave Winfield said, "Baseball was the top game in the country." He would go on to have among the widest range of choices any American athlete ever has had—baseball, basketball or football, for starters—which he would demonstrate as an athlete at the University of Minnesota.

Baseball won, and Winfield said it was because "it was just something I learned to love early on."

"I had good coaching," Winfield said. "A playground down the street, you'd play for free. Every waking hour we'd play. By the time I was twelve I said, 'I want to play professional baseball.' They said, 'Yeah, sure.' I got my college education, I got to play professional baseball for twenty-plus years. I lived my dream." His heroes included Willie Mays, who had the best all-around skillset of any Major League player.

"What attracted me, I liked the physical part of it. Running. I could field very well. Always had a great arm. And the coach used to always talk about, 'Attack the ball!' So my goal was to see how *hard* I could hit it. Not how far, or how many home runs, but how *hard* I could hit it. That kind of carried with me throughout my life."

When I think of Winfield throughout his Hall of Fame baseball career, two visuals come to me most notably. One is his unique combination of agile grace and steaming locomotive rounding second and heading for third. Two is that hard, punishing swing, ripping ball after ball and eventually settling with 3,110.

During the 2012 All-Star Week in Kansas City, I was around Winfield and took two or three ineffective stabs at asking him to identify a hit that meant the most to him. He was there for the annual Legends & Celebrities Softball Game, and even during preparation for that, I could see a familiar intensity and a certain inapproachability. I tried again at the MLB Players Alumni Association's annual fundraising dinner later that year in November. Removed from adoring fans and noise, he sifted through a distinguished career to find the one hit that had mattered most.

If you've never seen that expansive brightness of a Dave Winfield smile, it is as if he had just swung and connected.

He took me back to the night of October 24, 1992.

"Double in the World Series," he began. "Oh, I mean, I hit some incredible shots, but the most important one, the double I pulled down the line that drove in two runs, put us up in the World Series and we beat Atlanta."

That was Game Six at Atlanta-Fulton County Stadium. Otis Nixon had forced extras with a two-out RBI single off Blue Jays closer Tom Henke, and Atlanta manager Bobby Cox summoned Charlie Leibrandt to pitch in the 10th and 11th innings. With one out, Leibrandt hit leadoff man Devon White with a pitch. Future Hall of Famer Roberto Alomar singled, putting runners on first and second. After a fly out to center by Joe Carter—who would become an even bigger favorite in Canada one full year later—Winfield came up. He worked the count full, and then swung hard to make it 4–2. Atlanta scored once in the bottom of the 11th, but Jimmy Key got Otis Nixon this time and it was all over. I remember Winfield towering over everyone in the clubhouse champagne celebration—when six-foot six-inch mesomorphs were still less than common in baseball—after he had just delivered an entire nation its first Major League Baseball championship.

"I tell ya, it's like you prepare as best you can every day," Winfield said, wearing his 1992 ring as we spoke. "From a kid, we used to finish our practices or playing in the sandlot, with, 'I'm up to bat, men on base, end of the game, it's on you.' Boom. You get a hit. Then you go home. You don't go up, swing and miss at a pitch, go home. It took me twenty years in the Major Leagues to finally achieve something I'd dreamed about for many, many years. It's a great thing. It brings tears to your eyes. It makes you humble. It makes you happy and fulfilled and a lot of great things."

He felt certain that he had made the right choice in sports, going on to dedicate himself to helping others get the opportunity.

"More people still attend baseball games than any other sport," Winfield said. "Over seventy million people come. Minor League, forty million. Football can't match, basketball can't match . . . baseball is still the game."

JOE CHARBONEAU

The legend of Super Joe Charboneau begins, technically, on his first day in the big leagues. His most important hit came on that Friday night in his home state of California. A phenomenon was about to occur for the Indians.

"I think my first Major League hit. It was my second at-bat. I hit a home run at Anaheim Stadium, and I never thought the day, that opportunity, would come," he said on the morning of the 2016 World Series opener in Cleveland, where he was invited by the Indians and MLB to help give kids a youth clinic at a Boys & Girls Club. "I was a low-round draft choice. Got released in the Minor Leagues, got back, I was traded a couple times, played for three teams, Cleveland being the third team before I made the big leagues. So I think that first Major League hit, it was special.

"I never thought I was going to get a hit. I was so nervous my first at-bat, I hit a ground ball to third base, Carney Lansford backhanded it, kind of robbed me of a hit. And I grew up playing ball against Carney Lansford—Little League, high school, all the way through—so it wasn't the first time he robbed me of a base hit. It felt like I was never going to get my first Major League hit."

Dave Frost had won 16 games, matching Nolan Ryan for the most on the 1979 Angels, and this was his 1980 opener against Cleveland. In the top of the fifth, he was cruising with a 5–0 shutout, retiring Ron Hassey to start that inning. Up stepped Charboneau, whose legend was about to begin in that moment.

"I faced Dave Frost. Low and away slider," he recalled. "I was a low-ball hitter, and I hit it to right center. So it was special. [Indians reliever] Sid Monge ran out. Anaheim was under construction, and he ran out into the construction and got the ball for me.

"It was just that all the hard work you put in, all the effort I put into getting to the big leagues. It was summed up in my first hit, second at-bat, a home run in the big leagues. I was lucky enough that all my family and friends were there in Anaheim. It was very special to me. It paid off for me."

Charboneau had broken out in Double A ball with Chattanooga the year before, batting .352, and an injury to Indians slugger Andre Thornton opened a door that he charged right through. A blast with his bat and his personality, "Super Joe" Charboneau became a sensation, even the subject of a "Go Joe Charboneau" song, and he was named AL Rookie of the Year after batting .289/.358/.488 with 23 home runs and 87 RBIs. Charboneau was never the same after that, injuring his back the next spring and then scuffling for a couple more seasons before his exit from the scene. His legend, however, remains long after, and there was one other specific hit worth asking about.

On June 28, 1980, the sixth-place Indians were visiting the AL East-leading Yankees, and the home team put two runs on the board in the ninth for an 11–10 win. But what stood out was something the rookie slugger did leading off the second inning against Yankees' starter Tom Underwood. He sent a 3–1 pitch high into no-man's-land: the third deck in right field. Only Hall of Famer Jimmie Foxx and Frank Howard had done that before. Charboneau looked up at that distant landing spot as he was about to make the turn at second base during his trot, in awe himself.

Considering the first-hit response that he already had given me for this book, I felt compelled to at least remind him about that fabled blast.

"I was going to bring that up," he said with a smile. "That was a once-in-a-lifetime. I'd never hit a ball like that before. I never had that feeling. When I hit a ball like that, it was like all the stars were aligned; it was perfect. I never hit a ball that far in my life. It was amazing.

"That was amazing. I think the first hit meant a little more, but I didn't realize how far that ball went—to hit it into the third deck—until Reggie Jackson came up to me the next day. Reggie and I have been friends since then, and he was very nice to me about that. He grabbed my forearms and muscles, and he goes, 'Wow, do you know how far you hit that?' And he talked to me about how to conduct myself in baseball, what to do. He gave me a lot of advice. Reggie was a good man to me. He walked up to me and I froze, because it was Reggie Jackson, and I was in awe. He put me at ease. He told me, 'Don't try to hit a ball like that all the time. That's not going to happen again for a long time.' And Reggie has hit some long home runs. He's had so many great hits, World Series hits, everything."

REGGIE JACKSON

With three home runs in one night,
who could doubt Reggie Jackson's biggest hits?

Courtesy of Jim Accordino

"Everything" indeed. Most notably, Reggie Jackson hit three home runs on three consecutive pitches for the Yankees in the decisive Game Six of the 1977 World Series, and I found a pair of unique perspectives in interviewing people for this book. Here are two views of what that historic night meant:

JOE PISCOPO

Joe Piscopo was a blossoming standup comedian in 1977, a few years before joining the second cast of "Saturday Night Live," and on October 18 of that year he was off to another trip at his local airport. Something happened that night that sticks with him now when I ask him for a hit.

"Reggie's three homers—clearly," he said. "Like it was yesterday. I was on the road as I always am, you know? Even back then. I watched it on TV at Newark airport, and I was just floored, watching his third home run. I was about to get on a plane, thinking, 'Jesus, I should be at this game!'

"When we were kids, we used to go to the bleacher seats because we couldn't afford good seats. We used to go down close to the field, and then when Reggie would get up to bat, he had these massive hands. So just watching him from the airport, even then, that was the one thing that really struck me. Third home run of the World Series, three straight pitches. It was like nothing else."

In his mind, Piscopo was there with the crowd, chanting "Reggie! Reggie!" It was Game Six of the World Series, Yankees over Dodgers. After walking his first time up, Reggie swung at the first offering from Dodgers starter Burt Hooton and sent it into the right field stands at Yankee Stadium for a two-run homer and a 4–3 lead. It knocked Hooton out of the game.

In his next at-bat in the fifth inning, Jackson faced reliever Elias Sosa and crushed the first pitch with a man on again, a liner into the right field seats. Piscopo and Yankees fans smelled their first world championship since 1962 at that point—a 15-year drought that remains the longest since Babe Ruth arrived—and they implored their superstar slugger to take a curtain call. He was too into the game to consider it.

Now Piscopo was engrossed. It could not happen again, not on three consecutive pitches. Could it? This time it was Charlie Hough's turn to stop Reggie, and that meant a knuckleball. It did not matter. The slugger crushed this one, a 450-foot blast to the empty black bleacher seats in deep center field, effectively ending all hopes for the Dodgers. Reggie agreed to the curtain call this time, with an 8–3 lead on the board, and with those three consecutive home runs and the "Reggie! Reggie! Reggie!" chants, it became official: This was Mr. October.

In Game Three of the 2011 World Series, Albert Pujols of the Cardinals became the first player to do that since Reggie, something only Ruth had done before (twice). Pujols's performance was even more historic, because he had a postseason-record 14 total bases and an amazing four-inning hitting streak within the game. But that was at Texas. Maybe part of it was seeing Reggie do this in front of chanting Yankees fans. There was only one Reggie.

"We love Pujols, and it was great," Piscopo says, "but with Reggie, it was just the power of the home runs. It was the third home run that really put me out. I said, 'Geez, that was great.' I got on the plane . . . celebrated by myself."

As Piscopo might have said in his classic sports commentary on SNL Newsbreak (now called "Weekend Update"): "The big story . . . Reggie . . . . Reggie . . . REGGIE."

TOM BROKAW

"I've got a lot of memories of being in the ballpark," the NBC News special correspondent and beloved longtime anchor said from his office inside 30 Rock. "I was with Hank Aaron the summer before he hit the big home run and got to be friends with him. I was at Yankee Stadium the night Reggie hit three in a row out in the World Series. I have a large black and white photograph of Ted Williams in the All-Star Game, autographed by him to 'Tom, MY number one.' And I have a baseball from Joe DiMaggio in which he said to our camera crew, 'Do you think Tom would like a baseball autographed by me?' Those are two pretty good treasures."

As we walked through the NBC News corridors, I asked: "So you were there for Reggie-Reggie-Reggie?" His eyes lit up, like I'd asked him about covering Watergate or interviewing Putin. It was the moment his daughters became baseball fans.

In 1976, Brokaw was named host of NBC's *Today* show, and it was during the Yankees-Dodgers World Series of that year that "I feel this big meaty hand on my shoulder and it's George Steinbrenner. I had never met him." Steinbrenner was the still relatively-new owner of the Bronx Bombers, who were playing the team Brokaw had long loved. Brokaw tells this story:

"'I watch you on the *Today* show every morning, I think you're the best,'" Steinbrenner said. "'You coming to the game tonight?'

"'I am.'

"'Well, you're gonna be my guest.'

"'Oh, Mr. Steinbrenner, I'm bringing my family.' Wasn't true, but why not?

"'How many?' Steinbrenner replied.

"'I got three daughters and my wife.'

"'OK, I've got five of you. I'll have a table for you at the Stadium Club and then you've got the box right behind the Dodgers. Great seats, you'll love them.'"

Brokaw says he never had met The Boss.

"I go home and see the kids, not a word about the Dodgers. I tell them, 'We're going to the Stadium tonight, and we're going to be Mr.

Do Something Memorable

Steinbrenner's guests.' So we did have a fantastic table. We go down to get in our seats. Reggie comes up. My oldest daughter says, 'Daddy, Reggie Jackson's gonna hit a home run.' Bang! Comes up a second time, bang! She says, 'He's going to do it again.' He comes up a third time, and I said, 'I give up.' So that's their first baseball game, watching Reggie hit three in a row out. That's one for the ages. By the eighth inning, she's a huge Thurman Munson fan. She wept the day he died in the plane crash. My middle daughter Andrea is still a huge Yankees fan, married to a Mets fan, unfortunately. They absolutely fell in love with baseball at that moment."

Brokaw has a great perspective on what Baseball has meant in the fabric of American society. He authored *The Greatest Generation*, so he knows how it is also interwoven with military history, how important the national pastime was during World War II.

"It's the most elegant game. That's what I think about baseball," he said. "I think no one wrote about it more eloquently than Bart Giamatti, the late commissioner, who had been president of the AL. He said it is a game designed to break your heart. If you didn't believe him, ask a Baltimore Orioles fan, or ask a Washington Nationals fan. We all get invested in it, with our own home teams, but when playoff time comes and the Series comes, then we're all fans again, and we pick a team and we kind of attach ourselves to it, and we ride the roller coaster of emotions."

MIKE SHANNON

Before going on the air as the tradition-rich Voice of the Cardinals at Game Five of the 2011 World Series in Texas, Mike Shannon was grabbing a hot dog and soft drink in the press box. On his way to the broadcast booth, the former Cardinal they called "Moon Man" had an obvious answer to the question.

"That would have to be the home run I hit off Whitey Ford in the first game of the '64 World Series," he said. "He was trying to throw me inside. He kept missing. He missed two in there, and then he hung the other one.

"Then when I went home that night, I stopped by the drug store with my wife and kids and tried to pick up something, and they already had the morning paper out, and it had big block letters, 'Shannon's Home Run something.' It was a nice feeling for a kid in my hometown. It was pretty good beating those guys, with Mantle and Maris."

Ford was the winningest pitcher in World Series history. He gave up that home run to Shannon with one out in the sixth and Ken Boyer on second

177

base. The Yankees were leading at the time, 4–2. Shannon's blast tied the game and started a four-run inning. Tim McCarver doubled right after Shannon and that chased Ford. The Cardinals would win Game One, 9–5, on their way to a seven-game triumph.

"He was probably at the end of his career, then," Shannon said of Ford. "I'm sure I wouldn't have gotten that five years previous."

Back at St. Louis for what would be one of the two best Game Sixes in World Series history, I saw Mike outside of the broadcast booth shortly before pregame ceremonies. He had thought about his response and had one thing to add:

"In the seventh game against the Tigers, I hit a home run with nobody on and two outs. I think I had two strikes on me, I'm not sure. And I got a letter from some bartender in Detroit. He had a thousand-dollar pool, and he was spending that money. He could see that, and I hit that home run. He wrote me the nastiest letter. I could just see him, nobody on, two out, he had the numbers. You know how they do that with a pool. So he asked me what the hell did I do that for. So I wrote him back, and I said, 'Well, if I would have struck out, would you have sent me $500?'"

JIM RICE

"I don't know if it meant the most to me, but the one they talked about was the one I hit off Steve Busby," Hall of Famer Jim Rice said while at Spaulding Rehabilitation Hospital in Boston for a veterans' community event on the day of Game Two at the 2013 World Series. "Mr. Yawkey said it was the longest ball he ever watched in that ballpark, the one hit over the flagpole. So that was probably that one, because that's the one people always talk about."

What do you remember most about it?

"I just know the ball went over the flagpole and Mr. Yawkey said it was the longest. Straightaway center over the flagpole, off of Steve Busby."

Was he tough?

"All guys are tough. You just gotta hit mistakes. Make a couple mistakes on a good ball club, and you've got a chance to score some runs. You can't give a good team four or five outs. You're in bad trouble."

It was July 18, 1975, a night game at Fenway. Busby had already allowed a two-run blast to Carl Yastrzemski in the first inning, and now he was facing Rice in the third. Yaz was in his 15th of 23 seasons with the Sox, and Rice was in his first. Busby tried to place the fastball inside, but did not get it inside far enough.

This was the rookie's defining moonshot, exiting Fenway not over the Green Monster in left, but rather the rear wall behind the bleacher seats. To Red Sox fans who were not in the ballpark that night, there was no visual because it was not televised. They heard play-by-play man Jim Woods say on the radio that the ball was "disappearing into the folds of the American flag." Peter Gammons wrote in the *Boston Globe* that the "ball was stopped by Canadian customs."

In 2009, Rice was "finally" inducted into the Hall of Fame, in his 15th and final year on the ballot. He got there without my own Hall vote, as I honestly had never viewed him as an elite of the elites during his career. Was I wrong? Probably. Years later, after submitting my ballot for the Class of 2017, I wrote a long analysis of why I was overhauling my own voting process, one that never would have allowed me to fail to vote for Jim Rice. I became a voter who used the entire 10 maximum boxes, embracing the kind of advanced analytics that would have made Rice's Hall candidacy more obvious had they been available to us back then. Ironically, there I was with Rice, staying in the same Cooperstown motel with him and then walking through the Hall the next day for his customary electee orientation tour, appreciating the kind nature of this stunning power hitter, a few months before he gave a warm Hall speech.

In that speech, Rice told the crowd:

"You always feel that after every great once-in-a-lifetime moment, there cannot be anything else to top it."

That definitely applies to the home run he hit off Busby, to his answer for this book.

I told Rice what fellow Hall of Famer and contemporary slugger Dave Winfield had told me about just trying to hit it as hard as possible.

"I didn't have a philosophy. See it and hit it was my thing," Rice said. "That's what's wrong now—people think too much. You feel, you throw, you run, you make a play, you hit, and that's that. I don't think it should be that complicated. Just enjoy."

JIM SUNDBERG

I'm in the Texas Rangers dugout before the 2011 World Series Game Six classic, asking Jim Sundberg what it is like to play in a World Series Game Seven—just in case the Cardinals would win that night. He was forbidding the thought, of course, as the Rangers' senior executive vice president, but it would prove to be necessary after all.

"Sunny" had played in that other seven-game World Series against the Cardinals back in 1985, as the Royals' catcher—his ring as a player. But he said the one hit that mattered most to him had come in the seventh game of the series before that one.

"The hit that sticks out the most in my mind was a bases-loaded triple in the seventh game of the playoffs against Toronto in 1985," Sundberg said. "Bases loaded, hit the ball down the right field corner, and it hit right up on top of the fence and stayed in the ballpark. Otherwise it would have been a grand slam. That would be my single moment hit."

It was a huge hit, because that Game Seven was played at Toronto and the Blue Jays had the great Dave Stieb on the hill in the clincher. There were two out in the top of the sixth and Kansas City was clinging to a 2–1 lead when Sunny cleared the bases—the last batter Stieb would face that season. Sundberg would score on a subsequent single by Frank White off reliever Jim Acker, and that 6–2 victory would send the Royals into the Fall Classic and on their way toward a world championship.

MARK TEIXEIRA

We were literally in the shadows of giants at the 2009 World Series Media Day in the Great Hall of brand-new Yankee Stadium, with the large visage of Babe Ruth, Lou Gehrig, Yogi Berra, Mickey Mantle, and other Yankees greats looming over our heads as black-and-white immortal images on towering banners. Mark Teixeira had just finished obliging a barrage of interviews and got up from his interview table to head down toward the Yankees clubhouse for the team's workout in advance of Game One against the Philadelphia Phillies.

"Probably the walk-off home run to win Game Two of the [2009 American League] Division Series," he said matter-of-factly. "That's number one for me."

He had just walloped that memorable solo shot in the bottom of the 13th that same month—following Alex Rodriguez's homer off Joe Nathan to send it into extras—and that had given the Yankees a 2–0 series lead and sent them well on their way toward a world championship. Teixeira did not do much else that series, a classic postseason slump overall, but as a hitter you remember your successes, just as you do with any other profession.

Do Something Memorable

Teixeira's first hit was with Texas,
but he remembers a 2009 Yankee blast the best

The response was very "in the moment"—so much so that I decided at the time that I would not include it in this book. I decided that the best approach for this question is not at the ballpark during a postseason chase. It would be the worst time, I thought, especially considering the brevity of Teixeira's response. Johnny Damon's subsequent response about a hit that happened only two nights earlier only solidified my thoughts about this timing. Lesson learned; separate them from the moment.

Fast-forward six years. Immediately after the 2015 regular season ended, I was with Teixeira again, this time at his annual charity golf outing benefiting Harlem RBI, a part of Major League Baseball's longtime Reviving Baseball in Inner Cities (RBI) program to support kids. I interviewed him for an MLB.com story posted that day, about his unfortunate injury that ended an outstanding comeback season, and his teammates' postseason hopes, which would end dismally the next night in a Wild Card Game loss to Houston.

After our interview was done and we were just chatting, I said:

"I tried to ask you this question at the 2009 World Series Media Day and it was a bad time to get you. . ."

So now that he was completely separated from that moment—indeed from any moment due to his status rehabbing a leg fracture—this was the perfect time to delve into a 13-year career (at the time) that included 1,783 regular season hits, 34 postseason hits, and an All-Star body of work that included three Midsummer Classics.

Guess what? Teixeira went right back to the moment that had left such an impression on himself, and he smiled as he thought about just one hit.

"I think the walk-off home run against Minnesota in the ALDS, 2009," he replied. "It was my second postseason game with the Yankees, it was a great hit we really needed to win, and hitting an extra-inning walk-off home run was a feeling that you can't describe."

"Yes . . . and what was that feeling like?" I answered.

"Just the exhilaration. . . I still kind of get chills thinking about it, because you know how important every game in the postseason is, and to hit a walk-off in the postseason, hearing the crowd screaming, just the excitement of that moment—I haven't had many moments in my career like that."

Then he added: "There are a few home runs that kind of stick out in my career. I hit a home run in the World Series, a [decisive] home run in the [2005] All-Star Game. Those are probably the three that stick out in my mind."

Fast-forward again to August 5, 2016. I had just finished listening to him speak to media at his news conference to announce his retirement upon season's end. He was right back there at Yankee Stadium, the same place where he had once claimed an '09 hit.

This was an emotional address, as the retiring star repeatedly choked back tears. Teixeira was asked what he remembered most that he did on the field, and after initially telling reporters he would leave it up to them, he went back one last time: "A few of my biggest home runs—my first home run, the home run in my first All-Star Game, and then in 2009 the walk-off home run against the Twins. A walk-off home run at Yankee Stadium, in the playoffs? That's something you can't even dream about."

We'll just make it official with that last one, even moreso because of something else he emphasized in the news conference.

"If you play for another team, you always look at the Yankees different. There's something about the Yankees, and once I put on the pinstripes, I just felt it, I understood it. '09 was a whirlwind, it really was. I move into a new place and a new stadium. I probably didn't appreciate it at the time. You realize how difficult it was. The '09 season was special, it was magical. Looking back now, I can appreciate it much more because I know how special it is."

He was also six years into his streak of eight seasons with at least 30 homers and 100 RBIs, so that postseason walk-off shot represented his term of greatness. He left a lasting impression, especially in that 2009 moment, which symbolized his commitment to be known as "a switch-hitter with power" (in addition to sparkling defense and an incredibly positive impact on youth in the community).

Teixeira is only one of four switch-hitters in history with at least 400 doubles and 400 home runs, joining Eddie Murray, Chipper Jones, and Carlos Beltran. In his farewell announcement, Tex mentioned growing up a fan of Murray and the Orioles as a boy in the Baltimore area, and he credited his father with teaching him to hit from both sides of the plate like Steady Eddie.

"Being a switch-hitter is a special thing, but a switch-hitter with power is a rare thing in baseball," Teixeira said. "Mickey Mantle, Eddie Murray, Chipper Jones, and Carlos Beltran, these are guys I am proud to join. Your entire career flashes in front of your eyes when that happens.

"The most proud thing from a career standpoint is eight seasons in a row of thirty and 100. As a power hitter, you want to get to thirty and 100. You've made it. To do it eight seasons in a row, it means you were productive and durable, and I am proud to have done it."

BUCKY DENT

While Aaron Boone does not single out the home run he hit for the Yankees in 2003 to beat the Red Sox for the American League pennant, Bucky Dent absolutely goes that route with the one he hit a quarter-century earlier for the Yankees to beat the Red Sox for the AL pennant.

Sometimes there is no exception. Or perhaps it was because when we spoke in 2012, he was under siege from autograph seekers at Grand Central Station in New York—Yankees fans who still love to talk about the day in 1978 when a light-hitting shortstop beat the rivals on their home turf.

"It was the hit in Boston, when I hit the home run in '78," Dent said. "Because it was a one-game playoff, and it put us in the lead, and we went on to win the game."

Just to be sure, I told him that Boone and Carlton Fisk were among those whose most replayed hits were not the ones they wanted to discuss.

"If you're asking me which is the biggest hit, that was it," he said.

12

ORDER THE PRESENT

Anxiety for the future time disposeth men to inquire into the causes of things; because the knowledge of them maketh men the better able to order the present to their best advantage. —**Thomas Hobbes**, *Leviathan*

Darryl Strawberry felt prepared throughout his career, analyzing games from the on-deck circle and knowing what he wanted to do when he stepped into the box. Tony Gwynn and Stan Musial had completely different methods of preparing for pitchers, but they had so much else in common to share in an unforgettable roundtable discussion one summer day at the ballpark. The Alomar brothers grew up around the game as the sons of an All-Star player, and the lessons they absorbed back then allowed them to order the present to their best advantage. Tino Martinez knew what was coming in a huge World Series situation, because he prepared for a first-pitch fastball. Steve Finley had visualized a moment so often that it was second nature when it happened to win a division. Ivan Rodriguez and Mike Lowell were teammates on the Marlins' 2003 World Series championship club, and we'll find out whether either of them chose a hit from that Wild Card run. Kenny Lofton knew what to expect from Cardinals reliever Steve Kline in an October moment of truth. Anxiety for the future is the cause, and preparation is rewarded for those who seek knowledge now.

DARRYL STRAWBERRY

The first time I ever met Darryl Strawberry was at Spring Training 1984 in a cramped locker room in West Palm Beach, Florida. The long and lean outfielder from Crenshaw High in Los Angeles was the reigning National League Rookie of the Year for the Mets, and he was suiting up for a Grapefruit League exhibition against either the Montreal Expos or Atlanta Braves, who shared the West Palm facility in those days. What I remember is that he did not look or sound like his headlines up in New York. He seemed quiet and unassuming to me in that interview for a *Miami Herald* story, with such a purpose and focus. Then, as if it were all so sudden, three decades had gone by and we were talking again, and I was reminding him about our first meeting and the setting. It is a surreal but beautiful thing when that happens, no matter how old it makes you feel.

"Hitting was fun. It was easy for me, because of my IQ for the game," the Straw told me as we stood on the floor of the 2013 First-Year Player Draft at MLB Network, where he was a Mets club representative. "I understood the game. I always looked at the game from the on-deck circle and analyzed the game before I got up to the plate. So I always prepared myself. I think that's why I made it so easy, because before I got in the batter's box, I always had an idea what I wanted to do."

What he looks back on today really is the same thing he was telling me in his baseball dawn, that he had to prepare and go after it, be a student of the game. After our 1984 chat, he proceeded to make eight consecutive NL All-Star teams; win three World Series rings, in 1986 with the Mets and then again in 1996 and '99 with the Yankees; and finish with 335 home runs and 1,401 overall hits in a 17-year career.

Of course, we got around to his one most important hit of all, and at the time it was one that became even more galvanized because of his subsequent residence: the St. Louis area.

"Probably a home run I hit in St. Louis, in a nothing-nothing ball game, Ron Darling pitching, and we needed to win," Strawberry said. "I hit one off the clock, a hanging breaking ball off of Ken Dayley."

Strawberry was living in St. Peters, Missouri, when we spoke, and he said people always reminded him of that homer. But he has subsequently moved to the Orlando area, where he runs Darryl Strawberry Recovery Centers.

It was October 1, 1985, a happy month for Cardinals fans because it brought them a world championship. That month began with such a classic flourish. Darling had pitched nine scoreless innings, and John Tudor had countered with a shutout through 10. The Mets were seen by Cardinals fans in those days as the rival, generally abhorred, with "Pond Scum" T-shirts the order of the day.

Dayley came on in the top of the 11th and immediately struck out Keith Hernandez and Gary Carter. The digital clock on the scoreboard at old Busch read 10:44 when Strawberry slammed a Dayley pitch into it, an estimated 440 yards, as right fielder Andy Van Slyke just watched the flight of the slugger's 28th homer of the season. Strawberry ambled around the bases like it was any other homer, because he was not one to typically watch his own blasts and show up the opponent. Jesse Orosco got the save that night, the Mets beat the Cardinals again the next day to cut the NL East deficit to just one game, but the Cardinals took that series finale and then went all the way.

"We needed to go in there and sweep the Cardinals. We didn't end up sweeping them that year, but it was a highlight that I'll probably always remember," Strawberry said.

Mets fans will remind you that Strawberry often struggled mightily against left-handed pitchers. He fed off of righties. That probably fortified his choice for this hit.

"Ken Dayley was a tough lefty," Strawberry said. "Most people probably kid him about that, but he hardly ever hung a breaking ball. That breaking ball I hit, I mean, it got out of the ballpark so fast. There was a big celebration in our dugout when I came around, because it was a tough game, a nothing-nothing ball game. I think a lot of the other guys teased him about it, but he's probably got me out more times than I got him. That was just one big minute.

"The Mets were 'Pond Scum' every time I went in there. It was always exciting going in there. That was part of it. It's just the strangest thing. Then here I am ten years later, and I'm living in the city where they hated us. The fans there were so pleasant, they told me they never hated me personally, that I was a great ballplayer, they just hated the Mets."

STAN MUSIAL AND TONY GWYNN

One of the greatest days of my life was two hours with Stan Musial and Tony Gwynn, turning on a tape recorder as they talked hitting.

There is a beloved glossy 8x10 photograph on my desk at work that was taken in the summer of 1997 inside Busch Stadium II in St. Louis, where those two Hall of Famers gathered for an amazing roundtable discussion. Along with Gwynn and Musial were John Rawlings, then Editor of *The Sporting News*; Dick Zitzmann, Stan's longtime friend and business partner, who facilitated the event; and me. I had started *The Sporting News*' online operation in the previous year but was still writing and was responsible for compiling the transcript into a popular cover story in the July 28, 1997 issue. John and I simply provided the prompts; Musial and Gwynn were a virtuoso Carnegie Hall duet.

Tony was batting .398 when he arrived that day. You could have charged any price of admission to have fans sit in on that conversation. It was mind-blowing as they talked about seeing the different spins of the baseball coming toward a plate, what thoughts had gone through their mind, what hitting meant then. Here was a visiting San Diego player being welcomed with open arms in the home team clubhouse, off of which we used a room for the discussion. This was Stan the Man's town, after all.

When you think about preparation, in my mind no one ever personified that more than Tony Gwynn. He was fondly known by some as "Captain Video" because of his penchant for scouting opposing pitchers on a VCR. I asked Tony about that and he discussed at length his reasons and habits for studying up with technology. Then I asked Stan the Man how much time he had prepared for pitchers, and he smiled and said, "Oh, I start about the time I walk out of the on-deck circle."

They talked that day about the subject of hitting .400, something no batter has attained since Ted Williams—who advised Gwynn to swing more for the fence in right field—batted .406 in 1941.

"Thinking about hitting .400, you've got to be very determined, because look at the amount of times you've come to bat by September," Stan told Tony. "If you're not already up to .400, you have to get two hits every day."

"Absolutely," Gwynn replied.

The Hall of Famers talked about bat size, and on the subject of whether they would guess at certain pitches, Gwynn said he never guessed but rather "anticipated." On the subject of anticipation, Gwynn told a story about one particular hit.

It was the 1994 All-Star Game in Pittsburgh, three years before our conversation. David Cone, that year's AL Cy Young winner for Kansas City, replaced Greg Maddux on the mound for the AL in the bottom of the third inning. With one out, Jeff Bagwell singled and then Cone hit Gregg Jeffries with a pitch to put men at first and second. That brought up Gwynn, and he said in that roundtable chat that he was anticipating a forkball from Cone in that situation. That is exactly what he got, and Gwynn laced it down the line for a two-run double on the way to an NL victory.

"Lots of times I stand on first or second and just [wonder,] 'Where did that come from?'" Gwynn told us.

"Yeah, I know what you're talking about," Musial said.

They just fed off each other that day, and transcribing those two hours—I had to change mini-cassette tapes at least a couple of times—was a joy.

But that was 1997. I wish today that we had been able to ask each of them my nine-word question. We lost them in 2013 (Musial) and 2014 (Gwynn), and what a void they left. Tony was in the area for an event I was working one day in 2012, but as always, deadline writing was the priority, so rather than wait around for him, I figured there would always be another time. We are never guaranteed that later date. It is one of the lessons learned in the pursuit of one hit throughout these pages, perhaps appropriate for the "Seize the Moment" chapter. If you want to learn something from someone who has lived a successful life, ask and ask right now! Don't be bashful, especially in idle moments. If you think you have too many idle moments (as sportswriters do by the nature of the profession), fill them up! I think about Ralph Kiner and what proved to be his final interview one afternoon, a time to treasure. That roundtable discussion for a "Man to Man" cover will remain timeless, forever a chronicle of their thoughts about hits. But still I have wondered what they might have said to this question. Fortunately, I have been able to do the next best thing in this journey of discovery and ask surviving family members what they thought a particular hitting legend might have said. This happened in the case of Tony Gwynn.

Major League Baseball held the 2016 All-Star Week in San Diego, where you can find statues of Tony Gwynn and cherished memories of the hero they called Mr. Padre. I had been lucky beyond words to cover the historic, crowd-record-smashing 2007 Hall of Fame Induction of Gwynn and Cal Ripken Jr., and now I was in Gwynn's backyard, two years after his passing. One of the official All-Star events was new, a yoga event that drew 1,000 participants. The Gwynn family was represented there, by Tony's brother (and former teammate) Chris and Tony's son, Tony Jr.—both of them former big-league outfielders. I told Chris about my book and how sad I was that I had not been able to ask Tony this question. He had plenty of memories to share.

Let's start with Chris Gwynn's own hit. He played in the Majors from 1987–96 and was known mostly for his Dodgers days, spending his first five seasons with them, then two with Kansas City and two more with the Dodgers again. But his last stop was something fitting—a chance to team with his brother in San Diego.

"For me it would be '96, when I got a hit to win the pennant," Chris said. "We were playing the Dodgers, which is the team I came up with and spent a lot of my time with. We were in the eleventh inning, the last game of the year, and I was able to get a double to score Ken Caminiti and Steve Finley to win the division. That would definitely be my most memorable and probably most meaningful.

"It was the first time really that I ever played with Tony, because of our age difference. It was our last year. I struggled most of the year, fighting injuries, on and off the DL. I had flashes of things I did that were well, but for the most part it wasn't a great year. Just to be able to pull it together in that series, because we had to sweep them in order to win the division. The loser was going to play the Braves in the first year with their rotation. That was part of it. And then I remember Caminiti, the first game, he hit a long home run to win the game. Tony got the next hit to win the second game. And then I got the hit to clinch it. So that was in '96. A lot of the fans here, I only played one year in San Diego, and a lot of fans still thank me."

That was a dozen years after the hit he said Tony would have chosen.

"I don't know, and I'd be crazy to guess, but I would think in 1984 he got a big double off of Rick Sutcliffe in the LCS," Chris said. "To me, it kind of catapulted him onto his career. That would be one that I think is the most memorable, but for him I can't say for sure."

That double broke a 3–3 tie in Game Five against the Cubs, helping the Padres complete a comeback from 0–2 in the series to advance to the Fall Classic against Detroit.

"In that same series, I also remember the ball Tony hit that just ate up Ryno [Ryne Sandberg] at second base, so he had no chance to field it," Chris said. "It was the bottom of the ninth, tied 5–5, and he got the hit off Lee Smith. That set up Steve Garvey's big home run to make it a 2–2 series before they went on to clinch it. I was in college here at the time, and that's why I remember it."

He was referring to the same 1984 NLCS Game Four that Garvey drew from for his own response in this book.

Tony Gwynn would have had 3,141 regular season hits to choose from, another 33 in the postseason, and plenty more in All-Star Games, had I been able to ask him the question directly. Maybe he would have repeated that David Cone story from the 1994 All-Star Game, the one he told us on a day for the ages. It was a study in preparation, anticipating a forkball.

"When you step up to the plate, you've got to believe that you can handle whatever you're going to see," Tony said in those magical moments with Stan the Man—a pair of one-team, cheerful, batting-title legends who are missed so much these days. It was never more fun to transcribe a tape-recorder interview, because to mere mortals as John and I were at that roundtable, the challenge was to comprehend their shared banter about life atop Olympus, and then to pick up things you missed when you went back and listened to the full conversation again. Life is like that.

"How dedicated you are to trying to get the most out of yourself, I think kind of determines how good you are and for how long," Gwynn said. "As long as you prepare yourself every day to go out there and give it your absolute best effort to get it done, you can look at yourself in the mirror when it's over."

ROBERTO ALOMAR

Nolan Ryan was 41 and in the final year of his tenure with the Astros when he took the mound at San Diego's Jack Murphy Stadium on April 22, 1988. He was still throwing smoke, in the second year of a four-year streak of leading the Majors in strikeouts—a title he would hold 11 times in his career. And for a mustachioed, 20-year-old hitter from Puerto Rico named Roberto Alomar, that was no big deal.

Alomar knew exactly what to expect the first time he faced Ryan, because he had grown up around the game while his father, Sandy Alomar Sr., was an infielder behind Ryan on Angels teams from 1972–74, Ryan's winningest seasons.

"I know Nolan Ryan since he was a kid," Alomar told me in 2014 just before the start of MLB's Baseball Assistance Team dinner in New York. He laughed, still finding it unbelievable as well. "I know how he pitched."

Sandy Sr. would let his sons Sandy Jr. and Robbie join him during summers when school was out back home in Puerto Rico. They would shag outfield flies, hang around the clubhouse, and soak up the essence of the game from learned veterans. In fact, during his 2011 Hall of Fame Induction speech, Roberto thanked his sister "for taking care of my mom when we used to go to the United States to play the game of baseball." Sandy Sr. had been behind Ryan for the first of his seven no-hitters, and Ryan had once helped coach Roberto, age four, when his goal in life was to be a pitcher.

"They used to observe the game a lot. They asked a lot of questions," Sandy Sr. recently told the Cleveland *Plain Dealer.*

Roberto said, "It was awesome, as a young boy, to have the chance to be around big-league players."

That preparation meant everything. It gave them confidence to go along with their inherited skills. It gave Roberto an assurance on April 22, 1988, as a mustachioed rookie stepped into the box against a pitcher who was the king of preparation himself.

The Astros had won all three of Ryan's starts so far that April. In the bottom of the first, he gave up a single to that year's NL batting champ, Tony Gwynn. That brought up the other future Hall of Famer in Alomar, who had watched attentively on deck, still keeping his own mental scorebook. Ryan was quickly ahead in the count, 0–2. But Alomar, a switch-hitter batting lefty, swatted a grounder toward shortstop and beat it out, the first of 2,724 hits.

The next time up, Alomar was set down by Ryan on three pitches. That's the thing about their story together. They both knew about each other. Forward three years, when Nolan Ryan was pitching for Texas and threw the record seventh and final no-hitter of his career. That one ended with a fastball for a strike against the same Roberto Alomar.

"I've known that kid since he was a two-year-old toddler," Ryan said afterwards.

Alomar's preparation even helped there. He was anything but an easy final out. Alomar fouled off three pitches before finally whiffing on the eighth pitch.

"A stubborn, young hitter hangs in with him," the play-by-play announcer said after the third and last foul. Then his booth mate said, "You have that right—give some credit to Roberto Alomar, who battles and battles and battles here."

Alomar could have chosen many other hits, maybe the two-run home run in 1992 off A's closer Dennis Eckersley—that's year's AL Cy Young winner—in the top of the ninth inning of Game Four of the AL Championship Series at Oakland. That rocket to right enabled Toronto to take a 3–1 series lead instead of knotting it at 2–2. Oakland would win Game Five, before the Blue Jays clinched their first World Series berth.

Alomar was named the MVP of that ALCS, batting .423 (11-for-26) with two homers, four RBIs and four runs scored. Were it not for that home run off Eck, who knows if Toronto would have made it to its first Fall Classic. Then who knows if general manager Pat Gillick would have tinkered with his Toronto club in the same way, as the Blue Jays not only won in '92 or repeated in '93? That home run easily could have been a logical answer to mention here.

But after growing up around the greats like Ryan, it only made sense for Alomar to most fondly remember what happened the day he finally had a chance to be a big-leaguer himself.

"I wanted to be the best," he said in his Hall speech, "and I played the game only one way: to win."

SANDY ALOMAR JR.

It would have been nice if Roberto Alomar could have been joined on the stage for that Hall of Fame Induction by his brother, Sandy Jr.—something Roberto mentioned in his speech. I would have liked to have checked both on my ballot. Both of them received their first Major League call-ups by the Padres in that 1988 season. Through the 1998 season, both of them had been selected as All-Stars at least six times. But injuries hampered Sandy in the second half of his own 17-year career.

Instead, I am going to at least make sure these brothers are side-by-side right here.

"I have to say the home run against Mariano in the playoffs here, because it gave us a chance to play a Game Five against the Yankees and later on go and play Baltimore to go to the World Series," Alomar responded. "So a hit that puts you in a situation to go further in the postseason, that to me is the most important one."

We spoke just feet away from where it had happened nearly two decades earlier. This was the night of Game Six at the thrilling 2016 World Series between the Cubs and Indians in Cleveland, and Alomar was the Indians' first base coach. He came out onto the field in front of his team's dugout, and we caught up about 1997.

That had been his year. In 1997, the Puerto Rican catcher had his best career season with a .324/.354/.545 slash line, a career-best .900 OPS, 37 doubles, 21 homers, and 83 RBIs. Number 15 could have chosen a hit in that summer's All-Star Game—his fifth of six in his career—because he hit the game-deciding two-run homer off NL pitcher Shawn Estes and received the game's MVP award right there at his home ballpark.

"As a player, that was a fantastic event to be a part of the All-Star Game in your own backyard," Alomar said. "Just being part of the game was good enough, but to have a chance to perform in the game and win the game and win MVP was a surreal moment."

Alomar also had a 30-game hitting streak that season, and he was had the distinction of playing a heroic role in consecutive postseason Game Fours.

His second favorite hit was his walk-off single off closer Armando Benitez to beat his brother's team, Baltimore, on the way to that '97 pennant. But it was the first one he holds dearest, that shot off the greatest closer—and maybe greatest pitcher—of all-time.

"I didn't think I was going to hit a home run," Alomar recalled, "but I was prepared to do the best I could to help my team win in that situation."

It was a classic cutter, one Rivera was not afraid to throw in a 2–0 count, and it caught too much of the plate. The right-handed batter reached out and got the barrel on it, lining the ball over the wall in right. Rivera immediately looked down, realizing he had lost that battle. It is about being in charge of an at-bat, and Alomar won.

As with his brother, Sandy had grown up around the game, breathing in the ballpark atmosphere and as many of its advantages that a youth could handle. He developed a baseball mind, and he was prepared for Rivera.

"In the regular season, I had done well against him," Alomar said. "I just went up there with a plan, and I was good enough to be ahead in the count and able to make him throw me a pitch that I was looking for."

TINO MARTINEZ

When I talked to Tino Martinez for this book, he was in Lower Manhattan, only a handful of blocks away from Ground Zero. It was the fall of 2016, and he had been one of those who played a key role in bringing a city back to its feet 15 years earlier. Not surprisingly, perhaps, he went back to that moment.

"Oh, boy. I mean, first Major League hit was amazing because of the work I put in just to make the big leagues, and to get that first Major League hit. It was a special moment," the former Yankees first baseman began. "Then obviously the home run in Game Four of the World Series against the Diamondbacks. To tie the game with two outs in the bottom of the ninth was another big hit I'll never forget."

For formality's sake, I asked if he could narrow down those two.

"Oh, boy, it's tough. I mean, they were both great, both different feelings, but I guess the one that meant the most to the organization is the home run to tie the game. I remember Kim, the reliever, throwing first-pitch fastball to everybody. So I was looking first-pitch fastball. My goal was to get a good pitch, hit it hard somewhere, and keep the rally going. Fortunately, I hit it perfect, and it went out of the park."

In the only Halloween game ever played to that point, Curt Schilling had thrown seven strong innings for Arizona, leaving the game with a 3–1 lead. South Korean sidearm closer Byung-Hyun Kim had come in and struck out the Yankee side in the eighth, all on full-count pitches. When Martinez came to the plate in the ninth, there were two outs, Paul O'Neill was on first, and not only was a sellout crowd at old Yankee Stadium pulling with its collective heart, but curiously enough, so were most baseball fans across the nation. The Yankees had taken pride in how they were booed so often on the road, due simply to their dominance and giant payroll, and all of a sudden a lot of people wanted to see them four-peat.

That was because of what happened 50 days earlier, when the Twin Towers collapsed as part of a 9/11 terrorist attack on the U.S. by airline hijackers. So there was much more than usual on the line as the Yankees tried to avoid falling behind, three games to one, in that World Series.

That home run by the "BamTino," as Yankees radio man John Sterling would say it in his signature call, tied Game Four at 3–3 and set the stage for Derek Jeter's "Mr. November" walk-off heroics after the clock struck midnight in the 10th inning. "That was as loud as I've heard Yankee Stadium," Jeter said of the Martinez-homer celebration. After the game, Martinez went to the Midtown hotel where about 30 family members were staying, and the family all watched the TV replays of his smash to right-center. Martinez said he slept little because he was so eager to get back to the ballpark, where Scott Brosius would take his turn in Game Five and send the series back to Arizona with a 3–2 Yankees lead.

Even though the Diamondbacks were the eventual champions in a seven-game series in which the home team won every time, that three-game sweep at Yankee Stadium saw the return of a much-needed happiness. It brought relief, a gradual confidence in public leisure activity for New Yorkers who were tragically shaken to the core. They could gather together at a ballpark for a major event, with everyone watching. Life would never be the same, of course, but the developments in the World Series helped bring not only the city, but also the nation, back together so the healing process could begin. Martinez had played a key role in that precious time. His Rawlings Big Stick, used for that home run, is displayed in Cooperstown.

When you look at it today, farther and farther in the past, you think back and wonder how 9/11 could possibly have happened, and you remember all of the people—the workers, the first responders—who lost their lives so senselessly. You were reminded what Baseball meant, the same sport that Franklin Delano Roosevelt asked to be played during World War II, as a way to give Americans relief and to remind them of their normal lives. Martinez thought about what happened in 2001 and just shook his head.

"It gave the fans a brief break from thinking about all the tragedy," he said.

STEVE FINLEY

As long as we are talking about Tino Martinez's majestic home run in Game Four of that 2001 World Series, now is a good place to bring up the guy who tried to scale the wall in a valiant but futile attempt to catch that blast.

I chatted with Finley during 2016 All-Star Week in San Diego, where he was appearing at an event in which MLB helped dedicate a facility that assists U.S. military veterans in their transition to civilian life. Finley spent 19 years in the bigs, from 1989–2007, and the subject he most wanted to discuss was preparation. Not just preparing military members for civilian life, but also the kind of preparation that had taken him through those two decades on the field.

"The walk-off grand slam to clinch the division when I was with the Dodgers in 2004," Finley said of his answer to this book's question. "We were down 3–0 in the ninth inning. We came back and tied it up, the bases were loaded, Wayne Franklin was pitching. I took the first pitch fastball, not nervous at all. I was actually excited to be at the plate. I knew I was going to get the game over with. I didn't realize it was going to be a home run, but I knew the game was over with, for my part. I was not going to fail. So I remember being very relaxed. When I hit the ball, I didn't know it was going to go out of the ballpark. I hit it well, and then when I got to first, it went out, and the celebration was on."

What can people learn from that?

"Preparation is everything," he replied. "I played that moment in my mind thousands and thousands of times. From a kid all the way through the big leagues, you want to be put in that moment. If you play it enough times, when it happens, it's like 'This is where I was meant to be.' Preparation, always preparation. Practice, practice, practice."

There was an also-ran to this question that was worth mentioning. Although it might have been better-suited to the "Retribution" chapter in this book had it been his primary hit recollection, I think it also shows what preparation meant for Finley and how it can help others. At Turner Field in 2000, he managed an RBI single off the great Mariano Rivera as a pinch-hitter in the bottom of the ninth. It merely reduced the AL's margin of victory to three runs instead of two, but more importantly to Finley it was a little payback and the result of going to school on a previous at-bat against Rivera.

"I remember my at-bat prior to that, it was in the ['98] World Series," Finley said, referring to the series in which he and the Padres were swept by the Yankees. "He blew me up about right here next to my hands. It was the first time I'd ever faced him. I had that memory in my head and I had to get that back. I was not going to let him beat me in the All-Star Game, I choked up about four inches and still got jammed, but I was able to squeak it out to center field."

IVAN RODRIGUEZ

On the morning of the 2012 First-Year Player Draft, I had a long talk with Pudge Rodriguez about that foreign yet inevitable life just on the other side of retirement. Rodriguez was now 40 and in the midst of his first season as a retired player, leaving the Majors with such records as most games caught and most hits by a catcher, as well as 13 Gold Gloves and 14 All-Star Game selections.

"It's kind of tough," he said, "but at the same time, I'm very happy, to spend time with my family. I've got a son who plays for the Twins organization, and I get a chance to come and see him. I'll be honest with you, I miss the game of baseball. But at the same time, I have a blast being able to spend time with my wife and kids and enjoy."

Well, so much for the quiet life of retirement. I received my annual Hall of Fame ballot after the 2016 season, and one of the first boxes I checked was that of Ivan Rodriguez. He made it in on that first ballot. Many retrospectives about his long, 21-year career were on the way, reel after reel of his highlights.

I asked him what hit had meant the most and why.

Like many others, he went all the way back to the beginning, in his case June 20, 1991. The setting was Comiskey Park II in Chicago, and the rookie catching phenom from Puerto Rico was batting last in the Rangers' order.

"The first hit in the Major Leagues—it was a game-winning hit," said Rodriguez, remembering all but the "game-winning" part correctly. "I can say that was a very good moment to me. It was first and third, it was late in the game, eighth inning, I got a hit in the gap in left field and we ended up winning by one."

"Black Jack" McDowell owned him for most of the game, retiring him in his first three Major League at-bats on a deep fly to center, a groundout to second, and then a strikeout swinging. In the top of the ninth, trailing 3–2 and facing the same Bobby Thigpen who had saved a record 57 games a year earlier, Texas sent its full batting order to the plate. Back-to-back jacks by Ruben Sierra and Julio Franco gave the Rangers a 5–3 lead.

Later in the inning, with two men in scoring position, Rodriguez came up to face reliever Mélido Perez, a fellow Caribbean from the Dominican Republic. On a 2–1 count, Pudge rifled one to the right side for a single, plating two more runners to produce the final 7–3 margin. Rodriguez would be an All-Star the next 10 consecutive summers after bursting upon the scene in Arlington that summer.

What amazes me about that particular selection is that both Pudges who are in the Hall of Fame and in this book were the catchers that day in Chicago. Rodriguez said he always looked up to Carlton Fisk, but he explained that he was not nicknamed for him, but rather by Chino Cadahia, a Rangers coach at the time, who coined it as a nod to Rodriguez's short and stocky frame.

Rodriguez said his hit was "like something out of a movie," but it was an altogether easy time. He was 19 when he was called up, and right before his Hall election was announced, he wrote a column for *The Players' Tribune* in which he revealed that the call-up messed with his plan to be married.

"I should've been happy," he wrote. "But it was actually a little depressing. . . . The day they called me up I was supposed to get married on the field down in Tulsa where I was playing Double A ball. The night before, we had done some rehearsals with all the players out on the field, and it went great.

"Then the next day my manager at the time, Bobby Jones, calls me into his office and says, 'Hey kid, I think we have a problem.' I didn't know what was going on. 'You're getting called up, so you have two choices. You can either get married here tonight, or you're going to Chicago with the Rangers. But you can't do both. If you're headed to the big leagues, we're going to have to delay the wedding.' So I went to Chicago."

He broke the news to his fiancée, and they wound up marrying during the following Spring Training. Ivan Rodriguez definitely paid his dues.

His response to my question is like so many others throughout this book, a personal journey that goes back to hit number one. Each time, I wondered how they could have possibly overlooked one that just seemed so much more fantastical and historic. That's where it gets personal in this book, and the players are the judge and jury here.

Still, I thought of one particular time when Rodriguez really made his mark at the plate—in two distinctly different ways, one most applicable here.

It was the 2003 NL Division Series. Rodriguez was catching for the Florida Marlins, who had split the first two games in San Francisco. In Game Three, Rodriguez already had delivered with a two-run homer off Kirk Reuter in the first inning, and now it was the bottom of the 11th, Giants up by one, bases loaded, two outs, and Todd Worrell stretching his relief appearance after entering for the 10th. It was the ultimate *mano a mano*, best versus best, and Worrell had Rodriguez on the brink with a 1–2 count.

Pudge lined a single to right to win the game, making it the only time other than the Kirk Gibson Miracle Homer of 1988 that a player hit a walk-off with his team one strike from losing the game. That set the stage for what happened the next game, when Rodriguez held his ground at the plate, tagging out J.T. Snow in dramatic fashion to end a playoff series like no other series had ended before. Rodriguez says that he prefers to talk about his defense over his hitting when looking back, so I have a feeling that the hit he told me about was the only one he would even consider discussing in hindsight.

MIKE LOWELL

Ivan Rodriguez might not have selected a passage from his memorable 2003 postseason chase, but that is exactly where this road led his teammate, Mike Lowell, that season. On the night of October 7, 2003, Lowell came off the bench in the top of the 11th inning and hit a home run off Mark Guthrie. It gave the Marlins a 9–8 victory over the Cubs in the opener of the NL Championship Series. I went down to the clubhouse to talk to Lowell and wrote my story for MLB.com.

There was no way to know what would happen a week later, when Lowell and the Marlins rallied for eight runs in the eighth inning of a game all Cubs fans would forever remember as the Steve Bartman Game. And there was no way to know that eight years later, almost to the day, two World Series rings and so many hits later, Lowell would be chatting with me at the MLB Network studios and going back to that very moment as the one hit in his career that he most wanted to talk about. In fact, after he told me the story, I Googled the game and came up with my own article, thus reminded of what I had typed on my laptop there in the half-light of a postgame calm in a soon-to-be-shocked city.

"I would say it was Game One of the NLCS in 2003," Lowell said. "I had broken my hand in late August of that year, and I was having the best year of my career, power-wise, with home runs and RBIs. I missed the whole month. I know there was some talk that there was a chance I was not going to be on the postseason roster, and I had to prove I was healthy. So I actually was ahead of the timetable a little, and I played in the last game of the season, but I played in a lot of pain, and I really didn't play in the Giants series, which was the NLDS.

"So when that first game goes into extra innings, I'm basically the 25th man. We used up all our pinch-hitters and everything. When I got a chance to hit in the 11th inning, I hit a home run in that at-bat, we won the game by one, and I basically didn't sit after that. So I think that was just a very satisfying moment for me to overcome the hand injury, then to be able to contribute, and the team made just a huge run to the world championship."

Lowell's home run was the last of an LCS-record seven struck during that game. He had been hit by a pitch on the hand at the end of August and missed the rest of the regular season with a fracture, and he proved so rusty during that Giants series that rookie Miguel Cabrera continued to start at third that night.

"I was just prepared to have the at-bat," Lowell said after that game. "I'm not used to the pinch-hitting thing. My main focus was to stay loose. I was running up and down the stairs, stretching and making some dry swings in the clubhouse to be loose, basically from the seventh inning on, because I didn't know. I can't say I knew it was going to be hit off Guthrie. I was just ready for the at-bat."

The Marlins went on to win that World Series, shocking everyone in the process as unstoppable Wild Cards. Then there was the 2007 World Series, where the Red Sox swept the Rockies and Lowell was named Series MVP. I told him that I a little surprised he did not go with Game Two of that Fall Classic, when he lined a two-out double that chased starter Ubaldo Jimenez and gave Boston a 2–1 lead that would hold up as the final score at Fenway Park. The Red Sox would leave home up 2–0, and that momentum would carry over into two more victories in Denver, with Lowell holding the MVP trophy. Out of 1,619 regular season hits and 29 more in the postseason, I told Lowell I thought he might have gone with the shot off Ubaldo that scored Big Papi.

"That's like Two-A," Lowell said.

That was Lofton's only season with the Giants, and to call it a "season" is stretching it. He was acquired from the White Sox at the Trade Deadline in 2002, a rental who paid off. I remember Lofton as an itinerant blur, an October fact of life with 438 postseason plate appearances. He had 622 steals, 116 triples, and six consecutive All-Star selections over his 17 big-league seasons. His 68.2 WAR is eighth among center fielders, just ahead of Duke Snider.

Lofton was a one-and-done on the Hall of Fame ballot, and although I did not seriously consider checking his name then, his is one of those names that must come up for further discussion upon committee review now that more emphasis is on sabermetric analysis. He was never in quite the right place to win a ring. Yes, he earned more than $60 million in his career, but in retrospect, this was a spectacular athlete who deserves a little more from historians.

KENNY LOFTON

On the morning of Cleveland's 2013 American League Wild Card game against Tampa Bay, MLB brought Kenny Lofton to a New York event meant to rekindle memories of when he helped return the Indians to a postseason after a long time away. Of course, Lofton was with a lot of clubs, and in the postseason with a lot of clubs. He played in 11 different postseasons, with six different teams. When I asked him about his most memorable hit, his memories headed west to a walk-off single he pulled to right that triggered a memorable celebration scene by the Bay.

"The most memorable hit was probably the hit when I was playing with the Giants in 2002," he said. "I got the base hit for the Giants to go to the World Series, against the Cardinals. I think that was one of my biggest hits.

"They brought in a lefty to face me, Steve Kline. They felt like he was going to get me out. I had an idea of what he was going to throw, and he probably had an idea what I was looking for. I ended up figuring it out, reversing the tables and flipping around what he was going to throw, and I ended up getting the base hit, and David Bell scored."

That was Lofton's only season with the Giants, and to call it a "season" is stretching it. He was acquired from the White Sox at the Trade Deadline in 2002, a rental who paid off. I remember Lofton as an itinerant blur, an October fact of life with 438 postseason plate appearances. He had 622 steals, 116 triples, and six consecutive All-Star selections over his 17 big-league seasons. His 68.2 WAR is eighth among center fielders, just ahead of Duke Snider.

Lofton was a one-and-done on the Hall of Fame ballot, and although I did not seriously consider checking his name then, his is one of those names that must come up for further discussion upon committee review now that more emphasis is on sabermetric analysis. He was never in quite the right place to win a ring. Yes, he earned more than $60 million in his career, but in retrospect, this was a spectacular athlete who deserves a little more from historians.

13

NEVER SURRENDER

Every hit that has found its way into this collection was the result of intensity, fortitude, persistence and a special kind of mental toughness. Yet there were some respondents who met a distinct challenge head-on with a special kind of resolve. Craig Biggio has lived his life like he did in the batter's box, showing children with cancer how to fight – and vice versa. Jorge Posada delivered an especially satisfying hit off Pedro Martinez amid the most raging rivalry in sports. Think about Dale Murphy homering off of Dwight Gooden despite an injured hand, or David Eckstein overcoming his latest challenge by getting the best of a 100-mph power pitcher on a World Series stage. Dmitri Young reveals for the first time why he had nightmares about Randy Johnson – and what it meant to ruin a 17-strikeout game by the future Hall of Famer. In examples such as these, there was no possibility for retreat, nothing to do but rise to the occasion and win the battle. In fact, we count the word "battle" four times in Torii Hunter's answer. These are the unintimidated warriors.

CRAIG BIGGIO

The 1991 season began with a two-city trip for the San Francisco Giants, back when I covered them for the *San Jose Mercury News*. We started at San Diego and then went to Houston, and the middle game of that weekend series at the Astrodome was a 16–2 slaughter for the Giants. Craig Biggio, Houston's young catcher, had that game off, but he was a commanding presence on getaway day by going 4-for-4, bringing his career hit total at that point to 302.

"Biggio twice got base hits at 0–2 in both big innings to keep them going," Roger Craig, then the Giants' manager, told us over a plate of food in his postgame manager's room briefing. "That really hurt us." Those words did not mean much to me at the time, but when I went back and researched it more than a quarter century later, it really was a stage being set for the future.

Craig Biggio went on to get five total hits
in the same game as his 3,000th hit

The Astros never batted in the ninth because of that easy home victory, so Biggio never came up for a chance at a fifth hit on that day. Yet here we were in 2017, talking about a five-hit game anyway. Biggio was one of the rare 3,000 Hit Club members who responded to our question with the hit that gained them entry into that club. It came in 2007, highlighting a spectacular evening in Houston in front of friends and family.

"When you play the game for twenty years, there are a lot of things you remember, and obviously a couple that stand out," Biggio said. "I know Boggsie said 3,000 for this question, and for me it's got to be 3,000 also. Not for me personally. It's for my family, obviously, and it was for my teammates and the organization, but most of all it was for the fans. Because I mean, I played my whole career here in Houston, a year and a half in the Minor Leagues, then twenty years in the bigs, and it became something where we were all going to enjoy this thing together.

"When we went into that year and were seventy shy, it took on a new meaning—a whole different animal. I saw how excited fans were to be able to get to such a magical number and an incredible milestone, but yet again it was one of *their* guys who did it for one city and one organization for twenty-plus years, and it was so exciting. So for me, I mean we got to the World Series in 2005 and I wish there was a home run in that World Series to include here, but it wasn't meant to be for us. But the 3000th hit will probably be the signature hit I will always remember, because of the excitement fans had from the beginning of the year and to the day it happened."

It happened on June 28, 2007, in the middle of Biggio's 20th and final season with the Astros. It was a Thursday night at Minute Maid Park, against a Rockies team and a starting pitcher, Aaron Cook, who would pitch in that year's World Series. A capacity crowd of 42,537 fans was on hand, and so was his family and his longtime teammate and future fellow Hall of Famer, Jeff Bagwell, who had retired a year earlier. There have been so many interesting ways that Major Leaguers have reached 3,000 hits—some of them recounted here in this book—and getting there with a five-hit night certainly made this moment especially unique.

"It was kind of nuts," Biggio recalled. "I grounded out to third my first at bat, then I got a hit [number 2,998], and then an infield hit [number 2,999], and I'm like, 'Damn, we're right there. You're knocking at the door.'"

What happened in the bottom of the seventh that night is amazing in hindsight, and it spoke volumes about the makeup of this gamer throughout his career. I think back now to what Roger Craig told us, in the bowels of that old dome amid the infancy of both a season and a Hall of Famer's career. That was the Craig Biggio, battling back from 0–2 repeatedly, never surrendering, whose spirit was so alive the moment number 3,000 became within reach. After all, just consider this fact: The Astros entered his milestone game in fifth place and 14 games behind Milwaukee in the National League Central standings—not even halfway through the season.

That the Astros still had fight in them was perhaps not surprising, considering they already had demonstrated a penchant for big second-half comebacks during the Phil Garner years. So when Biggio stepped to the plate a hit away from history, with Cook and the Rockies nursing a 1–0 lead and two out in the bottom of the seventh, it was as if this were September in the heat of a pennant race. Biggio was not about to take it easy.

"It was a 2–0 count, a legitimate single to right center," Biggio said. "Everybody said I tried to stretch it into a double, but I was actually just trying to play the game. I remember we were losing 1–0, and Brad Ausmus was on second and he would score on that hit. There were two outs. Willie Taveras throws great. I tried to force it and hopefully he makes a bad throw. He threw me out by 10 steps. Everybody said I tried to stretch it to a double, but if it weren't a close game, I would have stopped. I tried to make him force a bad throw."

Biggio was easily tagged out at second, and that RBI single that tied the score was an interesting cause for celebration. He got up, and the party began.

"The moment afterward was very cool, very special," he said. "To be able to enjoy it with all the fans, with my family coming onto the field, what a special moment it was. Then to put the icing on the cake, Baggy was in the ballpark and he came out and I said, 'Let's enjoy this together.' We went on the field, and it was pretty cool.

"I still have people come up to me and talk about it and how excited they were and how they were there when it happened. That makes me feel great, because we did it together," Biggio said. "Not for me personally, because I did it, but because it was to give back to them at the end and be able to say, 'Hey, thank you for supporting me and loving me. We were able to do this together.'"

With the score tied at 4–4 in his milestone game, Biggio led off the bottom of the ninth against reliever Manny Corpas and lined a leadoff single but Houston could not score. In the bottom of the 11th, this time facing closer Brian Fuentes, Biggio started a rally with a two-out single, and he would score on a grand slam by Carlos Lee. That made it five hits, on his way to a final sum of 3,030.

That same never-surrender grittiness that had struck an opposing manager many years earlier was going strong in his final year. I voted for him his first year on the ballot, and he entered Cooperstown on his third try. He was a model of consistency on the field, as he was in the community. He spent nearly his entire playing career as a supporter and lead spokesperson for the Sunshine Kids Foundation, helping children with cancer. In 2007, he received MLB's prestigious Roberto Clemente Award. Given his demeanor as a player, it is easy to see why he was so passionate about Sunshine Kids. He showed them how to never give up, and they only fueled his resolve to live life with this attitude.

Looking back on it all, Biggio said: "When you get a hit, it feels great. When you don't, it stinks. Hitting is so hard. As I get older, I go, 'Man, you had like 3,000 hits,' but you think about how many right turns you made and how many outs you made. Baseball is such a special game. It's a game of failure, and you've got to stay strong, and you've got to fight, and you've got to keep working hard. I've told kids in our clubhouses, 'Guys, I've stepped into the box and I've been 0-for-32 and I don't even know how to use this thing.' You appreciate the game for what it's worth, how hard it is, and honestly how lucky we are to be able to play it at the highest level, at these cathedral ballparks, with fans who love the game. When you get a hit, it's great, and when you don't, it stinks. I pinch myself all the time. I was just a little kid from Long Island, New York, who made it big here in Texas."

DALE MURPHY

"I didn't do very well in our only postseason appearance," said seven-time All-Star Dale Murphy, who played for Atlanta from 1976 through most of 1990, a great on teams that merely set the stage for the Braves' dominance in the '90s. We were talking postseason baseball, because it was mid-October of 2012 when we chatted. The Cardinals had eliminated Murphy and the Braves in the 1982 NLCS on the way to the world title. "We played three games, it was a best-out-of-five, I have not very good memories," he said. "I wish I could share a postseason experience."

I told him he could pick a hit from his entire life. There were 2,111 Major League hits from which to choose.

"I'll tell you one that comes up a lot, that people ask me about a lot," he answered. "I had a consecutive game streak that was almost ended because I went back to catch a fly ball and I cut my hand. I didn't start the next day because I had a few stitches—I've grown from a few stitches to about twenty nowadays, although I only had about three—and I took batting practice and it didn't feel that bad. Chuck Tanner said, 'Well, I won't start you but if I get a chance to pinch-hit, we'll put you in.' I said, 'OK.'

"I didn't start, and I got up to pinch-hit, and it was against Doc Gooden. I didn't have a lot of success against Doc Gooden. People were really appreciative of the fact that I kept the streak going, and then I got up and I pinch-hit a home run off Doc Gooden. My only career home run off of Doc Gooden."

It was Wednesday, the last day of April in 1986. Gooden would go on to win 17 games for the Mets that season, leading them to the World Series title. That 8–1 victory in front of 23,361 fans at old Atlanta-Fulton County Stadium made him 4–0 that season, and his decision was marred only by that dramatic long ball by Murph.

Murphy had injured his hand in the third inning a day before by ramming it into the plexiglass fence in center. He had been taken to Piedmont Hospital, and the Braves had said at the time that he probably would miss a week of games. He actually wore a protective sponge on his hand when he took that batting practice the next day, unable to throw. The pinch-hit appearance marked his 676th consecutive game, then the most among active Major Leaguers. It remains one of the most fabled moments in Braves history, and especially given the year Gooden was having.

"It was the only curveball in my career that he threw me that I could hit. That's the only thing I remember," Murphy said. "The interesting thing was, it didn't even win the game. What it did was it kept my playing streak going, and people thought I had my hand amputated or something, so I always make it sound more dramatic than it was. That was a pretty special thing. I think Doc was taking it easy on me that night."

During his career, Murphy used "a relatively small bat"—34 and a half inches, 32 ounces. "Not many guys use thirty-two [ounces] now," he said. "Most of them are thirty-three and above. I just liked a lighter bat. The bat I used had a small barrel. You don't have many ounces, so the small barrel is better."

It sent baseballs over the wall 398 times. He was NL MVP in 1982–83. I asked him if he misses that feeling of the barrel meeting ball.

"You never get it out of your system," he said. "You wish you could still get back out there. The Braves invite me back to Spring Training nowadays and I love going down to Spring Training, it keeps you young. I'm very thankful to play baseball and you never get it out of your system, you always miss it."

JORGE POSADA

One of the most surprising responses came just three months after the Yankees' catching great officially called it a career. Looking back with fresh eyes, Posada was standing on a red carpet and I was thrusting a tape recorder toward him, asking him to make a rather difficult choice with limited time. He did not refer to the first home run anyone ever hit at new Yankee Stadium, nor one of the grand slams he smashed in back-to-back games in 2010, nor any of the 30 home runs he hit in 2003 as he tied Yogi Berra for most long balls by a catcher in club history. As of 2017, Posada ranked second to Derek Jeter in most postseason games with 125, third in at-bats with 416, and fourth in hits with 103. Considering that and his five rings, perhaps I should have anticipated an October hit, but which of all those October moments would he choose?

"I would say the bloop double against the Red Sox to tie the ball game, in the playoffs," Posada said. "It tied the ball game. We're in the seventh game of a really important playoff. I remember that one; that sticks out in my mind right now.

"Getting to the World Series, Aaron Boone wins the ballgame later on."

Think back to a time when "Who's your Daddy?" applied to Pedro Martinez, the Red Sox' ace. It was the bottom of the eighth, and Boston was protecting a 5–2 lead. He was still pitching at Yankee Stadium in

Game Seven of that ALCS. The Red Sox were so close to what could be something unthinkable—a trip to the World Series and a chance to finally reverse the Curse of the Bambino. Grady Little, the Red Sox' manager, could have gone to his bullpen, but he let Martinez go back out to the mound for the eighth. Nick Johnson led off for New York and popped to shortstop. Boston was five outs away.

Derek Jeter doubled to right and scored on Bernie Williams' single. It was 5–3, and Little still refused to pull his starter. Hideki Matsui stepped in and knocked a ground-rule double, with Williams forced to stop at third. First base was open. Still, Little stayed with Pedro. Given all the history, for the masses it seemed only a matter of time before Boston would find a way to lose. It always happened. Why would this night be any different? Up to the plate comes the number six hitter, Posada. Martinez had mowed him down so far that night: Fly out to center to start the second, groundout to first to end the fourth, lineout to center in the seventh. Little sure as hell was not going to intentionally walk Posada to get to Jason Giambi, who had just homered in his last two at-bats.

It was Martinez versus Posada, and a New York-Boston rivalry was on fire. These were two teams that hated each other, and Game Three had caused the volcano to erupt. Martinez plunked Karim Garcia in that game, causing players to rush in from the dugouts and bullpens. At one point, Posada pointed at Pedro and shouted at him, and Pedro gestured back to the catcher in what looked like a threat at the time. During the ensuing melee, 72-year-old Yankees bench coach (and former player) Don Zimmer rushed toward Martinez as if he was going to settle the matter himself. Pedro stepped aside like a matador and tossed Zimmer to the ground. Zimmer required assistance, elevating the hysteria. Yankee relievers had to be closely guarded by police back in their outfield bullpen, to protect them from fans. Posada had an entirely new level of vengeance, and he was not going to forget it.

In that crucial moment of Game Seven, Martinez lofted a 2-1 curve and an amped-up Posada swung through it for a strike, almost coming out of his spikes. Then came the fastball. It was middle-in, good pitch, but Posada's head was locked in and he got his hands through and blooped it toward center field. Plop—right in front of an incoming Johnny Damon. Williams scored, then Matsui crossed behind him with a hook slide. It was 5–5, the Yankee Stadium crowd was in delirium, and never to be forgotten was that roaring celebration of Posada as he stood on second. It was the end of the night at last for Martinez—Alan Embree replaced him—and the precursor to Aaron Boone's 11th-inning walk-off. That feeling Posada had on second base at that moment was the kind of satisfaction you hold onto after your career is over and someone asks you to tell a story about one hit in your life.

After the game that night, Posada was asked if his hit had been vindication for Martinez's actions in Game Three, when the pitcher had gestured to suggest that a pitch might be coming at his head in due time.

"Not even come to my head," Posada said. "What comes to my head is we tie the game. He was pretty tough. To tie it with a big hit is pretty special. It really tells a lot about this team. We didn't die down. We kept coming. The double by Jeter, the base hit by Bernie, and the double by Matsui gives me a chance to tie the game."

DAVID ECKSTEIN

David Eckstein won World Series with the Angels in 2002 and the Cardinals in 2006, and he was MVP of the latter Fall Classic against Detroit. When he returned to throw out the first pitch before historic Game Six of the 2011 World Series, his first full year away from the field, the scrappy shortstop from the University of Florida said he never would forget what he did in that 2006 series against reliever Joel Zumaya, then baseball's hardest-throwing pitcher. Zumaya routinely reached 100 miles per hour on the radar gun—at a time before Aroldis Chapman, when triple digits were still rarified air.

"Probably the biggest was the one in Game Four against Zumaya when it was a tie game, a hit to left center that put us ahead. That was the biggest hit in my career," Eckstein said.

He was 4-for-5 that night as the Cardinals' leadoff man, and his fourth hit was the big one. St. Louis and Detroit had split the first two games at Comerica Park, and we were all at Busch for Game Three to watch Cardinals ace Chris Carpenter string zeroes in a 5–0 victory. Two trends then were starting to emerge: bad weather, which pushed Game Four back a day, and an apparent seesaw Fall Classic. In Game Four, the Tigers took an early 3–0 lead, then fell behind, 4–3, then tied it on Brandon Inge's RBI double in the top of the eighth of closer Adam Wainwright. Where was all this going?

"Before Game Four, I was talking to some high school kids. [I] had a friend back in Gainesville, they had me on the phone, they said, 'How is it to hit Zumaya?'" Eckstein remembered. "I said, 'Tough, but I love the challenge.' Then I was up there, that was the thought process, and I wanted to come through. He throws so hard, I wanted to make sure I got on top, got my hands above the baseball."

Bottom of the eighth, Zumaya comes out of the bullpen and starts off by walking Yadier Molina on four pitches. Aaron Miles grounds into a 5–4 force play. Juan Encarnacion, who had come in to play right field during a double switch by manager Tony La Russa in the top of the inning, strikes out swinging, but Miles advances to second base on the wild pitch. Zumaya's legend was growing so fast, fans back in Detroit were wearing ski caps that read "Zoom Zoom," and the Yankees' Alex Rodriguez had said he never saw the ball when facing him in the prior AL Division Series. In St. Louis, his fastball readout was in the 80s and 90s, creating some buzz and making even him wonder if the home team was manipulating his readout for psychological purposes. One thing is clear: Zumaya took it all personally and Eckstein was a fighter.

On a 3–1 pitch, Eckstein lined a double to left that glanced off the glove of Craig Monroe, driving in the decisive run. The Cardinals would take a 3–1 series lead, and they would clinch the following night as Eckstein drove in two more. It was the first time since the Yankees in 1923 that a Major League team won it all in a brand-new ballpark.

"Right now I'm very angry," Zumaya said after the game, before reportedly walking the mile to his hotel by himself, livid and surrounded by Redbird fans. "We played hard today. Just some things happened that we really didn't want to happen."

That night, La Russa said of Eckstein: "He's the definition of a clutch player. Then you try to give an example of what that means—a game-winning hit against a guy throwing 100, and that's all you need to know . . . the toughest guy I've ever seen in uniform."

During the 2006 World Series champagne celebration scene in the Cardinals clubhouse, I watched as Eckstein was forced to down a shot of whiskey at the behest of teammate Scott Spiezio, who had also been his teammate in the 2002 title run. Or at least I thought it was whiskey.

"Tequila," Eckstein corrected me during our 2011 chat. "He got me to do that after we won in Anaheim, so that was a moment of tradition. Most people know I don't drink, and it's funny because after that I was on drunkathletes.com."

TORII HUNTER

Torii Hunter had just wrapped up his 15th year of Major League Baseball service, and so many of those were spent patrolling center field during his first stint with the Twins. He created so many big memories there, but ask him about one hit that meant the most to him at that point in his career, and he goes to his best postseason moment.

"Game One in 2009, we're playing the Red Sox in the playoffs," he said. "The Angels haven't beaten the Red Sox in like eleven postseason appearances over the last eleven years. So I was able to hit a three-run homer off Jon Lester and it kind of got the momentum going, and we ended up winning that Division Series, 3–0. They kept saying it, they kept saying it: we hadn't beaten the Red Sox. And I'm like, 'We're about to win this today.'"

It was the bottom of the fifth, scoreless opener, Lester and John Lackey in a pitcher's duel, with 45,070 fans at the Big A. Erick Aybar was on third and Bobby Abreu had just walked to put Angels on the corners with one out. Then came the hit that ranks number one for Hunter out of the 2,452 he had in regular seasons and the 51 more he had in postseason play.

"I remember Joe West behind the plate, I remember Jon Lester battling," Hunter told me after the 2011 season. "We got to a 3–2 count, we just battled and battled. He made a pretty good pitch, it was low and away, but it was a really good pitch for two strikes. I didn't swing, and Joe said, 'Ball.' That made it 3–2, so I battled and battled, and then—boom!—he threw a fastball, and I was able to hit it over the center-field wall. It was the greatest feeling in the world. That place went crazy. I think that built a lot of confidence for the fans, the organization, and the team. For me, too."

DMITRI YOUNG

Randy Johnson once struck out 17 Reds in a game, and the most amazing part is that batting against him that day is seen now as a literal dream come true. Just ask Dmitri Young.

"Wow. June 30, 1999. I call it The Hit That Saved My Career," Young said at a 2011 Baseball Assistance Team fundraising dinner in New York. "I had a dream back then. We were playing the Arizona Diamondbacks. They had a 6-foot-11 pitcher, left-handed guy. At the time I had one homer, like nine RBIs, hitting .220. That's when I started out with hair blond, then I brought it back black. Anyway, I had a dream that I hit a home run off Randy Johnson.

"The next day, we're facing Randy Johnson. Three-two count, working him, he tried to brush me off the plate. Gives me the stare down, but it doesn't bother me. I'm staring him down and laughing. He doesn't intimidate me. So 3–2, he throws me a slider and leaves it up. At old Cinergy Field, they had the red deck, and they had the brown. Four-hundred thirty-nine feet. I haven't shared that with anybody since then. But that's the answer to your question."

Despite the 17 strikeouts that day by Johnson, the future Hall of Famer, the Reds won, 2–0. Young's solo blast to left in the first inning was the only thing that mattered. It remains important to him now because it helped him turn around a season that had been a letdown from the one before. Young had batted .310 with 14 homers and 83 RBIs in 1998, his first season with Cincinnati.

"In '99, I wound up with 14 homers, 56 ribbies, average was up to .300, and helped the team get to that one-game playoff against the Mets. I had the good year in '98 with the Reds, and then I came there and was doing oddball stuff—you know, young-and-stupid stuff. The blond hair, it's just not me. Lost my starting job. So I was trying to work my way back. That was the turnaround, that hit, a dream come true."

GOOSE GOSLIN

In September of 1928, Goslin's big summer-long lead in the AL batting race was being gradually winnowed by Heinie Manush of the St. Louis Browns. It was down to just a fraction of a point going into the final day of the season. The teams played each other in that finale, the batting-race contenders each started in left field, and it went down to Goslin's final at-bat for Washington.

Manush's average was .378, and Goslin's was a fraction above. If Goslin is out, Manush wins. If Goslin gets a hit, he wins. Goslin knew that only because a sportswriter sent down the information to him before that at-bat, in a note that read: "If you go to bat and make an out, Manush will win the batting title. Best thing to do is don't get up to bat at all, and then you've got it made."

That would have been fine, except this was baseball, bravado, and boys being boys. Senators manager Bucky Harris told Goslin it was up to him, and offered to have someone pinch hit for him. Goslin's first inclination was to take him up on that offer, but teammate Joe Judge, who finished third in the AL MVP race that year, advised: "You better watch out or they'll call you yellow."

Goslin asked what he meant by that, and Judge replied: "Well, there's Manush right out there in left field. What do you think he'll figure if you win the title by sitting on the bench?" That seemed to do the trick. Goslin stepped in—and proceeded to fall into a quick 0-and-2 hole in his final plate appearance of 1928. One strike away from losing the batting title. Then he got another idea.

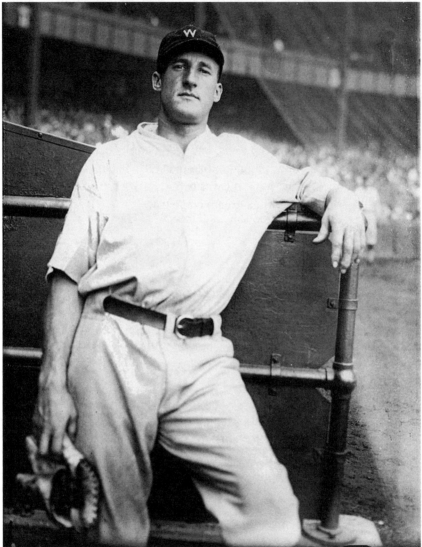

Goose Goslin won the batting title, though only by one hit

Have the ump throw him out. Bill Guthrie was umpire, and Goslin worked him as best he could. "Why those pitches weren't even close," Goslin said, proceeding to utter every word he could think of for a sure ejection. If it worked, then it would not go down as an official plate appearance—but he would have risen to the challenge in Manush's eyes. Only one problem: Guthrie was not about to let it happen. "You're not going to get thrown out of this game no matter what you do," the ump commanded. Not only that, he told Goslin that there was no way he was going to call a base on balls.

Back into the box stepped Goslin. Here it was—nothing on the line for the teams, but everything seemingly at stake for two individuals.

Goslin got a hit, finishing at .379.

"I heard him," he said of the ump. "And gee, you know—I got a lucky hit. Saved me. I guess that hit was the biggest thrill I ever got. Even bigger than that single that won the World Series in 1935."

We know Goslin had a homer and a double that day, going by the box score, but there was no recorded play by play. Lawrence Ritter's oft-cited book, *The Glory of Their Times*, discussed that final day, but it never said specifically what kind of hit that was to win the title. Based on the "lucky hit" comment by Goslin, I believe it was a double.

DRIVE THEM CRAZY

No one wants to be stereotyped, and that includes a baseball player. Of course, in reality it happens all the time. It happens from the first scouting report delivered to the front office, from the reputation that is built through peers, media, and fans. Breaking free of that box and altering public perception often can be a driving force, for better or worse, and not surprisingly the moments when that happened result in some most memorable hits here. Ozzie Smith was known as The Wizard for his defensive prowess, so an offensive spectacle stays readily in his mind. Same goes for Jim Palmer, of all people. Ralph Kiner hit home runs for a living, and because it usually happened for a losing team in Pittsburgh, he became expendable and recalled how it felt to go deep amongst All-Star brethren one summer. Davey Lopes, Prince Fielder, and Barry Lyons each embrace the memory of a time they did something no one could imagine—not even themselves. Their common thread is the mere sake of mattering in some unique regard, a relevance they welcomed, a surprise they gave everyone, at least temporarily changing the very way people looked at them.

OZZIE SMITH

When I think of Ozzie Smith's playing career, I often think of the Cardinals' annual media guide and how impressive it was to see the list of The Wizard's greatest plays at shortstop. They were ranked, and doing so was no easy task for the team's public relations department given the volume of highlights. For the purposes of this book, I was wondering what he ranked at the top of his own offensive moments in that Hall of Fame career.

"I guess that would have to be the home run that I hit in the playoffs in 1985 against the Dodgers, because I think up until that time people looked at me notably as just a defensive player," he said in 2011. "That one hit kind of changed the way people looked at me. It made people start to look at me as more of a complete player as opposed to a one-dimensional defensive player. That would be the one that stands out, the one people talk a lot about when I'm out—about that home run. Especially Cardinals fans, they talk about where they were. In your life, there are certainly things that happen and you remember exactly where you were and what you were doing at that particular time. That for me was certainly it."

Ozzie Smith and Bruce Sutter share a laugh as they wait to board a truck as Grand Marshals for the 2009 All-Star Game Red Carpet Parade

Photograph by author

The switch-hitter had batted left-handed 3,009 times in his career without a home run going into that Game Five of the National League Championship Series at old Busch Stadium in St. Louis. He smashed this one on a 1–2 pitch from Tom Niedenfuer, knocking the ball off a concrete pillar behind the right-field wall. There was a mob scene at home plate, the kind now commonplace after walk-offs. The Cardinals had lost the first two games of the series at Dodger Stadium, and that homer gave them a 3–2 series lead with the reassuring feeling of 21-game winners Joaquin Andujar and John Tudor lined up for the next two games as needed. Niedenfuer also would surrender the three-run homer to Jack Clark in the top of the ninth in the Game Six clincher back in LA, but it was the long ball by the guy Andujar called "the little midget" that is most remembered today.

One reason, even Ozzie acknowledges, is the way fans heard about it. There was only one Jack Buck, and that was one of the most replayed calls by the legendary Redbird broadcaster.

"You know, it's great when you can have a *great* making one of those calls," Ozzie told me. "It's all improvisational at that particular time. Of course, Jack is: 'There's one hit down the line . . . it could go, it could go . . .' and 'Go Crazy, folks, Go Crazy!' That's the way I sign a lot of autographs these days, because Jack was on the mic that particular time and he made that call and he saw the crowd go crazy."

JIM PALMER

Coincidentally, I interviewed Hall of Famer Jim Palmer because he was at our MLB.com studios in Manhattan in June of 2016 to promote a new book, *Nine Innings to Success*. I asked him The Question after our interview, and he eagerly and immediately offered his own entry about a subject—hitting!—that too few people care to broach with this legendary former Orioles right-hander. Palmer said matter-of-factly: "The homer off Jim Bouton."

"It was May, a Sunday afternoon. Man on first," he continued. "My first manager was Hank Bauer, and he had played with Don Larsen, who was my teammate then and another good guy that I asked a lot of questions about. Harvey Haddix, I was his teammate in that '65 season, which was his last. Sherm Lollar, he was our bullpen coach. I had a lot of people around to learn from. That day, I had come on in relief, and Davey Johnson's on first. Bouton had won eighteen games with the Yankees the year before. They were looking for a bunt.

"I never heard it, but twenty-five years later, when I was on a show with Bob Costas, he actually asked Joe Garagiola, who was doing radio that day, and told me the call: 'Clete Boyer sneaking in at third, [Joe] Pepitone sneaking in at first, here's the pitch, it's a high drive to right field . . . nineteen-year-old Jim Palmer has just homered over the right-center field fence! Clete Boyer was so close to home, if Palmer would have pulled the ball, they would have had to pick him up with a spatula.' I mean, it's vintage. I never heard the call of the game. But it was a room-service curveball. That was my first Major League win."

Mickey Mantle's two-run single in the top of the third had chased Baltimore starter Dave McNally in a 4–1 game, so Palmer was the reliever. Norm Siebern's homer off Bouton had made it 2–2 in the bottom of the third, and then that two-run blast by Palmer tied the score at 4–4. Palmer struggled in the sixth as Tony Kubek touched him for a go-ahead single, and despite the display of power, Palmer was replaced by a pinch-hitter in the bottom of the sixth. Luis Aparicio hit a two-run homer for the Orioles in that same half-inning, so Palmer still stood to record his first Major League win. It was Larsen, who was among the first to offer the young righty advice as they sat out in the bullpen those days, who relieved Palmer for the seventh and got the hold as Baltimore took that game by a 7–5 score.

"When I won my first start the next year, when I threw one hundred seventy-seven pitches, I hit another home run. It was so far over the left-field wall . . ."

Palmer wanted to keep talking, but more book promotion duty intervened, so we left it at that. He was proud of his bat as a pitcher. It was clear at this particular at-bat that Palmer was not going to be stereotyped as just another lame-hitting pitcher. In fact, once you scroll past his stellar pitching record (268 wins, three AL Cy Youngs), you can look at his batting record and see that by 1972, he was no slouch with a career-high .224 average (22-for-98) and .516 OPS (on-base percentage plus slugging average). Then, suddenly, just as he was becoming a legitimate concern at the plate, his bat was methodically removed from his very hands. The 1973 season brought the designated hitter to the AL.

Save for an 0-for-4 appearance during the 1979 World Series against Pittsburgh, Palmer, the only pitcher ever to win a World Series title in three different decades (1966, '70, and '83), never officially batted again in his remaining 12 years in the Majors.

Palmer told story after story that day: about his "stupidstitious" ritual of eating pancakes on start days (thus the early nickname "Cakes"); about the abuse he withstood for years from Orioles manager Earl Weaver, his renowned alter-ego; about the lessons he learned over the years and why he wanted to impart them; about his broadcasting career; about the AL East as it stood then; about his stepson's autism; about pitching mechanics and why his pitching coach in 1966 wanted him to get his pitch count down from 177 to "130 or 140"—imagine that! But I do think I saw a particular glint in those legendary eyes as we spoke briefly on the subject of hitting, and on that Sunday afternoon he served notice that he was handy enough with a bat to do more than bunt.

DAVEY LOPES

I was in the Phillies dugout before Game Two of the 2009 World Series at Yankee Stadium, and Davey Lopes, then a Phillies coach, was talking about the day he once knocked three balls out for the Dodgers on the road against the Cubs. He told me he remembered the three home runs he hit out at Wrigley Field. I asked what he remembered *most* about that day, and he got this surprised look on his face and then repeated himself:

"My third home run in Wrigley Field!

"That's what I remember about it. Not too many guys hit three home runs in one ball game. That was a pretty special day. If you ever said to me that I was going to hit three home runs in one ball game in my career, I would have said you were absolutely nuts. I don't think most people expect that, especially if you aren't known as a home run hitter. It's a rare feat, and that's why it kind of stands out. Even power hitters will tell you it's a special feat to do. You go ask them. There's not many people that can say they hit three home runs in one ball game. It's not very easy to do. You've got to factor in how many people played Major League Baseball. Then see how rare it is."

On August 20, 1974, during an 18–8 rout of the Cubs, the Dodgers collected 24 hits and set a franchise record with 48 total bases. Lopes did much of that damage by himself, and fittingly the first at-bat of the day at Wrigley was a Lopes homer off Tom Dettore, a Cubs right-hander who had just been acquired in a trade for Pittsburgh's Paul Popovich. The next inning began pretty much the same way, with Dodgers pitcher Don Sutton leading off (and grounding out), and with Lopes proceeding to slug another homer off Dettore, ending the pitcher's afternoon. It did not matter who Lopes was facing that day, though. In the third inning, Lopes faced reliever Dave LaRoche and doubled to center. In the fourth inning, the Dodgers nearly batted around, and Lopes was the final batter. He singled off LaRoche and drove in Ron Cey before Steve Yeager was thrown out at third to end the inning.

Think about this: The game was not half over, and Lopes already had two home runs, a double and a single—13 total bases. What a day he was having.

LaRoche made it through the fifth inning somehow without facing Lopes, facing four batters, but it was more of the same in the sixth, as Lopes hit his third homer of the day. It was a solo shot, one of three Dodger homers in that seven-run inning. He was 5-for-5 with three homers and there was plenty of baseball still to play.

In the top of the seventh, reliever Jim Kremmel finally retired Lopes, ending a one-two-three inning with a groundout to third. His turn to bat again never came around, as the game finished while he was in the hole. So Lopes finished 5-for-6. That lifted his batting average from .251 to .260, a decent jump when a little more than a month is remaining in a regular season. It exactly doubled the number of home runs he had hit to date that season. His 15 total bases set a Major League record for a leadoff hitter.

Lopes was speed, the wheels on the bases with all those great Dodgers hitters like Bill Russell, Steve Garvey, and Ron Cey hitting behind him. This was typical of what I encountered in asking some of the best players about one hit they remembered most. They often think of contrast, because of the surprise it brought to others, because of something they proved to themselves. In Lopes's case, his one hit was not a drag bunt that he beat out, not a single that put him aboard to set up a steal, but the day he showed the pop of a cleanup hitter, capping it with the third long ball in the Friendly Confines and getting a suddenly familiar handshake from Tommy Lasorda as he rounded third base.

PRINCE FIELDER

On the early afternoon of his triumphant 2009 Home Run Derby performance, Prince Fielder was seated at an interview table in the St. Louis Hyatt, and I was across from him with two or three other media members. I asked Fielder about his chances in the Derby, and I asked him what he remembered about his father Cecil's Home Run Derby days. Prince told me he remembered his Dad's shot off the restaurant glass at Toronto's SkyDome. Then after asking him work-related questions, I asked him if there was one hit in his lifetime that meant the most to him. Here is what he told me there in the National League All-Star interview room on that important day in his life:

"Uh, yeah...man, that's a tough one. I guess uh...I don't know, that's a good one. When I first got drafted, I got an infield single. So I thought that was pretty cool. Especially a power kid drafted out of high school, and my first hit was an infield single down the third base line. To me, that was pretty cool. It showed I had some kind of speed, I guess."

"Didn't you homer that game, too?" piped in another media member who was listening.

"Yeah. So it was perfect," Prince said. "Got it all knocked out."

Plenty of people went back and re-examined how Fielder had entered professional baseball on June 19, 2002, but this is probably the only place you will hear anything about his little infield single that literally got the ball rolling. People talk about his "smashing debut" when he crushed an opposite-field grand slam to help the Ogden (Utah) Raptors of the Pioneer

League tie its game against Idaho Falls at 9–9, before Ogden went on to a 12–9 victory. It was all about that Prince Fielder power.

Had I asked Fielder the same question one day later, I would not have been surprised if he would have cited his 503-foot blast in that Home Run Derby. But again, as you saw in the previous example of Davey Lopes, athletes often want to discuss contrast, to give some props to a part of their game overlooked by others. That's the great thing about my nine-word question: it is personal to the player.

BARRY LYONS

Barry Lyons had a cup of coffee with the Mets club that won the 1986 World Series, and went on to play seven seasons, all but two games in the National League. He went through a horrific circumstance in 2005 when Hurricane Katrina wiped out his home—along with so many others on the Gulf Coast—and received help from MLB's Baseball Assistance Team (BAT) for more than a year. He basically lost everything in that storm surge. One thing they could not take away was this memory, which he shared with me during a B.A.T. event late in the 2011 season:

"I had a few, but I could come up with one. Actually, August 20, 1987, I came to bat with the bases loaded, and went on to hit a grand slam that got us ahead in the game in which we eventually won over the San Francisco Giants. That one obviously stands out the most in my mind.

"Thursday afternoon. That was during the corked-bat era, when HoJo [Mets teammate Howard Johnson] and others were suspected. Whitey Herzog and Hal Lanier, NL managers then, they were confiscating bats and there were all kinds of issues during that time. During that bat, I fouled the ball down the third-base line and realized that my bat had cracked. So I went back and got another bat from the batboy. There was a comment after the game whether Roger Craig was going to ask to check my bat to see whether I might have had Howard's bat or something."

I asked Lyons if the Giants' manager pursued it.

"He didn't. I told him I would have been honored if he had checked it," he said.

"That was a very memorable day for me. It was the highlight as far as a particular hit in my career, as that was my only grand slam."

RALPH KINER

Courtesy of Michael Papariella

Ralph Kiner led the National League in homers
in each of his first seven seasons

The 1950 All-Star Game was played at original Comiskey Park in Chicago, and that was the scene of what Hall of Famer Ralph Kiner considered his most memorable hit. He was in the midst of one of the most dominant stretches any slugger ever has put together before or since, leading

221

the National League in home runs for seven straight years with the Pirates from his 1946 rookie season through 1952. It should have been no surprise that he chose to talk about a homer when we reminisced during the final week of the 2011 season, shortly before his 89th birthday.

"Really, it's so difficult to narrow it down to one hit. Unfortunately, I didn't get a chance to play in the World Series. We didn't have any winning teams in those days," he said. "My real participation was the All-Star Game. It was the 1950 All-Star Game. I had a hit that tied the game in the ninth inning, a home run. The National League went on to win the game in the 14th inning when Red Schoendienst hit a home run. We turned the evolution of the American League winning into the National League at that time."

Entering that game, the AL had been 12–4 and was riding a four-game winning streak in the event, which had started at that very ballpark back in 1933. The AL had come from behind and was on the verge of making it five in a row with a 3–2 lead when Kiner led off the top of the ninth against Tigers right-hander Art Houtteman. Joe DiMaggio had just entered the game as a replacement for Hoot Evers in right field. "Ralph Kiner can wipe out your lead with one swing," Warren Spahn said at the time, and indeed that is exactly what happened. Kiner hit a long homer to start a three-inning pitcher's duel, and it was Schoendienst from the Cardinals who would decide it with a solo shot in the top of the 14th.

Kiner's homer kept his league alive in a game that meant nothing in the standings, but as he stood there with a rich stock from which to choose, it was fairly clear to him. During our conversation, he thought it was worth mentioning an out earlier during that game that became very memorable to him as well.

"In that game, as a matter of fact, I made an out that proved to be a very important out to a guy named Ted Williams," he said. "He broke his elbow [in the first inning] catching my drive against the scoreboard in left-center field, and took a base hit away from me. And he said after that, he never could hit. All he did was hit .388 from then on." Then, with tongue firmly in cheek, he added: "Really unfortunate."

Kiner was elected into the Hall of Fame in 1975 and would spend a half-century as a Mets broadcaster. In fact, when I talked to him for this book, he was at an event to promote an upcoming Baseball Assistance Team fundraising dinner to help take care of members of the Baseball Family, and the theme of the dinner would be 50 years of Mets baseball. He thought back to those days before he took the microphone, to the unmatched feeling of swinging a steel-strong bat, when he symbolized power in the game before giving way to a back problem that cut his career short.

"There's no thrill like winning ball games with home runs," Kiner said. "I was a home run hitter. Until the era of the steroids, I was second to Babe Ruth in percentage of home runs hit per times at bat. That was a really big accomplishment to me, to be in that order. I led the league in home runs seven consecutive years, and that started from my first year in baseball. No one's ever done that. That was always a great thrill.

"It wasn't so important to a guy named Branch Rickey, who I never really enjoyed. He kept my salary after leading the league seven years in a row, twenty-five percent [raise]. In those days, twenty-five percent was a lot of money, compared to what they make in baseball now."

Rickey was the Pirates' general manager during the first half of the '50s, following his tenure in which he famously had made Jackie Robinson the first black player in the Majors. Kiner did not think much of Dickey as far as player/GM relationship, explaining his departure this way:

"He said to me, 'Son, where did we finish?'"

"I said, 'We finished last.'"

"And he said, 'We can finish last without you.'"

If you let Ralph Kiner talk long enough, he would tell you about another hit. Just for the record:

"My first [homer] was off Howie Pollet. He was [a 21-game winner] with the St. Louis Cardinals in 1946. Someone asked me, who did you hit for your *last* home run? I said I have no idea, because I didn't expect it to be my last.

"I got down to where I really couldn't play every day, and I wanted to get into something that was a little more permanent. As long as I couldn't be a part of the game in total games played, I accepted something else. I ended up being the GM of the San Diego Padres of the PCL."

We said goodbye, and I told Ralph what a pleasure it was to talk to him and to have known him. A little over two years later, he was gone, like Musial, Gwynn, and others that I and so many people had the good fortune of knowing at least just for a bit. Oh, to have asked Ernie Banks that one question when he was right there one day within arm's reach in San Francisco. Oh, to have asked Mickey Mantle that one question when he was signing that baseball in Atlantic City.

Living life without regret and with curiosity and passion, this explains why I have asked the persistent question of every legendary hitter before me in recent times. Why wonder when you can know? These men have been a cherished part of life, a fabled combination of gods and fellow citizens, real people like us except for the moments when their spikes settled into a chalked rectangle of dirt and they prepared for the fastball. Their hits connect us all, the ones we remember and the ones they hold dearest, and their lessons last forever.

ABOUT THE AUTHOR

Mark Newman is a recipient of the National Magazine Award for General Excellence and has been a baseball writer since 1990, including nearly the last two decades with Major League Baseball Advanced Media (MLB.com). This is his second book, in addition to *Hard to Believe: A Year Inside Red Sox Nation*, which followed the 2004 World Series and was MLBAM's first-ever e-book. The Indiana University graduate is a Hall of Fame voting member of the Baseball Writers' Association of America. Before MLBAM, he co-founded and oversaw content at digital ventures including Sporting News Online, NASCAR.com, and MAX Broadcasting Network. Before that, he was an award-winning pro sports beat writer for *The Miami Herald*, *Fort Worth Star-Telegram*, and *San Jose Mercury News*. Newman and his wife Lisa live in Piermont, NY, combining for four children (Matt, Ben, Josh, and Rachel) and an English Bulldog named Bingley.

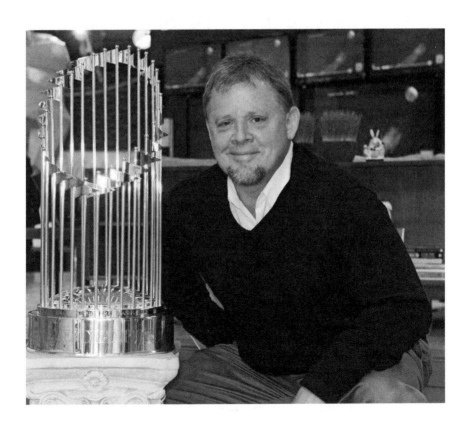

PLAYER ROSTER

*Active Player, stats as of end of 2016 season.

Team and position correlate to the hits that meant the most to them.

All-Star Games only noted if more than a dozen selections.

HANK AARON HOF: 1982 Page 133

Position: Center Field — Team: Milwaukee Braves

Bats: Right — At-bats: 12364

RBIs: 2297 — Hits: 3771

Home runs: 755 — MVP: 1957 NL

Total Bases: 6856 — Batting Average: .305

All-Star Games: 25 (1955, 1956, 1957, 1958, 1959-1, 1959-2, 1960-1, 1960-2, 1961-1, 1961-2, 1962-1, 1962-2, 1963, 1964, 1965, 1966, 1967, 1968, 1969, 1970, 1971, 1972, 1973, 1974, 1975)

ROBERTO ALOMAR HOF: 2011 Page 190

Position: Second Base — Team: San Diego Padres

Bats: Both — Runs: 150

RBIs: 1134 — Batting Average: .300

All-Star Games: 12 (1990, 1991, 1992, 1993, 1994, 1995, 1996, 1997, 1998, 1999, 2000, 2001)

SANDY ALOMAR, JR. Page 192

Position: Catcher — Team: Cleveland Indians

Bats: Right — RBIs: 588

Home runs: 112 — Batting Average: .273

CARLOS BAERGA Page 50

Position: Second Base — Team: Cleveland Indians

Bats: Both — RBIs: 771

Home runs: 134 — Batting Average: .291

HAROLD BAINES Page 122

Position: Right Field — Team: Chicago White Sox

Bats: Left — RBIs: 1628

Hits: 2866 — Batting Average: .289

DUSTY BAKER Page 137

Position: Center Field
Team: Los Angeles Dodgers
Bats: Right
RBIs: 1013
Home runs: 242
Batting Average: .278

CARLOS BELTRAN* Page 167

Position: Center Field
Team: Kansas City Royals
Bats: Both
At-bats: 9595
RBIs: 1571
Hits: 2685
Home runs: 432
Batting Average: .280

JOHNNY BENCH   HOF: 1989 Page 16

Position: Catcher
Team: Cincinnati Reds
Bats: Right
RBIs: 1376
Hits: 2048
Home runs: 389
MVP: 1970, 1972 NL
Batting Average: .247
All-Star Games: 14 (1968, 1969, 1970, 1971, 1972, 1973, 1974, 1975, 1976, 1977, 1978, 1979, 1980, 1983)

CRAIG BIGGIO   HOF: 2015 Page 201

Position: Second Base
Team: Houston Astros
Bats: Right
At-bats: 10876
Runs: 1844
Home runs: 291
Hits: 3060
Batting Average: .281

WADE BOGGS   HOF: 2005 Page 94

Position: Third Base
Team: Boston Red Sox
Bats: Left
At-bats: 9180
Runs: 1513
Home runs: 118
Hits: 3010
Batting Average: .328
All-Star Games: 12 (1985, 1986, 1987, 1988, 1989, 1990, 1991, 1992, 1993, 1994, 1995, 1996)

AARON BOONE Page 36

Position: Third Base
Team: Cincinnati Reds
Bats: Right
At-bats: 3871
RBIs: 555
Batting Average: .263

GEORGE BRETT   HOF: 1999   Page 90

Position: Third Base   Team: Kansas City Royals
Bats: Left   At-bats: 10349
Runs: 1583   RBIs: 1596
Home runs: 317   Hits: 3154
MVP: 1980 AL   Batting Average: .305
All-Star Games: 13 (1976, 1977, 1978, 1979, 1980, 1981, 1982, 1983, 1984, 1985, 1986, 1987, 1988)

LOU BROCK   HOF: 1985   Page 42

Position: Left Field   Team: St. Louis Cardinals
Bats: Left   At-bats: 10332
Hits: 3023   Batting Average: .293

BOBBY BROWN   Page 131

Position: Pinch Hitter   Team: New York Yankees
Bats: Left   At-bats: 1619
RBIs: 237   Batting Average: .279

JOE CARTER   Page 32

Position: Left Field   Team: Toronto Blue Jays
Bats: Right   RBIs: 1445
Home runs: 396   Batting Average: .259

ORLANDO CEPEDA   HOF: 1999   Page 14

Position: First Base   Team: San Francisco Giants
Bats: Right   At-bats: 7927
Runs: 1131   RBIs: 1365
Hits: 7927   Home runs: 379
MVP: 1967 NL   Batting Average: .297

CHRIS CHAMBLISS   Page 96

Position: First Base   Team: New York Yankees
Bats: Left   RBIs: 972
Home runs: 185   Batting Average: .279

JOE CHARBONEAU
Position: Left Field, Designated Hitter Team: Cleveland Indians
Bats: Right   Home runs: 29
Hits: 172   Batting Average: .266

WILL CLARK
Position: First Base   Team: San Francisco Giants
Bats: Left   RBIs: 1205
Home runs: 284   Batting Average: .303

ROBERTO CLEMENTE HOF: 1973
Position: Right Field   Team: Pittsburgh Pirates
Bats: Right   At-bats: 9454
Runs: 1416   Hits: 3000
MVP: 1966 NL   Batting Average: .317
All-Star Games: 15 (1960-1, 1960-2, 1961-1, 1961-2, 1962-1, 1962-2, 1963, 1964, 1965, 1966, 1967, 1969, 1970, 1971, 1972)

ERIC DAVIS
Position: Center Field   Team: Cincinnati Reds
Bats: Right   Runs: 938
RBIs: 934   Batting Average: .269

ANDRE DAWSON HOF: 2010
Position: Center Field   Team: Montreal Expos
Bats: Right   At-bats: 9927
RBIs: 1591   Home runs: 438
MVP: 1987 NL   Batting Average: .279

BUCKY DENT
Position: Shortstop   Team: New York Yankees
Bats: Right   Runs: 451
Home runs: 40   Batting Average: .247

DAVID ECKSTEIN
Position: Shortstop   Team: St. Louis Cardinals
Bats: Right   Runs: 701
RBIs: 392   Batting Average: .280

JIM EDMONDS
Page 116

Position: Pinch Hitter

Bats: Left

RBIs: 1199

Team: Anaheim Angels

Runs: 1251

Batting Average: .284

JIM EISENREICH
Page 100

Position: Left Field

Bats: Left

Home runs: 52

Team: Kansas City Royals

Runs: 492

Batting Average: .290

PRINCE FIELDER
Page 219

Position: First Base

Bats: Left

RBIs: 1028

Team: Ogden Raptors

Runs: 862

Batting Average: .283

STEVE FINLEY
Page 195

Position: Center Field

Bats: Left

Home runs: 304

Team: Los Angeles Dodgers

Runs: 1443

Batting Average: .271

CARLTON FISK   HOF: 2000
Page 30

Position: Catcher

Bats: Right

Home runs: 376

Team: Boston Red Sox

RBIs: 1330

Batting Average: .269

STEVE GARVEY
Page 160

Position: First Base

Bats: Right

MVP: 1974 NL

Team: San Diego Padres

Home runs: 272

Batting Average: .294

LUIS GONZALEZ
Page 34

Position: Left Field

Bats: Left

RBIs: 1439

Team: Arizona Diamondbacks

Runs: 1412

Batting Average: .283

JOHNNY GORYL

Position: Second Base   Team: Minnesota Twins
Bats: Right   Home runs: 16
Hits: 134   Batting Average: .225

GOOSE GOSLIN   HOF: 1968

Position: Left Field   Team: Washington Senators
Bats: Left   RBIs: 1612
Hits: 2735   Batting Average: .316

CURTIS GRANDERSON*

Position: Center Field   Team: Detroit Tigers
Bats: Left   Runs: 1082
RBIs: 838   Batting Average: .254

KEN GRIFFEY JR.   HOF: 2016

Position: Center Field   Team: Seattle Mariners
Bats: Left   At-bats: 9801
Runs: 1662   RBIs: 1836
Hits: 2781   Home runs: 630
MVP: 1997 AL   Batting Average: .284
All-Star Games: 13 (1990, 1991, 1992, 1993, 1994, 1995, 1996, 1997, 1998, 1999, 2000, 2004, 2007)

KEN GRIFFEY SR.

Position: Left Field   Team: Seattle Mariners
Bats: Left   Runs: 1129
RBIs: 859   Batting Average: .296

MARQUIS GRISSOM

Position: Center Field   Team: Montreal Expos
Bats: Right   Runs: 1187
Home runs: 227   Batting Average: .272

CHRIS GWYNN

Position: Pinch Hitter   Team: San Diego Padres
Bats: Left   Runs: 119
RBIs: 118   Batting Average: .261

TONY GWYNN   HOF: 2007   Page 186

Position: Right Field   Team: San Diego Padres
Bats: Left   Runs: 1383
Hits: 3141   Batting Average: .338
All-Star Games: 15 (1984, 1985, 1986, 1987, 1989, 1990, 1991, 1992, 1993, 1994, 1995, 1996, 1997, 1998, 1999)

JOSH HAMILTON   Page 63

Position: Right Field   Team: Texas Rangers
Bats: Left   Home runs: 200
MVP: 2010 AL   Batting Average: .290

BRAD HAWPE   Page 22

Position: Pinch Hitter   Team: Colorado Rockies
Bats: Left   Runs: 400
RBIs: 492   Batting Average: .275

RICKEY HENDERSON   HOF: 2009   Page 93

Position: Left Field   Team: San Diego Padres
Bats: Right   At-bats: 10961
Runs: 2295   Stolen Bases: 1406
Hits: 3055   Home runs: 297
MVP: 1990 AL   Batting Average: .279

TORII HUNTER   Page 209

Position: Center Field   Team: Anaheim Angels
Bats: Right   RBIs: 1391
Home runs: 353   Batting Average: .277

CLINT HURDLE   Page 45

Position: Right Field   Team: Kansas City Royals
Bats: Left   RBIs: 193
Home runs: 32   Batting Average: .259

REGGIE JACKSON   HOF: 1993   Page 174

Position: Right Field   Team: New York Yankees
Bats: Left   At-bats: 9864
Runs: 1551   RBIs: 1702

Strikeouts: 2597   Home runs: 563

MVP: 1973 AL   Batting Average: .262

All-Star Games: 14 (1969, 1971, 1972, 1973, 1974, 1975, 1977, 1978, 1979, 1980, 1981, 1982, 1983, 1984)

FERGUSON JENKINS   HOF: 1991   Page 157

Position: Pitcher   Team: Chicago Cubs

Bats: Right   At-bats: 896

Home runs: 13   Batting Average: .165

DEREK JETER   Page 9

Position: Shortstop   Team: New York Yankees

Bats: Right   At-bats: 11195

Runs: 1923   Home runs: 260

Hits: 3465   Batting Average: .310

All-Star Games: 14 (1998, 1999, 2000, 2001, 2002, 2004, 2006, 2007, 2008, 2009, 2010, 2011, 2012, 2014)

CHIPPER JONES   Page 88

Position: Third Base   Team: Atlanta Braves

Bats: Both   Runs: 1619

RBIs: 1623   Home runs: 468

MVP: 1999 NL   Batting Average: .303

JIM KAAT   Page 118

Position: Pitcher   Team: Minnesota Twins

Bats: Left   Runs: 117

Hits: 232   Batting Average: .185

DON KESSINGER   Page 49

Position: Shortstop   Team: Chicago Cubs

Bats: Both   Runs: 899

Hits: 1931   Batting Average: .252

RALPH KINER   HOF: 1975   Page 221

Position: Left Field   Team: Pittsburgh Pirates

Bats: Right   RBIs: 1015

Home runs: 369   Batting Average: .279

ED KRANEPOOL
Page 165

Position: First Base

Team: New York Mets

Bats: Left

Runs: 536

RBIs: 614

Batting Average: .261

ABRAHAM LINCOLN
Page 145

16th President of the United States

KENNY LOFTON
Page 200

Position: Center Field

Team: San Francisco Giants

Bats: Left

Runs: 1528

RBIs: 781

Batting Average: .299

EVAN LONGORIA*
Page 146

Position: Third Base

Team: Tampa Bay Rays

Bats: Right

RBIs: 861

Home runs: 254

Batting Average: .271

DAVEY LOPES
Page 217

Position: Second Base

Team: Los Angeles Dodgers

Bats: Right

Hits: 1671

Runs: 1025

Batting Average: .263

MIKE LOWELL
Page 198

Position: Pinch Hitter

Team: Florida Marlins

Bats: Right

RBIs: 952

Home runs: 223

Batting Average: .279

BARRY LYONS
Page 220

Position: Catcher

Team: New York Mets

Bats: Right

At-bats: 628

Home runs: 15

Batting Average: .239

MICKEY MANTLE
HOF: 1974
Page 141

Position: Right Field

Team: New York Yankees

Bats: Both

At-bats: 8102

RBI: 1509

Runs: 1676

Hits: 2415

Home runs: 536

MVP: 1956, 1957, 1962 AL   Batting Average: .298

All-Star Games: 20 (1952, 1953, 1954, 1955, 1956, 1957, 1958, 1959-2, 1960-1, 1960-2, 1961-1, 1961-2, 1962-1, 1963, 1964, 1965, 1967, 1968)

EDGAR MARTINEZ   Page 7

Position: Designated Hitter   Team: Seattle Mariners
Bats: Right   At-bats: 7213
RBIs: 1261   Batting Average: .312

TINO MARTINEZ   Page 193

Position: First Base   Team: New York Yankees
Bats: Left   RBIs: 1271
Home runs: 339   Batting Average: .271

DON MATTINGLY   Page 80

Position: First Base   Team: New York Yankees
Bats: Left   Hits: 2153
MVP: 1985 AL   Batting Average: .307

CARLOS MAY   Page 161

Position: Left Field   Team: Chicago White Sox
Bats: Left   Runs: 545
Home runs: 90   Batting Average: .274

JOHN MAYBERRY   Page 165

Position: First Base   Team: Kansas City Royals
Bats: Left   Runs: 733
RBIs: 879   Batting Average: .253

BRIAN MCCANN*   Page 84

Position: Catcher   Team: Atlanta Braves
Bats: Left   RBIs: 934
Home runs: 256   Batting Average: .265

TIM MCCARVER   Page 17

Position: Catcher   Team: St. Louis Cardinals
Bats: Left   RBIs: 645
Home runs: 97   Batting Average: .271

FELIX MILLAN HOF: 1983

Page 58

Position: Second Base
Bats: Right
MVP: 1973 NL

Team: Atlanta Braves
Home runs: 22
Batting Average: .279

JOE MORGAN HOF: 1990

Page 111

Position: Second Base
Bats: Left
Runs: 1650
MVP: 1975, 1976 NL

Team: Cincinnati Reds
At-bats: 9277
Hits: 2517
Batting Average: .271

DALE MURPHY

Page 205

Position: Pinch Hitter
Bats: Right
Hits: 2111
MVP: 1982, 1983 NL

Team: Atlanta Braves
RBIs: 1266
Home runs: 398
Batting Average: .265

STAN MUSIAL HOF: 1969

Page 186

Position: First Base, Outfield
Bats: Left
Runs: 1949
Hits: 3630
MVP: 1943, 1946, 1948 AL

Team: St. Louis Cardinals
At-bats: 10972
RBIs: 1951
Home runs: 475
Batting Average: .331

All-Star Games: 24 (1943, 1944, 1946, 1947, 1948, 1949, 1950, 1951, 1952, 1953, 1954, 1955, 1956, 1957, 1958, 1959-1, 1959-2, 1960-1, 1960-2, 1961-1, 1961-2, 1962-1, 1962-2, 1963)

MATT NEWMAN

Page 102

Position: Center Field

Bats: Right

JIM PALMER HOF: 1990

Page 216

Position: Pitcher
Bats: Right
Hits: 85

Team: Baltimore Orioles
Home runs: 3
Batting Average: .174

DAVE PARKER

Page 99

Position: Designated Hitter
Bats: Left

Team: Oakland Athletics
At-bats: 9358

Hits: 2712

Home runs: 339

MVP: 1978 NL

Batting Average: .290

JAKE PEAVY*   Page 162

Position: Pitcher

Team: San Diego Padres

Bats: Right

Home runs: 3

Hits: 87

Batting Average: .168

TONY PEREZ   HOF: 2000   Page 55

Position: Third Base

Team: Cincinnati Reds

Bats: Right

RBIs: 1652

Home runs: 379

Batting Average: .279

MIKE PIAZZA   HOF: 2016   Page 24

Position: Catcher

Team: New York Mets

Bats: Right

RBIs: 1335

Hits: 2127

Batting Average: .308

All-Star Games: 12 (1993, 1994, 1995, 1996, 1997, 1998, 1999, 2000, 2001, 2002, 2004, 2005)

JORGE POSADA   Page 206

Position: Catcher

Team: New York Yankees

Bats: Both

Runs: 900

RBIs: 1065

Batting Average: .273

ALBERT PUJOLS*   Page 109

Position: First Base

Team: St. Louis Cardinals

Bats: Right

At-bats: 9478

Runs: 1698

RBIs: 1873

Home runs: 591

MVP: 2005, 2008, 2009 NL

Batting Average: .305

JIM RICE   HOF: 2009   Page 178

Position: Left Field

Team: Boston Red Sox

Bats: Right

RBIs: 1451

Hits: 2452

Home runs: 382

MVP: 1978 AL

Batting Average: .298

BOBBY RICHARDSON
Page 75

Position: Second Base
Team: New York Yankees
Bats: Right
Runs: 643
Home runs: 34
Batting Average: .266

CAL RIPKEN JR.   HOF: 2007
Page 155

Position: Shortstop
Team: Baltimore Orioles
Bats: Right
At-bats: 11551
Runs: 1647
RBIs: 1695
Hits: 3184
Home runs: 431
MVP: 1983, 1991 AL
Batting Average: .276
All-Star Games: 19 (1983, 1984, 1985, 1986, 1987, 1988, 1989, 1990, 1991, 1992, 1993, 1994, 1995, 1996, 1997, 1998, 1999, 2000, 2001)

BROOKS ROBINSON   HOF: 1983
Page 74

Position: Third Base
Team: Baltimore Orioles
Bats: Right
At-bats: 10654
RBIs: 1357
Hits: 2848
MVP: 1964 AL
Batting Average: .267
All-Star Games: 18 (1960-1, 1960-2, 1961-1, 1961-2, 1962-1, 1962-2, 1963, 1964, 1965, 1966, 1967, 1968, 1969, 1970, 1971, 1972, 1973, 1974)

FRANK ROBINSON   HOF: 1982
Page 78

Position: Left Field
Team: Cincinnati Reds
Bats: Right
At-bats: 10006
Runs: 1829
RBIs: 1812
Hits: 2943
Home runs: 586
MVP: 1961 NL, 1966 AL
Batting Average: .294
All-Star Games: 15 (1956, 1957, 1959-1, 1959-2, 1961-1, 1961-2, 1962-1, 1962-2, 1965, 1966, 1967, 1969, 1970, 1971, 1974)

ALEX RODRIGUEZ
Page 47

Position: Third Base
Team: New York Yankees
Bats: Right
At-bats: 10566
Runs: 2021
RBIs: 2086
Home runs: 696
Hits: 3115

MVP: 2003, 2005, 2007 AL   Batting Average: .295

All-Star Games: 14 (1996, 1997, 1998, 2000, 2001, 2002, 2003, 2004, 2005, 2006, 2007, 2008, 2010, 2011)

IVAN RODRIGUEZ   HOF: 2017   Page 196

Position: Catcher   Team: Texas Rangers

Bats: Right   RBIs: 2844

MVP: 1999 AL   Batting Average: .296

All-Star Games: 14 (1992, 1993, 1994, 1995, 1996, 1997, 1998, 1999, 2000, 2001, 2004, 2005, 2006, 2007)

PETE ROSE   Page 65

Position: First Base   Team: Cincinnati Reds

Bats: Both   At-bats: 14053

Runs: 2165   RBIs: 1314

Hits: 4256   Home runs: 160

MVP: 1973 NL   Batting Average: .303

All-Star Games: 17 (1965, 1967, 1968, 1969, 1970, 1971, 1973, 1974, 1975, 1976, 1977, 1978, 1979, 1980, 1981, 1982, 1985)

BABE RUTH   HOF: 1936   Page 148

Position: Right Field   Team: New York Yankees

Bats: Left   At-bats: 8399

Runs: 2174   RBIs: 2214

Hits: 2873   Home runs: 714

MVP: 1923 AL   Batting Average: .342

TIM SALMON   Page 113

Position: Right Field   Team: Anaheim Angels

Bats: Right   RBIs: 1016

Home runs: 299   Batting Average: .282

REGGIE SANDERS   Page 147

Position: Designated Hitter   Team: Kansas City Royals

Bats: Right   Runs: 1037

Home runs: 305   Batting Average: .267

MIKE SCHMIDT   HOF: 1995   Page 77

Position: Third Base   Team: Philadelphia Phillies
Bats: Right   Runs: 1506
RBIs: 1595   Home runs: 548
MVP: 1980, 1981, 1986 NL   Batting Average: .267
All-Star Games: 12 (1974, 1976, 1977, 1978, 1980, 1981, 1982, 1983, 1984, 1986, 1987, 1989)

MIKE SHANNON   Page 177

Position: Right Field   Team: St. Louis Cardinals
Bats: Right   RBIs: 367
Home runs: 68   Batting Average: .255

OZZIE SMITH   HOF: 2002   Page 214

Position: Shortstop   Team: St. Louis Cardinals
Bats: Both   Runs: 1257
Home runs: 28   Batting Average: .262
All-Star Games: 15 (1981, 1982, 1983, 1984, 1985, 1986, 1987, 1988, 1989, 1990, 1991, 1992, 1994, 1995, 1996)

REGGIE SMITH   Page 85

Position: Center Field   Team: Boston Red Sox
Bats: Both   Runs: 1123
RBIs: 1092   Batting Average: .287

RUSTY STAUB   Page 28

Position: Right Field   Team: Houston Astros
Bats: Left   Runs: 1189
RBIs: 1466   Batting Average: .279

DARRYL STRAWBERRY   Page 184

Position: Right Field   Team: New York Mets
Bats: Left   RBIs: 1000
Home runs: 335   Batting Average: .259

JIM SUNDBERG
Position: Catcher
Bats: Right
RBIs: 624
Team: Kansas City Royals
Runs: 621
Batting Average: .248

RON SWOBODA
Position: Right Field
Bats: Right
RBIs: 344
Team: New York Mets
Runs: 285
Batting Average: .242

MARK TEIXEIRA
Position: First Base
Bats: Both
Home runs: 409
Team: New York Yankees
RBIs: 1298
Batting Average: .268

MIGUEL TEJADA
Position: Shortstop
Bats: Right
RBIs: 1302
MVP: 2002 AL
Team: Baltimore Orioles
At-bats: 8434
Home runs: 307
Batting Average: .285

FRANK THOMAS   HOF: 2014
Position: First Base
Bats: Right
RBIs: 1704
MVP: 1993, 1994 AL
Team: Chicago White Sox
At-bats: 8199
Home runs: 521
Batting Average: .301

JIM THOME
Position: Designated Hitter
Bats: Left
Hits: 2328
Team: Chicago White Sox
Home runs: 612
Batting Average: .276

ALAN TRAMMELL
Position: Shortstop
Bats: Right
Hits: 2365
Team: Detroit Tigers
Home runs: 185
Batting Average: .285

JUSTIN UPTON* Page 101
Position: Right Field   Team: Arizona Diamondbacks
Bats: Right   Runs: 829
Home runs: 236   Batting Average: .269

BOB WATSON Page 112
Position: First Base   Team: Houston Astros
Bats: Right   RBIs: 989
Home runs: 184   Batting Average: .295

ROY WHITE Page 17
Position: Left Field   Team: New York Yankees
Bats: Both   Runs: 964
Home runs: 160   Batting Average: .271

BERNIE WILLIAMS Page 60
Position: Center Field   Team: New York Yankees
Bats: Both   RBIs: 1257
Home runs: 287   Batting Average: .297

MAURY WILLS Page 52
Position: Shortstop   Team: Los Angeles Dodgers
Bats: Both   Runs: 1067
MVP: 1962 NL   Batting Average: .281

MOOKIE WILSON Page 62
Position: Center Field   Team: New York Mets
Bats: Both   Runs: 731
Home runs: 67   Batting Average: .274

DAVE WINFIELD HOF: 2001 Page 170
Position: Right Field   Team: Toronto Blue Jays
Bats: Right   At-bats: 11003
RBIs: 1833   Home runs: 465
Hits: 3110   Batting Average: .283
All-Star Games: 12 (1977, 1978, 1979, 1980, 1981, 1982, 1983, 1984, 1985, 1986, 1987, 1988)

DAVID WRIGHT*   Page 163

Position: Third Base   Team: New York Mets
Bats: Right   Runs: 949
RBIs: 970   Batting Average: .296

CARL YASTRZEMSKI   HOF: 1989   Page 40

Position: Left Field   Team: Boston Red Sox
Bats: Left   At-bats: 11988
Runs: 1816   RBIs: 1844
Hits: 3419   Home runs: 452
MVP: 1967 AL   Batting Average: .285
All-Star Games: 18 (1963, 1965, 1966, 1967, 1968, 1969, 1970, 1971, 1972, 1973, 1974, 1975, 1976, 1977, 1978, 1982, 1983)

DMITRI YOUNG   Page 210

Position: First Base   Team: Cincinnati Reds
Bats: Both   RBIs: 683
Home runs: 171   Batting Average: .292

ROBIN YOUNT   HOF: 1999   Page 106

Position: Shortstop   Team: Milwaukee Brewers
Bats: Right   At-bats: 11008
Runs: 1632   RBIs: 1406
Hits: 3142   Home runs: 251
MVP: 1982, 1989 AL   Batting Average: .285